National Council for the Social Studies
8555 Sixteenth Street • Suite 500 • Silver Spring, Maryland 20910 • socialstudies.org

NCSS BOARD OF DIRECTORS, 2025–2026
OFFICERS

Tina M. Ellsworth, Ph.D.
PRESIDENT
University of Central Missouri
Warrensburg, MO

David Kendrick
VICE PRESIDENT
Loganville High School
Loganville, GA

Joe Schmidt
PRESIDENT-ELECT
Bill of Rights Institute
Augusta, ME

Jennifer Morgan
PAST PRESIDENT
West Salem Middle School
West Salem, WI

BOARD OF DIRECTORS

CherylAnne Amendola
Montclair Kimberley Academy
Montclair, NJ (2027)

Stephen Masyada
Lou Frey Institute and the Florida
Joint Center for Citizenship
Orlando, FL (2027)

Marc Turner
Spring Hill High School
Columbia, SC (2026)

Alex Cuenca, Ph.D.
Indiana University
Bloomington, IN (2026)

Heather Nice
The Colonial Williamsburg
Foundation
Williamsburg, VA (2026)

Anne Walker
Edison High School
Alexandria, VA (2028)

Carly Donick
Cabrillo Middle School
Ventura, CA (2026)

Gabriel Valdez
Fort Worth Independent
School District
Fort Worth, TX (2028)

Terrell Fleming
Prince Edward County Public Schools
Farmville, VA (2027)

Stephanie Nichols
Narragansett Elementary School
Gorham, ME (2028)

Renita Parks
Memphis, TN (2028)

Kimberly Huffman
Wayne County Schools
Smithville, OH (2024)

NCSS EXECUTIVE DIRECTOR Kelly McFarland Stratman

EDITORIAL STAFF ON THIS PUBLICATION Laura Godfrey, Nancy Driver
DESIGN AND PRODUCTION Rich Palmer

© 2025 National Council for the Social Studies
Silver Spring, MD

Library of Congress Cataloging-in-Publication Data

Names: Nance, Starlynn R. editor | Roberts, Scott L. editor
Title: The C3 framework and film : bringing Hollywood to the social studies classroom as a catalyst for teaching inquiry / edited by Starlynn Nance and Scott L. Roberts.
Description: First edition. | Silver Spring : National Council for the Social Studies, 2025. | Includes bibliographical references and index. | Summary: The C3 Framework and Film: Bringing Hollywood to the Social Studies Classroom as a Catalyst for Teaching Inquiry incorporates the C3 Framework with the use of film so that elementary and secondary pre-service and practicing teachers can use film in their social studies inquiries in a productive manner. This book contains teacher-made, classroom-ready units and Inquiry Design Model (IDM) blueprints that accompany and supplement these units. The strategies offered in this book show teachers how students can become active viewers of film across all major social studies content areas"—Provided by publisher.
Identifiers: LCCN 2024052733 | ISBN 9780879861292 paperback
Subjects: LCSH: Motion pictures in education | Social sciences—Study and teaching | Inquiry-based learning | Motion pictures—Study and teaching
Classification: LCC LB1044 .C22 2025 | DDC 300.71/2—dc23/eng/20250511
LC record available at https://lccn.loc.gov/2024052733

Table of Contents

Foreword 9
A Screen Onto the Past and Present
Scott Alan Metzger

About the Editors 6

Contributors 7

Preface 13
Starlynn Nance and *Scott L. Roberts*

Chapter 1 18
Introduction
Welcome to C3 and Film
Scott L. Roberts

Chapter 2 23
C3 Inquiry, Film, and Applying Disciplinary Concepts and Tools
Starlynn Nance

Chapter 3 28
Elementary Teachers' Experience With Using the C3 Dimensions With Geography and Film
How Did Geography Contribute to the Differences in Early American Colonies?
Sean Boyle and *Lori Boyle*

Chapter 4 40
Elementary Teacher's Experience With Using the C3 Dimensions With Civics and Film
Rock the House: Learning Legislation
Samantha Faivor

Chapter 5 52
Elementary Teacher's Experience With Using the C3 Dimensions With United States History and Film
Teaching Indigenous Resilience and Sovereignty Through Lacrosse History and Culture
Kate Van Haren

Chapter 6 65

Secondary Teachers' Experience With Using the C3 Dimensions With World History and Film

The Silk Road and the 21st Century: Co-Teaching Ancient China as a Map to the Present

Starlynn Nance and *Taylor Hawes-Guldenpfennig*

Chapter 7 82

Secondary Teacher's Experience With Using the C3 Dimensions With Economics and Film

Exploring the Economic Dynamics of WWII: An Inquiry Into the Home Fronts of an Axis Power and Allied Power

Cameron Pack

Chapter 8 96

Secondary Teacher's Experience With Using the C3 Dimensions With Social Science Integration and Film

Teaching Students to See the World Through Another's Eyes: An Online Course

Taylor Hawes-Guldenpfennig

Chapter 9 113

Ready-Made Lessons for Elementary and Secondary Teachers

Introduction

   How Did Geography Contribute to the Differences in Early American Colonies? 114
   Sean Boyle and Lori Boyle

   How Can We Make a Difference in Our Community? 123
   Samantha Faivor

   How Do Indigenous Athletes, Like Those Who Play Lacrosse, Teach Others About the Resilience of Indigenous Cultures and Sovereignty? 139
   Kate Van Haren

   Does China Make the World Flat? 151
   Starlynn Nance and Taylor Hawes-Guldenpfennig

   Can the Home Front Determine a War? 158
   Cameron Pack

Can You See the World Through Others' Eyes? 176
Taylor Hawes-Guldenpfennig

Chapter 10 187
Additional Lessons for Elementary and Secondary Teachers
Introduction

Did the Filmmakers of Pocahontas *Rewrite History?* 189
Nancy B. Sardone

How Has Migration and Immigration Affected the World, in the Past, Present, and Future? 199
Meghan Beauchamp and Chloe Thompson

What Did the Lost Generation Lose? 213
Cameron Pack

How Did a Vacation Start a War? 221
Jackson Magargee

Under What Circumstances Would Breaking the Law Be Justified? 233
Starlynn Nance and Katie Engemann

Index 242

About the Editors

Starlynn R. Nance is a Professor of Education in the Sociology, Anthropology, and Social Studies Department at the University of Central Missouri (UCM). She received her doctoral degree from the University of Oklahoma in 2012. Prior to this position, she was the Middle School Program director at Fitchburg State University in Massachusetts. Before becoming a professor, she taught on-level and advanced placement social studies classes at public and private schools. She is the director of the nationally recognized Social Studies Program at UCM and teaches all social studies courses including Methods in Social Studies. She is the author of *Hollywood or History? An Inquiry-Based Strategy for Using Television Shows to Teach Issue-Centered Curriculum* and was the editor of the special issue, Using Film, Television Shows, and/or Documentaries to Teach Narratives verses Counter Narratives in History Classes, of *Oregon Journal of Social Studies* and co-editor of the special issue, Effective Use of Films in the Social Studies Classroom, of *Social Studies Research and Practice*. She has been published in *Middle Grades Research Journal, Oregon Journal of Social Studies, Teaching Social Studies, Ohio Social Studies Review* and has contributed to several edited books such as the *Hollywood or History?* series, *Teaching Social Studies: A Methods Book for Methods Teachers* and *Cinematic Social Studies: A Resource for Teaching and Learning Social Studies in Film*. She has presented at the College University Faculty Assembly, the National Council for the Social Studies (NCSS), the Missouri Council for the Social Studies, the Oklahoma Council for the Social Studies, the Oklahoma Council for History Education, Teacher Education, and the International Society for the Social Studies Conferences. She is a former board member of the Oklahoma and Missouri Council of the Social Studies and was a former delegate for Oklahoma at NCSS. She has won the Region 7 Certificate of Merit for Outstanding Faculty Advisor from the National Academic Advising Association, Outstanding Advisor for the Missouri Academic Advising Association, Outstanding Advisor for UCM, and New Faculty Award for the College of Arts and Humanities at UCM. She was on the US Parallel History team that wrote the curriculum for the Civil Rights Movement and recently received an International Society for Technology Education (ISTE) certificate for Artificial Intelligence where her final project was showcased on the ISTE website. Her research interests are culturally responsive teaching, history education, and literacy in social studies classes.

Scott L. Roberts currently serves as Professor of Social Studies Education at Central Michigan University. He teaches courses in elementary social studies education and research methods. He has served as board member of the Michigan Council for Social Studies, on several committees for the National Council for the Social Studies, on the editorial board of *Social Studies and the Young Learner*, and was named the Georgia Council for the Social Studies' Gwen Hutchinson Outstanding Social Studies Educator in 2012. A former middle school teacher, he received his doctorate from the University of Georgia in social studies education in 2009. He is the author of multiple publications concerning history and social studies education and is the co-editor of the *Hollywood or History?* book series for Information Age Publishing. His research interests include state history, discussion-based strategies, history education, and educational technology.

Contributors

Meghan Beauchamp graduated with her bachelor's degree in Elementary Education, grades PreK–6, from Central Michigan University in December 2024. She cares for many young children in her life, and her interests include place-based learning and Michigan history.

Lori Boyle holds a degree in Elementary Education and a master's degree in Teaching and Learning from Nova Southeastern University in Fort Lauderdale, Florida. With twenty years of experience, she is certified in seven areas and currently teaches at Central Michigan University. She is pursuing a doctorate in Educational Technology.

Sean Boyle, a former social worker, earned his bachelor's degree in Secondary Education and History from Central Michigan University in 2023 and teaches at Chippewa Hills Schools, Michigan. He employs experiential and project-based learning to engage students.

Katherine Engemann graduated with her bachelor's degree in Secondary Social Studies Education with a minor in history from the University of Central Missouri in 2020. She has taught for four years in Hermann, Missouri. Her interests include Holocaust and other genocide studies and differentiated instruction.

Samantha Faivor graduated with her bachelor's degree in Elementary Education from Central Michigan University in 2024 and teaches fourth grade at Riley Elementary in St. Johns, Michigan. Her interests include curriculum development and place-based learning.

Taylor Hawes-Guldenpfennig graduated with a bachelor of science in education, social studies, from the University of Central Missouri and a master's degree in K–12 Educational Leadership. She has taught for five years and is currently teaching Ancient World History at Pleasant Lea Middle School in Lee's Summit, Missouri. She is the 2024 Missouri Council for the Social Studies Teacher of the Year.

Jackson Magargee is a senior in the Social Studies Program at the University of Central Missouri and will graduate in 2025. He coaches high school basketball and has taught content and disciplinary literacies, AI, and culturally responsive lessons during his internships.

Cameron Pack is a tenth-grade World History high school teacher, head wrestling coach, and Staff Sergeant in the U.S. Army Reserve. He graduated from the University of Central Missouri and is currently finishing his master's degree in history. He is the Outstanding History Teacher of 2025 for the state of Missouri from the Daughters of the American Revolution and the 2025 Missouri Council of Social Studies Teacher of the Year.

Nancy B. Sardone received a master's degree and a doctoral degree from New York University. She holds a bachelor's degree from University of Massachusetts at Amherst in Resource Economics. Nancy teaches social studies methods and other courses at Georgian Court University in Lakewood, New Jersey.

Chloe Thompson graduated with a bachelor's degree in Elementary Education PreK–6 from Central Michigan University in December 2024 and is currently pursuing a Master of Arts in Teaching: Early Childhood Classroom Teaching at Saginaw Valley State University in Michigan. She is a kindergarten-prep teacher at Sacred Heart Academy in Mount Pleasant, Michigan, and has worked with elementary students in various roles. Her interests include Michigan history, movement-based learning, and early childhood education.

Kate Van Haren is a current doctoral candidate at Penn State University. She also teaches fourth- and fifth-grade social studies and literacy at Pittsville Elementary School in Wisconsin. Her interests include advocating for elementary social studies and teaching history with a decolonizing lens.

Foreword

A Screen Onto the Past and Present

Scott Alan Metzger, The Pennsylvania State University

In 1890, American inventor Thomas Edison's company developed the technology that would become the modern motion picture camera. One of the first films made was the 34-second *Blacksmith Scene* (1893), with actors performing the role of commonplace workers. By 1895, desperate to reverse the flagging novelty of the new technology, Edison produced what can be seen as the first professional movie with hired actors, period costumes, and even special effects—*The Execution of Mary Stuart*, an 18-second reenactment of the 1587 event culminating with the display of her severed head. Less than one decade after their advent, nascent American motion pictures had already begun representing both the social present and the historical past.

Cinema quickly spread across the globe. In France, the Lumière brothers made the landmark 1896 film *Arrival of the Train at La Ciotat Station* that gave rise to the evocative urban legend of Parisian viewers ducking in fear from the screen image of a locomotive speeding toward them. In 1902, Georges Méliès made perhaps the greatest early film and first true literary screen adaptation, *A Trip to the Moon*, based on a Jules Verne science-fiction story. In the following decades, a film industry also emerged in Germany but was overshadowed by the Nazi era's notorious propaganda films made by Leni Riefenstahl. German cinema never fully recovered from World War II. At the same time, a film industry developed in Japan that survived the war. Led by Akira Kurosawa's famed historical samurai movies, Japanese cinema became influential worldwide and today enjoys massive global popularity due in no small part to its animation (anime). The success of Japan is mirrored in the increased success of cinema from South Korea, China, Turkey, and India. Thanks to the streaming service Netflix, the market for films made by and about diverse international cultures is greater than ever.

This whirlwind tour of film history demonstrates that filmmaking from its earliest years embraced historical and contemporary social/political issues and cultural representations. Movies have always served as a screen onto which our world's historical past and contemporary present are projected. The historical, the social/political, and the cultural are all part of the academic enterprise we now call social studies. Perhaps that is why educators have been drawn to movies for so long, evidenced by educational publications calling for the inclusion of film in the classroom (one of the earliest being Consitt's 1931 *The Value of Films in History Teaching*). This enthusiasm took a while to be realized, however, since film projectors, celluloid reels, and auditorium screens were prohibitively expensive. By the 1980s, lower prices for televisions and the advent of commercially released, affordable home video made it possible for movies to enter classrooms almost anywhere. Movies in schools proliferated in the 21st century with the even greater affordability of DVD/Blu-ray and easy access through digital streaming.

Scholarly interest in educational implications of popular film picked up in the 1990s—a decade known for award-winning blockbusters that included *Dances with Wolves*, *Schindler's List*, *Saving Private Ryan*, and *Gladiator*. This may be why interest began with history educators, inspired by the work of Peter Seixas (1993) on how watching Westerns influenced young peoples' thinking about Native-White relations in history. A new generation of doctoral students was attracted to the study of film and history at a talk given by the late Richard Paxton in 2002 on his informal study of high schoolers watching history movies. I was one of those new students in the audience, and over the coming years, a group of us joined Rich in publishing work for this growing field that included two books on history movies in the classroom (Marcus, 2006; Marcus et al., 2018). My final collaboration with Rich was for a chapter in *The Wiley International Handbook of History Teaching and Learning* (2018), which I coedited with Lauren Harris. Paxton and coauthor Alan Marcus reviewed decades of accumulated research on film media in history education and concluded by poignantly observing that new historical narratives compete in society and the minds of students partly through media and technology: "To give short shrift to this facet of modern life, or to ignore it altogether, would be a terrible abdication for the field" (Paxton & Marcus, 2018, p. 596).

I am happy to say that many others have taken up the field of film in education over the past two decades, including this volume's coeditors Starlynn Nance (2022) and Scott Roberts (Roberts & Elfer, 2018, 2021, 2025). Importantly, attention has extended beyond older teenagers to students in middle and elementary grades, too (Roberts et al., 2022; Van Haren & Roberts, 2021). Attention has not remained solely on film, as interest has grown in other technologies—for instance, recent work in this field has looked at video games and digital simulations (Metzger & Paxton, 2016; Wright-Maley et al., 2018). History may be predominant in the academic work on media in social studies education, but it is not exclusive. Prior scholarship also has examined civic and social issues through media, including documentary films as perspective-laden narratives (Hess, 2007). As Stoddard and Marcus (2017) note, "The research on media in social studies is as dynamic and diverse as the evolving and increasing role that media has in teaching and learning social studies itself" (p. 494).

Now the field has reached the second half of the 2020s, after a past decade that I think may be fairly described as tumultuous, both domestically within the US and globally. Additionally, education and schooling in the US (and many similar countries) have entered a divisive and demanding new era socially and politically. The National Council for the Social Studies' *College, Career, and Civic Life (C3) Framework for Social Studies State Standards* was released early in this tumultuous period. Like anything from the "before times," C3 could have wrecked on the shoals of partisan backlash and culture wars. However, it had something to steer its course over these difficult years: the Inquiry Arc. By calling for teachers and their students to investigate compelling questions by using disciplinary tools, concepts, and content to make evidence-backed interpretations and generalizations to apply in the real world, the C3 Inquiry Arc possesses lasting relevance and can weather the changing political storms sweeping through the school system.

The C3 Framework and Film: Bringing Hollywood to Social Studies Classrooms as a Catalyst for Teaching Inquiry is a valuable book for this moment. Modern digital technology has infused our lives with media perhaps like never before. Through media engagement, young people come to the classroom primed to see their world through narratives swirling around popular culture. While heated culture wars likely have made many teachers today more cautious about using "Hollywood" in the classroom than during the heady early 2000s, the good reasons for critically engaging with film media in the social studies classroom remain as compelling as ever. Young people are growing up in an increasingly media-saturated environment. Media have a definite relevance to their daily lives. It makes sense to tap this relevance as a way to engage students in inquiry into compelling questions and in critical thinking about media content and messaging. The C3 Inquiry Arc provides a cogent structure on which to engage with this kind of meaningful inquiry.

The book you are holding (or perhaps looking at on a screen!) makes a needed contribution to the social studies field by linking the longstanding interest in using film in the classroom to the durable and convincing inquiry goals of the C3 Framework. And this isn't just for high school history classrooms. Starlynn Nance and Scott Roberts have gathered educators from across diverse educational experiences, professional contexts, and content interests. You will find in this book not just history but also geography, civics, economics, and the social sciences and both secondary and elementary grade levels. Each chapter offers a detailed walk-through of a C3-aligned inquiry lesson based in a compelling question that uses film media in an academically responsible and cogent manner. These are the kinds of lessons that teachers can boldly show to administrators and parents to justify the time spent looking at movies in the classroom.

I hope teachers will draw from this book the confidence not to feel afraid to teach challenging inquiry through educational use of film media in the classroom. Times may be difficult for schools and teachers, but resources such as *The C3 Framework and Film* can equip you to transcend political and cultural discord by building bridges to a deeper understanding of each other, of our society, and of the historical moment we all live in.

References

Consitt, F. (1931). *The value of films in history teaching*. Bell.

Hess, D. (2007). From *Banished* to *Brother Outsider*, *Miss Navajo* to *An Inconvenient Truth*: Documentary films as perspective-laden narratives. *Social Education, 71* (4), 194–199.

Marcus, A. S. (Ed.) (2006). *Celluloid blackboard: Teaching history with film*. Information Age.

Marcus, A. S., Metzger, S. A., Paxton, R. J., & Stoddard, J. D. (2018). *Teaching history with film: Strategies for secondary social studies* (2nd ed.). Routledge. (First edition published 2010)

Metzger, S. A., & Harris, L. M. (Eds.) (2018). *The Wiley international handbook of history teaching and learning*. Wiley Blackwell.

Metzger, S. A., & Paxton, R. J. (2016). Gaming history: A framework for what video games teach about the past. *Theory & Research in Social Education, 44* (4), 532–564. **https://doi.org/10.1080/00933104.2016.1208596**

Nance, S. R. (2022). *Hollywood or history? An inquiry-based strategy for using television shows to teach issue-centered curriculum*. Information Age.

Paxton, R. J., & Marcus, A. S. (2018). Film media in history teaching and learning. In S. A. Metzger & L. M. Harris (Eds.), *The Wiley Handbook of History Teaching and Learning* (pp. 579–601). Wiley Blackwell.

Roberts, S. L., & Elfer, C. J. (2018). *Hollywood or history? An inquiry-based strategy for using film to teach United States history*. Information Age.

Roberts, S. L., & Elfer, C. J. (2021). *Hollywood or history? An inquiry-based strategy for using film to teach World History*. Information Age.

Roberts, S. L., & Elfer, C. J. (2025). *Hollywood or history? An inquiry-based strategy for using cartoons to teach topics in elementary and secondary social studies*. Information Age.

Roberts, S. L., Wellenreiter, B. R., Ferreras-Stone, J., Strachan, S. L., & Palmer, K. L. (2022). *Teaching middle level social studies: A practical guide for 4th–8th grade* (3rd ed.). Information Age.

Seixas, P. (1993). Popular film and young people's understanding of the history of Native American-White relations. *The History Teacher, 26* (3), 351–370. **https://doi.org/10.2307/494666**

Stoddard, J. D., & Marcus, A. S. (2017). Media and social studies education. In M. M. Manfra & C. M. Bolick (Eds.), *The Wiley Handbook of Social Studies Research* (pp. 477–498). Wiley Blackwell.

Van Haren, K., & Roberts, S. L. (2021). Hollywood film and the C3 framework: An inquiry-based lesson about immigration. *Social Studies and the Young Learner, 34* (2), 10–13.

Wright-Maley, C., Lee, J. K., & Friedman, A. (2018). Digital simulations and games in history education. In S. A. Metzger & L. M. Harris (Eds.), *The Wiley Handbook of History Teaching and Learning* (pp. 603–629). Wiley Blackwell.

Preface

The C3 Framework and Film: Bringing Hollywood to the Social Studies Classroom as a Catalyst to Teaching Inquiry is a book that has its origins through years of conversations and collaborations between Starlynn Nance and Scott Roberts. This book evolved from working together on the *Hollywood or History?* (HOH) series and presenting this strategy to teachers and professors nationwide (even being interviewed on several podcasts, one being from Northern Ireland). Using the strategy where film is part of the inquiry process, Starlynn incorporated it into her method's class. She focused the film and film clips into the NCSS C3 Inquiry Framework and not as a stand-alone lesson after or during a unit. Because Starlynn's program is nationally recognized by the Specialized Professional Association (SPA) which is the National Council for the Social Studies (NCSS), her curriculum revolves around the National Standards for the Preparation of Social Studies Teachers. Her curriculum is the C3 Inquiry Framework, and students are required to use it in their teaching as pre-service teachers. Using film was very easy to incorporate in her curriculum, and she felt it made the students' units stronger having this component added to the inquiry. Using this experience to write her HOH series book she incorporated the C3 Inquiry Framework in each chapter unit using sitcoms. However, the focus of the book was just for high school (and some middle school) social studies classrooms and not elementary. Knowing that social studies is mostly neglected in elementary, she wanted to include elementary teachers in her next book proposal (e.g., Au, 2009; Diliberti et al., 2023; Fitchett & Heafner, 2010; Fitchett et al., 2014a; Fitchett et al., 2014b; Heafner, 2018; Pace, 2012; Tyner & Kabourek, 2021; VanFossen, 2005; VanFossen & McGrew, 2008; Vogler et al., 2007; Whitlock & Brugar, 2019). Her goal was to have elementary teachers use inquiry and film to meet their standards (language arts, etc.) while adding more social studies content to their curriculum. Reaching out to Scott, she started a discourse explaining how the HOH fit nicely in the C3 Inquiry Framework and was being used in classrooms taught by her student teachers and former students (HOH even being adopted as electives in some school districts). She felt that bringing the C3 Inquiry Framework, the NCSS themes, and film (documentaries, TV, cartoons, etc.) together could be helpful in all social studies classrooms. But she wanted to be more inclusive and needed Scott's expertise with elementary teachers and pre-service students to develop a proposal for a book.

Scott has been working with elementary social studies teachers and teacher candidates for over a decade. While originally certified as a 6–12 social studies teacher, he gained valuable experience working with students and teachers in grades K–5 by earning both an ESL and Gifted endorsement as a classroom teacher. Later in his career he worked as a district K–12 Social Studies program specialist and for the past 11 years, he has taught elementary social studies methods courses at Central Michigan University. Scott worked closely with several elementary school teachers in developing and implementing lesson plans based on the ideas and concepts found in the social studies literature (Levstik & Barton, 2022; VanSledright, 2002) as well as on the elementary standards of the C3 Framework and ELA Common Core curriculum.

When Scott developed the *Hollywood or History?* strategy he knew that the inclusion of film in inquiry-based instruction would be just as effective for students in the elementary grades as it was in the secondary level. He has worked with several teachers, teacher candidates, and methods instructors over the years to make sure that those who worked with elementary level students had the same opportunities to critically analyze audio/visual media as those in the older grades (Pennington et al., 2024; Roberts et al., 2022; Roberts & Elfer, 2018; Roberts & Elfer, 2025; Van Haren & Roberts, 2021).

Both Starlynn and Scott agree that using film as a part of the C3 Inquiry Framework would be beneficial for elementary and secondary pre-service and practicing teachers. Teachers at the elementary level could incorporate film within language arts inquiries that would meet their standards but also bring in social studies content and more critical thinking. Secondary teachers could move away from passively showing a movie to introducing film clips as a part of the inquiry process allowing students to do history rather than be entertained. This book marries the C3 Inquiry Framework with the use of film (or documentaries, YouTube videos, instructional videos, cartoons, etc.) so teachers at the elementary and secondary levels can incorporate film in a productive manner as part of an inquiry strategy. It goes beyond standalone lessons using film by implementing sections or clips to enhance Dimensions 2 and 3. Students begin to analyze film and verify the historical story rather than being passive viewers of it. It is also important to focus on the major content areas identified in Dimension 2. Social studies classes usually have titles such as geography, economics, world history, etc. so this book demonstrates the major content areas through the elementary and secondary chapters. That focus was important to show all social studies teachers that they can create C3 Inquiry Framework units highlighting film no matter the subject area they are assigned.

Starlynn and Scott were adamant in bringing practicing teachers as contributors writing the chapters in the school year (2023–2024) prior to the publication of this book. Teacher and student voices are heard in each chapter and each teacher tells their story but also creates a unit for teachers to use in their classrooms. These teacher-made, classroom-ready units are written in the Inquiry Design Model (IDM) Framework template that is familiar to many teachers at all levels in public and private schools. In addition, we also acknowledge high school students are taking online courses and new technologies are being adapted to the classroom. In order to meet this style of learning, one chapter is written from an online high school teacher and two IDM units include enhancements for artificial intelligence.

Chapters 1 and 2 include an introduction about film, a brief explanation of C3, and how to implement film with the C3 Framework. Chapters 3 through 5 focus on elementary lessons while Chapters 6 through 8 focus on secondary lessons. All chapter IDMs can be found in Chapter 9 with additional film IDMs found in Chapter 10.

In Chapter 3, fifth-grade teacher Sean Boyle and special education professor Lori Boyle used a variety of YouTube clips about the development of the 13 British colonies to help students learn geography and history. In this inquiry-based lesson, students learn about the important geographic concepts that led to both Indigenous and colonial powers settling in these areas. Sean's students "took action" by developing their own colonies based on the four dimensions of the C3 Framework. In Chapter 4, third-grade student teacher Samantha Faivor describes how she based a civics lesson on the classic *School House Rock* favorite, "I'm Just a Bill." Using the cartoon as an activating activity, her students went through each Dimension of the C3 Framework to learn about the legislative process in the United States. They were able to "take action" by developing new laws for their own school. In Chapter 5, fourth- and fifth-grade teacher Kate Van Haren used the documentary *Spirit Game, Pride of a Nation*, and clips from YouTube to help students learn about the history of lacrosse and the significance of the sport to many Indigenous nations. More importantly, students learned about elements of tribal sovereignty through the story of the Haudenosaunee nation's pursuit of having its own lacrosse team in the 2028 Olympic Games. Kate's students "took action" by writing acrostic poems, and once the weather became better in Wisconsin, playing the game themselves.

For secondary, the teachers concentrated on world history, economics, and the social sciences with topics consisting of ancient China, World War II, and culture. In Chapter 6, Starlynn and Taylor Hawes-Guldenpfennig take a co-teaching approach to the Silk Road where students learn about trade, globalization, and culture in ancient times and compare it to what those concepts mean today. The students experience a firsthand account of sweat shop work in China through a teenager's eyes in the documentary *China Blue* (2005). This C3 inquiry takes the students on a journey from ancient China to the present that asks the students to answer the compelling question, "Does China make the world flat?" The IDM also includes an enhancement for artificial intelligence to converse with AI about current issues with sweat shops. Chapter 7 uses the lens of economics to evaluate home fronts during WWII. Using this different perspective, Cameron Pack compares and contrasts home fronts from an axis power and an allied power focusing on how policies (e.g., economic and propaganda) affected the war and the people. Cameron uses two films, produced during the time period, one by the British and the other by the Nazis, to teach how all aspects of the home front can affect the economy. Chapter 8 is written by Taylor Hawes-Guldenpfennig and is from her online sociology class. Her objective was to use a case study of Canadian residential schools to teach the concept of culture. This C3 inquiry was fully taught online and addressed all four dimensions. She also implemented the documentary film *We Were Children* (2012) into Dimension 3, comparing primary and secondary sources so students answer the compelling question, "Can you see the world through others' eyes?"

Using the C3 Framework with film can enhance the inquiry by giving visuals to students, allowing first-hand accounts to be heard, and determining fact from fiction. This addition to the C3 Framework is an exceptional example of how elementary and secondary teachers can move from traditional teaching to facilitating inquiry in the social studies classrooms.

Starlynn Nance
Scott L. Roberts

References

Au, W. (2009). Social studies, social justice: W(h)ither the social studies in high-stakes testing? *Teacher Education Quarterly, 36* (1), 43–58.

Diliberti, M. K, Woo, A., & Kaufman, J. H. (2023). *The missing infrastructure for elementary (K–5) social studies instruction: Findings from the 2022 American Instructional Resources Survey.* RAND Corporation. **www.rand.org/pubs/research_reports/RRA134-17.html**

Fitchett, P. G., & Heafner, T. L. (2010). A national perspective on the effects of high-stakes testing and standardization on elementary social studies marginalization. *Theory & Research in Social Education, 38* (1), 114–130.

Fitchett, P. G., Heafner, T. L., & Lambert, R. G. (2014a). Assessment, autonomy, and elementary social studies time. *Teachers College Record, 116* (10), 1–34.

Fitchett, P. G., Heafner, T. L., & Lambert, R. G. (2014b). Examining elementary social studies marginalization: A multilevel model. *Educational Policy, 28* (1), 40–68.

Heafner, T. L. (2018). More social studies? Examining instructional policies of time and testing in elementary schools. *The Journal of Social Studies Research, 42* (3), 229–237.

Levstik, L. S., & Barton, K. C. (2022). *Doing history: Investigating with children in elementary and middle schools* (6th ed.). Routledge.

Pace, J. L. (2012). Teaching literacy through social studies under No Child Left Behind. *Journal of Social Studies Research, 36* (4), 329–358.

Pennington, L. K., Fortune, D., Tackett, M. E., Horst, P. H., & Kessler, M.A. (2024). *Hollywood or history? An inquiry-based strategy for using film to teach salient social issues in elementary social studies.* Information Age Publishing.

Roberts, S. L., & Elfer, C. J. (2025). *Hollywood or History?: An inquiry-based strategy for using cartoons to teach topics in elementary and secondary social studies.* Information Age Publishing.

Roberts, S. L., & Elfer, C. J. (Eds.) (2018). *Hollywood or history? An inquiry-based strategy for using film to teach United States history.* Information Age Publishing.

Roberts, S. L., Wellenreiter, B., Ferreras-Stone, J., Strachan, S. L., & Palmer, K. L. (2022). *Teaching middle level social studies: A practical guide for 4th–8th grade* (3rd ed.). Information Age Publishing.

Tyner, A., & Kabourek, S. (2021). How social studies improves elementary literacy. *Social Education, 85* (1), 32–29.

Van Haren, K. & Roberts, S. L. (2021). Hollywood film and the C3 framework: An inquiry-based lesson about immigration. *Social Studies and the Young Learner, 34* (2), 10–13.

VanFossen, P. J. (2005). "Reading and math take so much of the time …": An overview of social studies instruction in elementary classrooms in Indiana. *Theory & Research in Social Education, 33* (3), 376–403.

VanFossen, P. J., & McGrew, C. (2008). Is the sky really falling?: An update on the status of social studies in the K–5 curriculum in Indiana. *International Journal of Social Education, 23* (1), 139–179.

VanSledright, B. (2002). *In search of America's past: Learning to read history in elementary school.* Teachers College Press.

Vogler, K. E., Lintner, T., Lipscomb, G. B., Knopf, H., Heafner, T. L., & Rock, T. C. (2007). Getting off the back burner: Impact of testing elementary social studies as part of a state-mandated accountability program. *Journal of Social Studies Research, 31*(2), 20–34.

Whitlock, A. M., & Brugar, K. A. (2019). Teaching elementary social studies during snack time and other unstructured spaces. *The Journal of Social Studies Research, 43* (3), 229–239.

Chapter 1

Introduction

Welcome to C3 and Film

Scott L. Roberts

The challenges of teaching and learning social studies are well documented in the social science education literature. For example, in the subject area of history, historical content is yearly multiplying and, over a period of time, decisions about what to emphasize become more and more opaque. In addition, social studies topics find themselves in competition with newer, more salient issues. Due to the political divide in the United States, battles over the social studies curriculum are often waged between various political ideologies all over the country (Dart, 2018; Hartman, 2017).

At the elementary level, social studies is being neglected with very little time being devoted to the subject. This is primarily due to the focus put on English/Language Arts and mathematics, a holdover from the No Child Left Behind and Common Core era. Though social studies courses such as American history, world history, geography, and government/civics are required at the middle and secondary level, they are still being taught using traditional and ineffective practices such as the sole use of textbooks, lecture, worksheets, or film with little evidence of inquiry-based practices (Roberts et al., 2022).

Thus, the rationale for the present text. For over a decade, Starlynn and I have practiced, researched, published, and presented on the effective use of Hollywood films and television programs in the social studies and history classroom. While classroom utility and teacher practice have remained our primary objectives in our work, we wanted to change the focus of this volume. Much of our prior work focused on allowing students to use inquiry-based practices to determine the accuracy of film based on evidence found in primary and secondary sources. While we discussed elements of the C3 Framework in the development of lesson plans focused on the use of film, in celebration of the 10th anniversary of the C3 Framework, first released in 2013, we wanted it to be the primary focus of the lesson plans in this book. In addition, we wanted K–12 social studies classroom teachers to develop lessons in this book that focus on the four primary disciplines of the social studies (i.e., civics, economics, geography, and history). We are encouraged by the possibilities and the capacity of this text to impact teaching of and learning about these disciplines using a popular form of visual media: film.

Problems and Possibilities of Using Film in the Social Studies Classroom

As we describe in our other publications, teaching and learning through Hollywood, or commercial, film productions is anything but a new strategy. In fact, it has been something of a mainstay in the American classroom for a century (Kaka, 2022; Nance, 2022; Roberts & Elfer, 2018, 2021; Yoder & Johnson, 2022). For example, Thomas Edison once forecast "that the motion picture projector might well replace the need for teachers and other instructional leaders" (Ball & Byrnes, 1960, p. 127). While Edison's predictions did not come to fruition, the use of film as a fixture in classrooms, especially social studies, is undeniable. Various research in the 20th century about the permanence of film in the K–12 classroom clearly attests to its importance and use (Dale & Ramseyer, 1937; Hoban & van Ormer, 1970; Horley, 1949; O'Connor & Jackson, 1974; Young, 1926).

Teaching with film in the social studies classroom has often been seen as a nearly fundamental instructional resource that classroom educators possess. For example, Russell (2012) reported, that in a study of social studies teachers' use of film, 100% claimed to use a movie at least once per month to teach content and concepts (p. 22). In another study, Marcus and Stoddard (2007) found that 71% of the high school social studies teachers surveyed used some portion of a Hollywood feature film in their classes at least "a few times a week" (p. 309). The expanded access to websites that many teachers have come to enjoy and rely upon (e.g., YouTube, TeacherTube) suggests that social studies educators may be using selected clips from commercial films in their teaching more often than ever before. This is due to the availability, ease of use, and the nature of the subject matter itself.

Not only is film a common pedagogical tool, but there is growing evidence to support its instructional value. For instance, in his guidebook for teachers of history and social studies, Russell (2007) highlights a number of possibilities which he believes characterize educational applications of film. Some of the beneficial attributes of film were the promotion of active viewership, higher order thinking skills, creative thought and inventiveness, and enhanced interest in historical figures and content (Russell, 2007, pp. 1–2). Others note that film has the special capacity to capture the student viewers' attention and to promote curiosity (Briley, 2002; Metzger, 2010; Roberts, 2014). Moreover, a number of scholars have commented on the applicability of film to the teaching of sensitive and critical social studies content. Russell (2012) has written that, within the domain of Holocaust education, the use of film to teach such critical and challenging historical subject matter holds as much utility and impact as guest speakers in the eyes of many educators (Donnelly, 2006). Similarly, Scheiner-Fischer and Russell (2012) argued that film is uniquely well-suited to the task of promoting gender equity in history and social studies instruction. In addition, Buchanan's (2015) work with pre-service social studies teachers suggests that film, particularly documentary film, offers new and meaningful avenues for teaching about the Civil Rights Movement at the elementary level.

Purposeful and effective instruction through film is not problem-free. There are many challenges that go with the classroom use of motion pictures. One of the most significant and well-documented obstacles surrounding the use of feature films in the classroom is that they reflect bias of the director or studio and are often unreliable sources of historical, geographical, and cultural information (Afflerbach & VanSledright, 2001; Metzger, 2010; Roberts & Elfer, 2018; Seixas, 1993; Wineburg et al., 2001). Films contain inaccuracies, biases, and misrepresentations about the topic(s) portrayed, a feature that is perhaps inextricable and inherent. Illustrations of this reality are evidenced in recent Hollywood films such as *Oppenheimer* (2023) and *Napoleon* (2023). Given these inaccuracies, simply showing films to students without any sort of structured activity or rationale limits students' opportunities to develop sound understanding of the topics under study. More importantly, even in those instances where students are generally informed about the inaccuracies present within a given film before or after viewing it, if not provided with opportunities to critically evaluate, reflect, and engage with the content of the film directly, the exercise remains passive. These types of lessons generally limit the potential for deeper content understanding and skill development (Marcus et al., 2018; Metzger, 2010).

Why This Book?

In response to the limitations associated with teaching through film, we sought to develop practical lesson ideas that might bridge gaps between theory and practice and assist teachers endeavoring to make effective use of film in their classrooms, especially lesson plans that meet the four dimensions of the C3 Framework. These lesson plans offer step-by-step instructions and, though focused on a specific grade level, can be adapted for a variety.

Films can also serve as a powerful tool in the social studies classroom and, if appropriately utilized, can foster critical thinking and civic mindedness. The College, Career, and Civic Life (C3) Framework, adopted by the National Council for the Social Studies in 2013, represents a renewed and formalized emphasis on the perennial social studies goals of deep thinking, reading, and writing. It should be noted that the C3 Framework is comprehensive and ambitious. However, we believe that as teachers endeavor to digest and implement the platform in schools and classrooms across the country, the desire for access to structured strategies that lead to more active and rigorous investigation in the social studies classroom will grow increasingly acute. Our hope is that the present volume might play a small role in the larger literature of supporting practitioners, specifically teachers of PreK–12 social studies disciplines, by offering a collection of classroom-ready lessons designed to foster social studies inquiry through the careful use of selected films.

References

Afflerbach, P., & VanSledright, B. (2001). Hath! Doth! What? Middle graders reading innovative history text. *Journal of Adolescent and Adult Literacy, 44* (8), 696–707.

Ball, J., & Byrnes, F.C. (Eds.). (1960). *Research, principles, and practices in visual communications.* National Association of State Universities and Land Grant Colleges.

Briley, R. (2002). Teaching film and history. *OAH Magazine of History, 16* (4), 3–4.

Buchanan, L. B. (2015). Fostering historical thinking toward the civil rights movement counter-narratives: Documentary film in elementary social studies. *The Social Studies, 106* (2), 47–56.

Dale, E., & Ramseyer, L. L. (1937). Teaching with motion pictures: A handbook of administrative practices. American Council on Education.

Dart, T. (2018, September 19). Classrooms: The latest battleground in Texas's culture wars. *The Guardian.* www.theguardian.com/us-news/2018/sep/19/ted-cruz-texas-board-of-education-curriculum-hillary-clinton

Donnelly, M. (2006). Educating students about the Holocaust: A survey of teaching practices. *Social Education, 70* (1), 51–54

Hartman, A. (2017, September 5). How the culture wars destroyed public education. *The Washington Post.* www.washingtonpost.com/news/made-by-history/wp/2017/09/05/how-the-culture-wars-destroyed-public-education/

Hoban, C. F., Jr., & van Ormer, E. B. (1970). *Instructional film research, 1918–1950.* Arno Press.

Horley, H. D. (1949). *The efficacy of motion pictures in teaching of Geography* (UMI No. EP55504) [Master's Thesis, University of Southern California]. ProQuest Dissertations and Theses Global.

Kaka, S. J. (Ed.). (2022). *Hollywood or history? An inquiry-based strategy for using film to teach about inequality and inequity throughout history.* Information Age.

Marcus, A. S., Metzger, S. A., Paxton, R. J., & Stoddard, J. D. (2018). *Teaching history with film: Strategies for secondary social studies* (2nd ed.). Taylor and Francis.

Marcus, A. S., & Stoddard, J. D. (2007). Tinsel Town as teacher: Hollywood film in the high school classroom. *The History Teacher, 40* (3), 303–330.

Metzger, S. A. (2010). Maximizing the educational power of history movies in the classroom. *The Social Studies, 101* (3), 127–136.

Nance, S. R. (2022). *Hollywood or history? An inquiry-based strategy for using television shows to teach issue-centered curriculum.* Information Age.

National Council for the Social Studies. (2013). *Social studies for the next generation: Purposes, practices, and implications of the college, career, and civic life (C3) framework for social studies state standards.*

O'Connor, J. E., & Jackson, M. A. (1974). *Teaching history with film.* American Historical Association.

Roberts, S. L. (2014). Effectively using social studies textbooks in historical inquiry. *Social Studies Research and Practice, 9*(1), 119–128.

Roberts, S. L., & Elfer, C. J. (2018). *Hollywood or history? An inquiry-based strategy for using film to teach United States history.* Information Age.

Roberts, S. L., & Elfer, C. J. (2021). *Hollywood or history? An inquiry-based strategy for using film to teach world history.* Information Age.

Roberts, S. L., Wellenreiter, B. R., Ferreras-Stone, J., Strachan, S. L., & Palmer, K. L. (2022). *Teaching middle level social studies: A practical guide for 4th–8th grade* (3rd ed.). Information Age.

Russell, W. B., III. (2007). *Using film in the social studies.* University Press of America.

Russell, W. B., III. (2012). The reel history of the world: Teaching world history with major motion pictures. *Social Education, 76* (1), 22–28.

Scheiner-Fisher, C., & Russell, W. B., III. (2012). Using historical films to promote gender equity in the history curriculum. *The Social Studies, 103* (6), 221–225.

Seixas, P. (1993). Popular film and young people's understanding of the history of Native American-White relations. *The History Teacher, 26* (3), 351–370.

Wineburg, S., Mosborg, S., & Porat, D. (2001). What can Forrest Gump tell us about students' historical understanding? *Social Education, 65* (1), 55–58.

Yoder, P. J., & Johnson, A. (2022). *Hollywood or history? An inquiry-based strategy for using film to acknowledge trauma in social studies.* Information Age.

Young, A. L. (1926). Teaching with motion pictures. *The Peabody Journal of Education, 3* (6), 321–326.

Chapter 2

C3 Inquiry, Film, and Applying Disciplinary Concepts and Tools

Starlynn Nance

As Scott mentioned in the introduction, we wanted to celebrate the 10th anniversary of the C3 Framework by creating a book that includes film as an integrated part of the C3 inquiry rather than a suggestion. In addition, it is also important that the inquiries presented in each chapter were created and taught by practicing teachers in elementary and secondary classrooms (in the 2023–2024 school year). The teachers' chapters are narratives that explore the implementation of a film-centered C3 inquiry and also highlight student voices and experiences. The chapters discuss all four dimensions, and each contributor created a classroom-ready Inquiry Design Model (IDM) for immediate use that corresponds to their chapter. This is a wonderful addition, but we also wanted our readers to have a chapter to return to, as a guide, to create film-centered inquiries that correlate with the individual teacher's curriculum. In this chapter, I will briefly explain the C3 Framework, describe the "Disciplinary Concepts and Tools" for the inquiry (Dimension 2), and suggest a "how-to" guide to create classroom inquiries with film.

The purpose of the C3 Framework is to help guide states in the preparation of students for college, career, and civic life and to expose students to "informed inquiry" (National Council for the Social Studies [NCSS], 2013, p. 17). Collectively, the four dimensions connect and encourage more reading and writing and to fully incorporate inquiry and literacy skills (content and disciplinary) in elementary and secondary social studies classes. Although the dimensions work together, Dimension 1, Developing Questions and Planning Inquiries, guides students in using supporting and compelling questions from the specific discipline to understand the content (facts, concepts, and generalizations). Dimension 2, Applying Disciplinary Concepts and Tools, is divided into core disciplines (i.e., history, civics, geography, and economics) and subsections to organize, think, and question that curricular knowledge. Students use a variety of content and skills from the specific discipline (curricular content) to decide what to use when answering the compelling question. Dimension 3, Evaluating Sources and Using Evidence, allows students to use skills to gather, analyze, and evaluate sources to use as evidence to support their claims or counterclaims in the final product. Dimension 4,

Communicating Conclusions and Taking Informed Action, moves the student to take informed action on public issues and develop citizenship skills as they implement their plan of action.

Incorporating all four dimensions in the social studies classroom can be an easy transition as shown in Chapters 3–8. Collectively, these chapters focus on the four core disciplinary subjects with the addition of world history and a social science. Our goal was to show teachers from elementary and secondary grade levels that it does not matter what grade or subject you teach; the C3 Framework can be used to develop inquiries that are film centered.

As teachers create C3 inquiries, they may notice that Dimension 2 is unique in its structure. This dimension has "an additional layer of three to four categories within each discipline subsection… [which] provide an organizing mechanism for the foundational content and skills" (NCSS, pp. 13–14). An example of history using the subsections comes from an NCSS professional development webinar by Elaine Carey (2015). Her presentation, *Teaching and Learning Like a Historian: The C3's Dimension 2*, emphasizes how this dimension is used to "organize knowledge" and use *what, why, where, when, who,* and *how* questions to develop historical skills using the content from the course. She stresses that it is important for students to realize where evidence (content) originates as they begin to develop claims and counterclaims and to answer supporting and compelling questions. Understanding curricular content knowledge is important but as students engage in more curricular and conceptual content, they develop skills such as chronological reasoning, perspective taking, and sourcing skills. She notes that teachers and students should "gather information from a wide array of sources and to ask questions of that evidence, whether it's documents, images, film, literature, or material culture" and begin to "consider the significance of the evidence and to form interpretations of the past that are relevant not only to understanding the past but understanding the present" (Carey, 2015, 38:40–38:58). Students need to grasp that history is an interpretation and argument not a description (Carey, 2015). Carey (2015) informs the audience that through this dimension students are seeing and understanding historical events through the subsections of (a) change, continuity, and context; (b) perspectives; (c) historical sources and evidence; and (d) causation and argumentation. During this professional development webinar, Carey was joined by other professionals who discussed the remaining three core disciplines.

As Carey mentions, film (see Chapter 1 for a description of the term "film" as used in this book) is a way to gather information about specific content, topics, or concepts. Each teacher-contributor produced a chapter that was specifically designed to use film and one of the four core disciplines to present real-life examples and experiences as an encouragement to all teachers to try a film-centered C3 inquiry in their classroom. However, sometimes it is easier to have a guide along with their real-life examples. The following is a suggested guide that can assist pre-service, beginning, and seasoned teachers to incorporate film-centered C3 inquiries in the classroom. This chapter will highlight the IDM format (C3 Teachers, n.d.) for continuity.

For this example, I describe the elements of the IDM for each of the four dimensions so teachers can think about them individually and then collectively (see Table 2.1).

Table 2.1 *Film-Centered Guide*

Dimension	Compelling Question	Supporting Questions	Formative Performance Tasks	Featured Sources	Summative Performance Task and Taking Informed Action
Dimension 1	Introduce the compelling question by staging the question as a "hook."				
Dimension 2	Use the compelling question as an exit ticket after the last formative performance task in Dimensions 1, 2, and 3.	Create supporting questions from daily objectives. Show film and/or relevant film clips.	Create formative tasks for students to assess knowledge of the supporting questions or daily objectives.	Use featured sources to answer the supporting question (e.g., specific clips in the film or a secondary source to annotate, source, and analyze). Sources are examples of the conceptual C3 Framework Indicators (NCSS, 2013).	
Dimension 3	Begin the class by reviewing the compelling question.	Create supporting questions from daily objectives, historical thinking skills, and the C3 Framework Indicators.	Create formative tasks for students to assess knowledge of the supporting questions or daily objectives (usually by using primary sources.)	Gather balanced primary sources.	After the lessons are completed, have the students answer the compelling question as an authentic assessment (e.g., P.E.E.L. paragraph).
Dimension 4 (Student Led, Teacher Facilitated) (Teachers *do not* create Formative or Summative Tasks during Dimension 4.)	Ask the students to compare the unit with current events in the community that need action. Ask the students to create their own compelling question about the topic chosen.	Have the students create supporting questions and answer the questions posed.	Have the students create an action proposal from the research.	Have the students create a bibliography of the sources used to answer the student-created supporting and compelling questions.	Have the students present the action plan and outcomes of its implementation to the appropriate audience (e.g., school board, city council members, etc.).

Before beginning the C3 inquiry, teachers should choose and watch the film to determine if it is an appropriate featured source for students to analyze. Teachers may ask themselves the following questions: Does it fit with the inquiry? Do the appropriate clips pique interest, meet standards, help answer the supporting and compelling questions, encourage critical literacy, and allow students to question the writer and director? Do the clips enhance curricular and conceptual (subsections of Dimension 2) content? Can the clips be verified or refuted by primary sources? These are some major considerations when choosing a film for the inquiry.

After the film has been chosen and vetted, the teacher will create the compelling question and develop Dimension 1 (or the "Staging the Question" section on the IDM blueprint). In Dimension 1, the goal is to get the students' attention on the topic and to introduce the compelling question. "Staging the Question" should develop an atmosphere for inquiry rather than just asking a question for a Teacher Talk. Create an engaging activity such as gamification, analyzing a music video, or acting out parts of a play (Nance, 2021, 2022; Swan et al. 2018a) to pique interest. Complete the activity and introduce the compelling question as an exit ticket to gauge students' knowledge and interest.

Moving into Dimension 2, collect the objectives for the required standards (curricular content) and the C3 Indicators (conceptual content). Use these two types of content to develop your supporting questions for each dimension (2–4). Dimensions can have a different number of supporting questions as deemed necessary by the teacher and by the chosen and/or required curriculum. The formative performance task assesses the students' grasp of the objectives (or supporting questions). Formative performance tasks could include creating a map, a simulation, centers, graphic organizer, answering content questions in collaborative groups, or annotating a secondary source. Coupled with the formative performance task are the featured sources. Students use the featured sources to answer the supporting questions and to begin developing claims and counterclaims with this evidence for the compelling question. Repeat this process, mostly using primary sources, as featured sources in Dimension 3.

Dimension 4 Indicators are especially helpful for getting students to move outside the classroom and practice citizenship skills (see D4.3.9–12, D4.6.9–12, D4.7.9–12, and D4.8.9–12 Indicators). The overview graphic in Table 2.1 is one option for Dimension 4 that brings curricular and conceptual content from the past to the present. This encourages a student-centered, student-driven action plan that is communicated to the appropriate audience and implemented by the students.

As Swan et al. (2018b) state, "teachers teach best the material that they mold around the needs of their particular students and the contexts in which they teach" (p. 5). This book—*The C3 Framework and Film: Bringing Hollywood to the Social Studies Classroom as a Catalyst for Teaching Inquiry*—aims to meet that expectation for teachers in the social studies classroom. By adding to the growing resources of the C3 Framework from the National Council for the Social Studies, state councils, and other teaching professionals, this book hopes to assist teachers in bringing the C3 inquiry alive for students. When film is taught in an academic fashion, rather than as an afterthought or filler of time, it can be an effective addition to inquiry and developing critical thinking skills (Roberts & Elfer, 2018). Using this text will hopefully embolden elementary and secondary teachers to "draw on their own wealth of teaching experience as they add activities, lessons, sources, and tasks that transform the inquiries into their own, individual pedagogical plans" (Swan et al., 2018b, p. 5)

References

C3 Teachers. (n.d.). *The inquiry design model.* https://c3teachers.org/inquiry-design-model/

Carey, E. (2015). Teaching and learning like a historian The C3's dimension 2. In P. Levine, P. VanFossen, J. Hauf, & E. Carey, *Dimension 2: Applying Disciplinary Concepts and Tools* [Webinar]. National Council for the Social Studies. **www.socialstudies.org/resources/dimension-2-applying-disciplinary-concepts-and-tools**

Nance, S. R. (2021). How to C3 series: Part I. *Oregon Journal of Social Studies 9* (2), 4–10.

Nance, S. R. (2022). *Hollywood or history? An inquiry-based strategy for using television shows to teach issue-centered curriculum.* Information Age.

National Council for the Social Studies. (2013). *College, Career, and Civic Life (C3) Framework for Social Studies State Standards: Guidance for Enhancing the Rigor of K-12 Civics, Economics, Geography, and History.* **www.socialstudies.org/c3**

Roberts, S. L., & Elfer, C. (2018). *Hollywood or history? An inquiry-based strategy for using film to teach United States history.* Information Age.

Swan, K., Lee, J., & Grant, S. G. (2018a). *Inquiry design model: Building inquiries in social studies.* National Council for the Social Studies; C3 Teachers.

Swan, K., Lee, J., & Grant, S. G. (2018b). *Teaching the college, career, and civic life (C3) framework: Part two.* National Council for the Social Studies.

Chapter 3

Elementary Teachers' Experience With Using the C3 Dimensions With Geography and Film

How Did Geography Contribute to the Differences in Early American Colonies?

Sean Boyle and Lori Boyle

In fifth grade, students are beginning to explore their place in the world, both geographically and conceptually. They understand their home in relation to their community and school, and some may know where their community fits within their state. A few students may even grasp their state's place within the country, and a couple may understand how their country fits into the global landscape. An exploratory unit in geography aligns with elementary social studies standards focused on the history of Native Americans and North American/United States colonization (see Table 3.1). Asking the question "How did geography contribute to the differences in early American colonies?" provides a foundation for understanding geographical concepts, such as settlement decisions, the use of local natural resources, and geographical patterns influencing individuals and communities. Through exploring these concepts, students develop an appreciation for the factors influencing survival and success in different environments.

Overview of the Lessons: How Did Geography Contribute to the Differences in Early American Colonies?

The evolving social studies standards in elementary education are especially evident in the upper grades (grades 4–5). The curriculum has shifted from basic concepts such as community principles, landforms, and local history to applying these concepts in the broader context of historical places and peoples. In fifth grade, students are enthusiastic to showcase their knowledge but also seek deeper insights into the significance of their learning. Although they might not explicitly ask, "Why does this matter?" addressing this question from the outset is crucial to maintaining their engagement and curiosity throughout the unit.

This lesson is designed to start and end with a hands-on simulation, aided by the use of YouTube videos, engaging students in the challenge of determining where to establish a settlement.

Dimension 1 introduces students to the task with minimal prior knowledge about the factors essential for survival and success. Through interactive discussions and activities, students are introduced to key terminology and explore the benefits and resources needed for a viable settlement.

Dimension 2 broadens their understanding by providing historical context about the land before colonial settlement. Students learn about the resources each region offered, the ways Native Americans utilized these resources, and the environmental factors they considered for their livelihoods before European colonization.

Dimension 3 delves deeper into the relationships between early settlers and Native Americans, highlighting the distinctions among the three regions of the 13 colonies. This dimension focuses on understanding how natural boundaries influenced settlement patterns. Students engage with a video that examines the success of settlements based on their geographical interactions and explore which of these settlements continue to thrive today.

To consolidate their learning, students create an edible map using chocolate chips for mountain ranges, licorice for rivers, and M&Ms for landmarks, allowing them to visualize and digest the knowledge they have acquired.

Dimension 4 revisits the initial simulation, challenging students to apply their enhanced understanding to determine the most suitable location for a long-term successful settlement on a map. They utilize the insights gained throughout the lesson to create a map of an imaginary settlement, demonstrating their comprehension of the essential elements for sustainable and successful settlements.

By engaging students in an inquiry-based and experiential learning process, this lesson not only answers the implicit question of why their learning matters but also empowers them to apply historical principles to practical and imaginative scenarios (see Table 3.2).

Dimension 1: Developing Questions and Planning Inquiries

To set the stage for our lesson, I (Sean) engaged my fifth-grade class with an interactive simulation game from the Michigan Social Studies Hub (Michigan Department of Education, n.d.). This platform offers simulations aligned with grade-level standards, designed to make social studies both engaging and informative. I chose the "Where should we locate our colonial town?" game for grades 5–6, which challenges students to evaluate geographic conditions and connections crucial to early American settlement.

I launched the game on our interactive whiteboard, allowing the entire class to participate collaboratively. As the game introduced the historical context—settling a new colonial town a century after Columbus's voyages—students were immediately curious about the factors influencing settlement decisions. I heard questions and comments like "Did they just settle wherever the boat arrived?" "They need trees for their forts and houses" and "Did they look for places with trees to cut down and build?" When a snippet of a map appeared, highlighting features like waterways and land formations, the room buzzed with discussions about their importance.

In small groups, students eagerly debated the advantages and disadvantages of five potential locations for the new colonial town: "They need fresh water!" "Near the ocean is good for fish or to go back to England!" and "You can't farm on a beach!" The game provided practical details, such as the area's size (33 miles) and travel challenges through hilly terrain, sparking animated conversations about the significance of these conditions. Vocabulary terms like "conditions" (physical and human characteristics) and "connections" (routes and relationships with other places) were introduced, and students quickly connected these terms to their decision-making process.

As they "explored" via the game further, students discovered additional geographic features of each location—swamps, rivers, and cropland—and their potential impact on settlers' decisions. These revelations led to deeper group discussions about balancing favorable conditions with strategic connections. Visual aids, including photographs of each potential settlement, prompted students to reassess their choices. One group, initially inclined to settle near a large river for easy access to water, reconsidered after learning about the frequent flooding in that area.

Throughout the game, students experienced a series of "aha" moments. They began to realize that successful colonization required more than just finding a suitable spot for landing. They needed to think critically about long-term survival, considering how geography would influence everything from food sources to trade routes. One student remarked, "I never thought about how swamps could be both good and bad—good for protection, but bad for building homes!"

By the end of this first lesson, students were more aware of the complexities involved in early American settlement. They applied historical knowledge to real-world scenarios, enhancing their understanding of geographic influences on human settlement and survival. This immersive, interactive approach captivated students, sharpening their critical thinking skills and deepening their appreciation for the strategic decisions that shaped early American colonization.

Dimension 2: Applying Disciplinary Concepts and Tools

Building on foundational concepts from Dimension 1, Dimension 2 deepened students' understanding of geographical factors, climate considerations, and the existing communities of Native American people in the regions explored by British colonists for settlement.

To start, students examined maps highlighting mountain ranges and bodies of water across the 13 colonies. As they observed these features, students discussed how natural elements like rivers and mountains often served as boundaries and strategic points for trade routes and travel. "Look how the mountains create a barrier here; it's like a natural fort!" one student noted, highlighting their understanding of geographical "conditions" and "connections."

Next, students were divided into groups and provided with blank maps of the original 13 colonies. They watched the YouTube video *Colonial America: 3 Regions of Colonies—U.S. History for Kids*, which guided them to categorize the colonies into three distinct regions—Southern, New England, and

Table 3.1 *C3 Framework Dimensions Overview: Grade 5 Geography*

C3 Framework Dimension and Standard(s)	Description and Resources
Dimension 1 **D1.2.3-5.** Identify disciplinary concepts and ideas associated with a compelling question that are open to different interpretations. **D1.5.3-5.** Determine the kinds of sources that will be helpful in answering compelling and supporting questions, taking into consideration the different opinions people have about how to answer the questions.	In Dimension 1, students interact with a simulation game to elicit a curiosity about considerations for colony locations. They begin to realize that features of the land and resources needed impact the possibilities and opportunities for early settlers. *Where should we locate our...?* game (Michigan Department of Education, n.d.)
Dimension 2 **D2.Geo.4.3-5.** Explain how culture influences the way people modify and adapt to their environments. **D2.Geo.8.3-5.** Explain how human settlements and movements relate to the locations and use of various natural resources.	In Dimension 2, students interact with maps and watch YouTube videos to understand the 13 colonies as divided into three regions with different resources and motivations for settlements as well as the ways the Native Americans lived on those lands and utilized those resources. For maps, see Britannica (n.d.), Smithsonian National Museum of the American Indian (2018), & Education.com (n.d.). For videos, see Harmony Square (2019) and Miacademy Learning Channel (2024).
Dimension 3 **D3.1.3-5.** Gather relevant information from multiple sources while using the origin, structure, and context to guide the selection. **D3.3.3-5.** Identify evidence that draws information from multiple sources in response to compelling questions.	In Dimension 3, students further explore the settlement and development of the three regions and the ways that geography and topography aided in the governance of cooperation of the colonies to eventually form a new nation. They create edible maps that show mountains, rivers, and landmark settlements. Appalachian Mountains media (Britannica, n.d.) Comparing colonies video (Civics Review, 2022) *The edible United States* lesson plan (A. W. Creations, 2019)
Dimension 4 **D4.3.3-5.** Present a summary of arguments and explanations to others outside the classroom using print and oral technologies (e.g., posters, essays, letters, debates, speeches, and reports) and digital technologies (e.g., Internet, social media, and digital documentary). **D4.6.3-5.** Draw on disciplinary concepts to explain the challenges people have faced and opportunities they have created, in addressing local, regional, and global problems at various times and places.	In Dimension 4, the understanding of resources, climate, conditions, and connections becomes evident as students create maps of their own settlements, explaining what is needed for survival and success *Where should we locate our...?* game (Michigan Department of Education, n.d.).

Mid-Atlantic—based on their characteristics. As the video paused, students labeled their maps and engaged in lively discussions about the motivations of early settlers in Virginia and Plymouth: "It's all about the money" and "No, the Pilgrims were focused on religion."

While learning about the Southern region, students were intrigued by its fertile soil, warm climate, and abundant rivers, ideal for farming cash crops like tobacco, rice, indigo, and cotton. "I can see why they chose this area—everything they need for farming is right here!" remarked a student, grasping the appeal of the Southern region. Discussions also highlighted the emergence of communities for religious and political gatherings and the economic impact of the slave trade, leading one student to reflect, "Why did slavery became a part of their lives so quickly after settling … Why couldn't they just bring more workers from England?"

In exploring the New England region, students discovered the challenges posed by rocky, infertile land and harsh winters, which led settlers to focus on industries like fishing, lumber, and trade. The emphasis on education and religious principles in governance resonated with students. "No wonder they had to become good at fishing and trading; farming was so hard there," a student observed, connecting the region's geography to its economic activities. The video then introduced the Mid-Atlantic region, known for its diversity and economic opportunities facilitated by cities like Manhattan (now part of present-day New York City) and Philadelphia. Students discussed the cultivation of staple crops and the development of thriving trade industries. "This region seems like a good mix of farming and trade—probably why it was so busy," a student commented, linking the area's geographic and economic diversity. They also considered the complexities of relationships with Native Americans and European stakeholders, leading to questions like, "How did they manage so many different cultures in one place?"

Following this exploration of colonial regions, students examined a map of North America labeled with tribal locations while watching the YouTube video, *Comparing the Lives of Native Peoples | Learn About the History and Culture of Native Peoples* (Harmony Square, 2019). I provided them with Venn diagrams to explore similarities and differences across Native American cultures, focusing on Indigenous nations such as the Wampanoag and Powhatan within the regions settled by Europeans. "It's amazing how each tribe adapted differently to their environment," one student noted, as they filled in their diagrams.

Facilitated discussions underscored how prior knowledge of Native American nations informed their understanding of settlement locations, farming practices, migration patterns, and cultural focuses. Students reflected on the challenges and limited cooperation between colonists and Native Americans due to conflicting goals and approaches to land and resources. "It must have been really tough to get along when they saw land so differently," a student reflected, showing empathy towards the historical context.

By integrating geographical considerations and historical context, Dimension 2 of our lesson deepened students' awareness of how environmental factors and cultural dynamics shaped early American colonization. This interactive approach not only reinforced academic content but also fostered critical thinking and empathy toward diverse historical perspectives.

Dimension 3: Evaluating Sources and Using Evidence

In Dimension 3, students delved into how climate and weather influence the success of settlements, building on concepts from science lessons. I began this lesson with a Quick Write formative assessment where students responded to the prompt, "Describe how climate influenced the formation of colonies." As students wrote independently, they reflected on agricultural patterns, seasonal activities, and survival strategies tied to regional weather, drawing from key points in earlier Dimension 2 videos. "I think the colonies near rivers had an advantage because they could grow crops easily and get water," one student noted, connecting climate factors to settlement success.

Following this, I guided students through a slideshow to facilitate group activities. They created T-charts to analyze the advantages and disadvantages of colonists forming relationships with Native Americans during settlement. As students shared their thoughts with each other, they realized how knowledge of suitable crops, planting times, and local natural resources could help establish successful colonies. One student remarked, "Knowing when to plant crops would be so important. They probably learned a lot from the Native Americans." The discussion also highlighted potential threats, with another student observing, "If the Native Americans felt threatened, they might not have helped, and the colonists could have failed."

Next, the class watched the YouTube video *Comparing New England, Middle, and Southern British Colonies* (Civics Review, 2022), which categorizes the 13 colonies into three distinct regions, each with unique characteristics. Students took notes on the geographical features, climate, economy, religion, notable individuals, and governance of each region. After the video, a mini quiz assessed their understanding of industry development in each region, its evolution over time, and the relevance of geographic features in the modern world. "It's cool to see how some industries from back then are still important today," one student commented during the quiz.

To conclude, students revisited maps showing physical features such as mountains, rivers, and waterways, examining colonial settlement locations in relation to these features. They discussed the advantages of proximity to natural features, such as their roles as boundaries, trade routes, and resources for industry. "Being close to a river would make it easier to trade and get supplies," a student noted, recognizing the strategic importance of waterways. In pairs, students created edible maps of the United States using dough and candy to represent mountain ranges (chocolate chips), rivers (licorice strands), lakes (blue frosting), and major cities (M&Ms). This hands-on activity deepened their understanding of the relationship between waterways, major settlements, and regional boundaries. "I never thought about how rivers connect different places—sometimes it is hard to see the rivers on a map, but this makes it easy to see how they are connected," one student reflected while placing licorice strands on their map.

Dimension 4: Communicating Conclusions and Taking Informed Action

In Dimension 4, the lesson culminated by revisiting and expanding upon concepts from Dimension 1. Based on the topic of study, I decided that it would be best for my students to "take action" inside the walls of the classroom. The session began with a collaborative activity during which the students and I created a list of important geographical features they had explored and the key factors to consider when selecting sites for settlement or developing new communities. Students contributed enthusiastically to the discussion. "Don't forget rivers—they're important for water and trade," one student suggested. Another added, "Mountains can be good for protection, but they might make it harder to travel." These insights set the stage for the day's activities.

Building on the discussion, I reintroduced the "Where Should We Locate Our Colonial Town?" simulation game from Dimension 1. This time, students applied their new understanding of settlement success and failure to make more informed decisions about the best locations for establishing new communities. As they engaged with the game, students debated their choices. "I think we should pick a location with a river for easy access to water and trade routes," one group decided. Another group focused on resources: "We need to be close to forests for building materials and hunting."

I then presented a brief PowerPoint presentation on the four essential components of a map: title, compass, key or legend, and scale. This provided the foundation for the students' final project. "A title to tell you what the map is about, a compass shows direction, and a scale shows distance," a student clarified, demonstrating their understanding.

For the culminating activity, students created maps of hypothetical new settlements. They were encouraged to design unique locations that highlight various geographical features and resources of the surrounding areas, rather than using existing locations. As students drew, colored, and labeled their maps, I circulated the room, engaging them in discussions about their choices (see Figure 3.1).

Figure 3.1 *Students Drawing, Coloring, and Labeling Maps*

During these interactions, I prompted students to think critically about their resources for water and food, nearby land formations, the extent of the area their map covered, and the climate or region of their settlement. "Why did you choose to put your settlement near the mountains?" I asked one student, who replied, "for protection and because we can get wood from the forests there." Another student was questioned about their water source: "I placed my settlement by a lake because it provides water and fish."

Students were reminded to incorporate the four essential map components—title, compass, key or legend, and scale—into their designs (see Figure 3.2). "Remember to add a scale so we know how far things are apart," a student reminded their group, reflecting the day's lesson.

Table 3.2 *Lessons Overview: Grade 5 Geography*

Dimension and Lesson	Description and Time Required
Dimension 1, Lesson 1 Where Should We Settle?	In the first lesson of Dimension 1, students are introduced to the compelling question for this unit, "How did geography contribute to the differences in early American colonies?" The teacher will lead the whole class through an online simulation game (Michigan Department of Education, n.d.). Students will interact in small groups to decide on plausible successful settlement locations (20 minutes). Students are introduced to the vocabulary terms "conditions" and "connections" and sort geographical features under these two terms (20 minutes).
Dimension 2, Lesson 1 Mapping the Terrain: Key Geographical Features of the 13 Colonies	This lesson starts with response to the question "What were major geographical features of the 13 colonies?" (5 minutes). While looking at a projected map, students focus on mountain ranges and bodies of water (rivers, lakes, etc.) followed by a Think-Pair-Share discussion (5 minutes).
Dimension 2, Lesson 2 Consider the Climate Differences	In this lesson, students have mini whiteboards and a blank map of the 13 colonies. While watching YouTube video *Colonial America: 3 Regions of Colonies – US History for Kids* (Mi-academy Learning Channel, 2024), the teacher will pause the video when the narrator asks questions about how climate would affect colonization. Students discuss their responses in groups and write responses on their white board. Students divide their maps into three distinct regions and make connections about the differences in the focus of the settlers from region to region (40 min).
Dimension 2, Lesson 3 First Americans	Students are given a map of where the Indigenous nations lived in the US and a blank Venn diagram. While watching the YouTube video, *Comparing the Lives of Native Peoples	Learn about the history and culture of Native Peoples* (Harmony Square, 2019), students make notations about similarities and differences among the nations (45 min). As an extension of the previous lesson, the teacher then leads a classroom discussion about how the nations in each region could have influenced or assisted the colonists (30 min).
Dimension 3, Lesson 1 Building a Nation	This lesson continues the conversation about the challenges of relationships between the Native Americans and the colonists. Using a T-chart labeled "Positive Outcomes" and "Negative Consequences," students consider not only how Native Americans assisted the colonists in utilizing the natural resources of the regions but also how the arrival and settlement efforts of the colonists were a threat to Native Americans (40 min).
Dimension 3, Lesson 2 Centers of Industry	In this lesson, the students watch the YouTube video, *Comparing New England, Middle, and Southern British Colonies* (Civics Review, 2022). The teacher will pause between narrated descriptions of each region and facilitate further exploration and conversation about how the colonists began building economies around industries that utilized the geographic features and resources of each region (30 min). If time allows, students and teacher can research and discuss if those industries still exist in those areas or regions today (20 min).
Dimension 3, Lesson 3 Water is Life	In this last lesson for this dimension, students get to interact in a multisensory activity. First, students will look again at a map of the 13 colonies, this time focusing on the physical features (especially the mountains, rivers, and lakes). (10 minutes) Then, students are paired up (or put into small groups) and given edible dough, licorice, chocolate chips, and M&Ms to create their own maps of the US. This allows students to demonstrate their awareness of the proximity of landmarks and cities to bodies of water and the ways that mountain ranges and rivers can create natural boundaries (30 minutes).

Dimension 4, Lesson 1 What Do We Need?	This lesson is an opportunity for the teacher to informally assess what students have learned or what may need to be retaught or reviewed. In groups, students will make a list of geographic features that are desirable for settlers (10 minutes). The teacher then revisits the simulation game from Dimension 1, having students play again, with new insights into conditions and connections to be aware of, and determine if they would select a different location than they did the first time they played the game (20 min).
Dimension 4, Lesson 2 The Perfect Place to Settle	The summative task for this unit begins with a teacher presentation about four needed parts of a map (title, compass, key or legend, and scale). (12 min) Students are then given blank sheets of white paper and instructed to create a map of their perfect settlement location with the desirable geographic features and the four needed parts of a map. On the back, students write a narrative description of their settlement, its resources, and geographic features (40 min).

Figure 3.2 *Student Maps*

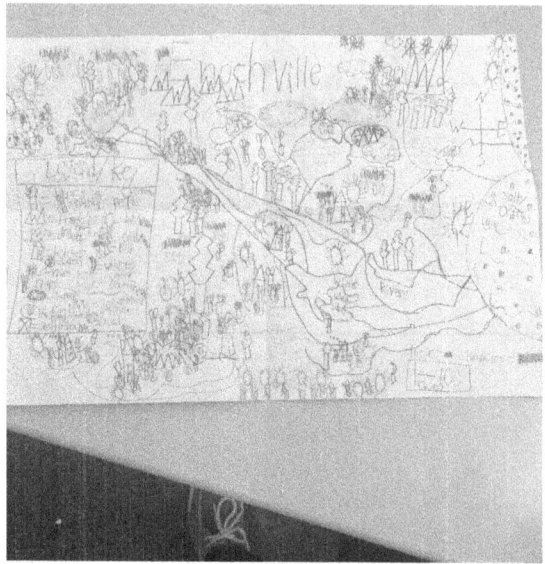

Upon completing their maps, students wrote summaries on the back, explaining their decision-making processes and detailing what their settlements had to offer. This reflective writing allowed them to articulate the reasoning behind their choices and to demonstrate their understanding of the geographic, economic, and climatic factors influencing successful settlements. "We chose this location because it has a river for water and transport and fertile land for growing crops," one student wrote, showing a comprehensive grasp of the factors involved (see Figure 3.3).

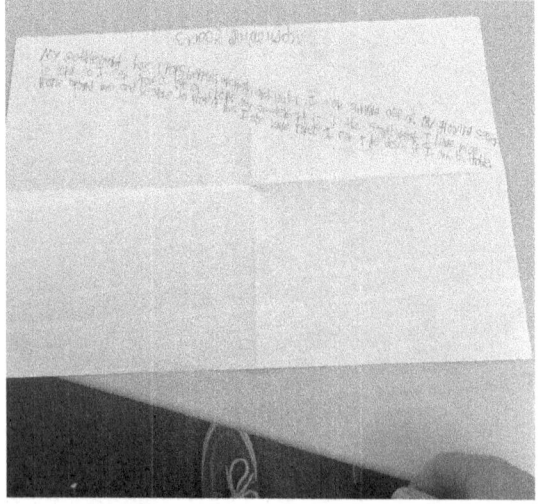

Figure 3.3 *Reflective Writing for Map in Figure 3.2*

Final Comments

This lesson effectively employed the C3 Framework's Inquiry Design Model to deepen students' understanding of settlement considerations, but it also revealed challenges in keeping students focused. The interactive simulations and engaging map activities were instrumental in exploring how geographical features and resources impact settlement success, though some students were more inclined to play with the simulation rather than engage with its learning aspects. To address this, it would be helpful to break up the videos into shorter clips to maintain attention spans, ensuring key points are emphasized effectively. Additionally, while creating edible maps was an enjoyable hands-on activity, it sometimes led to creative liberties that strayed from the lesson's objectives. Despite these challenges, this multifaceted approach successfully fostered a comprehensive sense of place and spatial awareness, illustrating the enduring relevance of geographic influences across different time periods.

References

A. W. Creations. (2019). *Social studies lesson plan: The edible United States.* Teachers Pay Teachers. www.teacherspayteachers.com/Product/Social-Studies-Lesson-Plan-The-Edible-United-States-4339694

Britannica. (n.d.). *Appalachian Mountains: Media.* www.britannica.com/place/Appalachian-Mountains/images-videos

Civics Review. (2022, November 9). *Comparing New England, Middle, and the Southern British colonies* [Video]. YouTube. www.youtube.com/watch?v=D_MUtWssRJE

Education.com. (n.d.). *The thirteen colonies.* www.education.com/worksheet/article/13-colonies/

Harmony Square—Educational Videos and Activities. (2019, October 9). *Comparing the lives of Native Peoples: Learn about the history and culture of Native Peoples* [Video]. YouTube. www.youtube.com/watch?v=NErXRVfm1uU

Miacademy Learning Channel. (2024, December 6). *Colonial America: 3 regions of colonies—U.S. history for kids* [Video]. YouTube. www.youtube.com/watch?v=7PXnraFcTnM

Michigan Department of Education. (n.d.). *Where should we locate our...?* www.misocialstudies.org/locationsimulations.html

National Council for the Social Studies. (2013). *The college, career, and civic life (C3) framework for social studies state standards: Guidance for enhancing the rigor of K–12 civics, economics, geography, and history.*

Smithsonian National Museum of the American Indian. (2018). *Northern Plains treaties: Is a treaty intended to be forever?* Native Knowledge 360° https://americanindian.si.edu/nk360/plains-treaties

Chapter 4

Elementary Teacher's Experience With Using the C3 Dimensions With Civics and Film

Rock the House: Learning Legislation

Samantha Faivor

At the onset of this lesson, third-grade students grappled with a deceptively simple question: "How can we make a difference in our community?" Their initial responses, while heartfelt, reflected a surface-level understanding of civic engagement—be kind, help each other, clean up litter, volunteer. However, as we began working with the C3 Framework, metamorphic thinking occurred. With each lesson, students underwent a great transformation, evolving from passive observers to active participants in the democratic process. Take, for instance, one typically reserved student who did not often show enthusiasm for school. However, through this project, the student demonstrated remarkable involvement, leading group discussions, producing and conveying new ideas, and debating what they felt was important. The student even expressed to their parents how excited they were to come to school and work on this project, which the parents were kind enough to share with me. In this lesson, students began to recognize the power of their voice and the importance of advocating for change.

    This comprehensive approach in civics education allowed students to see themselves as critical contributors to public discourse and action. They learned that their engagement could extend beyond traditional activities and include more dynamic interactions, such as drafting legislation or leading community initiatives. Through the curriculum, they discovered that "civics is not limited to the study of politics and society; it also encompasses [active] participation" within their communities (National Council for the Social Studies [NCSS], 2013, p. 31). For example, students could organize food drives, "adopt" families in need during the holiday season, or make blankets for a baby pantry or animal shelter. Additionally, students could create campaigns to raise awareness about important issues, like pollution and water conservation, or collaborate with local businesses to develop initiatives that benefit the community, such as creating a community garden. Students practiced "discussing issues and making choices and judgments with information and evidence," by engaging in structured debates, participating in mock legislative sessions, and collaborating in small groups to research and present their findings (NCSS, 2013, p. 31). This approach enabled students to advocate for school improvement initiatives they felt passionate about, such as enhancing playground facilities (a crowd favorite), improving technology schoolwide, creating outdoor learning spaces, and implementing an additional enrichment class focused on coding and robotics. This shift from simple community tasks to impactful civic action demonstrates the transformative power of civic studies, preparing students not only to understand the mechanisms of government and society but also to participate meaningfully and effectively, ensuring they are ready to take informed actions that contribute positively to their communities (Roberts et al., 2022).

Overview of the Lessons:
How Can We Make a Difference in Our Community?

Teaching civics in the middle grades is crucial as it introduces students to fundamental concepts of citizenship, governance, and community roles. At this developmental stage, students are increasingly capable of understanding societal structures and can begin to form their own opinions about personal responsibility and the common good. Introducing civics education at this point fosters a sense of civic duty and awareness that is hoped to encourage lifelong participation in the democratic process.

To engage students effectively, the Inquiry Design Model (IDM) unit incorporates a blend of literature supports, educational videos, and simulation activities. The video segment "I'm Just a Bill" from *Schoolhouse Rock* plays a foundational role by vividly illustrating the journey of a bill becoming a law (Schoolhouse Rock, 1976/2014). The use of film aided in making abstract concepts tangible and accessible for young learners. Following the video segment, students engaged in a legislative simulation, embodying roles as lawmakers to propose, debate, amend, and vote on bills. This hands-on approach not only deepened their understanding of lawmaking but also notably empowered them to see how individual ideas can influence broader community rules and policies.

This IDM unit aimed to refine students' understanding of government branches and roles in the legislative process in a manner that highlights citizen participation (see Table 4.1 and Table 4.2). A key goal was to empower students, emphasizing that everyone has the potential to contribute ideas that can lead to significant changes. This is facilitated by inquiry-based learning that encourages students to explore the origins of laws, emphasizing that many begin with just an *idea*.

Dimension 1: Developing Questions and Planning Inquiries

During the activities focused on the contributions citizens make to their community, the students came to recognize everyday actions that enhance the common good, the well-being and interests shared by everyone in a community. They identified various ways individuals contribute to the community they live in, from volunteering at local shelters to participating in community decision-making. This recognition instilled values foundational to a democratic society such as justice, equity, and respect.

Table 4.1 *C3 Framework Dimensions Overview: Grade 3 Civics*

C3 Framework Dimension and Standard(s)	Description and Resources
Dimension 1 **D1.2.3-5.** Identify disciplinary concepts and ideas associated with a compelling question that are open to different interpretations. **D1.3.3-5.** Identify disciplinary concepts and ideas associated with a supporting question that are open to different interpretations.	In Dimension 1, students investigate how individual actions contribute to community welfare and the importance of engaging in civic activities. They learn the role of advocacy in positive changes for the common good. In this dimension, students will be introduced to the compelling question for the C3 inquiry unit. *The Voice That Won the Vote* (Boxer, 2020)
Dimension 2 **D2.Civ.11.3-5.** Compare procedures for making decisions in a variety of settings, including classroom, school, government, and/or society. **D2.Civ.12.3-5.** Explain how rules and laws change society and how people change rules and laws.	This dimension involves teaching the core content through structured lessons that build upon students' initial inquiries. In Dimension 2, students explore the structure and function of laws in government and gain a comprehensive understanding of the legislative process. *The School With No Rules* (Moon, 2014) *I'm Just a Bill* (Schoolhouse Rock, 1976/2014) *Meet Michigan* (McConnell, 2009) *Michigan Studies* (Bradford et al., 2016) Supplemental: *What Do You Do With an Idea?* (Yamada, 2014)
Dimension 3 **D3.1.3-5.** Gather relevant information from multiple sources while using the origin, structure, and context to guide the selection. **D3.4.3-5.** Use evidence to develop claims in response to compelling questions.	Students investigate primary and secondary sources to verify and enrich their understanding of the concepts learned. In this dimension, students effectively craft arguments for school improvement, use evidence to support their ideas, and engage in persuasive advocacy to promote community improvements. The lessons for Dimension 3 will likely span four to five days. State Fossil: Mastodon, S.B. 397 (Mich. 2002) "Mastodon Named State Fossil" (University Record Archives, 2002) "Persuasive Writing for Kids" (Clark, 2024) "Writing a Bill" lesson plan (Anti-Defamation League, 2020)
Dimension 4 **D4.8.3-5.** Use a range of deliberative and democratic procedures to make decisions about and act on civic problems in their classrooms and schools. **D4.3.3-5.** Present a summary of arguments and explanations to others outside the classroom using print and oral technologies (e.g., posters, essays, letters, debates, speeches, and reports) and digital technologies (e.g., Internet, social media, and digital documentary).	This dimension focuses on students presenting their conclusions and taking informed action based on their learning. Students debate and vote on the bills they have created, communicating their conclusions through persuasive arguments. The successful bills are presented to an "executive panel" like the principal for approval, mirroring real-world legislative action. Student-generated resources

The literature investigation of *The Voice That Won the Vote* (Boxer, 2020) further enriched student understanding of the power of our voices. This segment allowed students to explore the concept of advocacy and its critical role in driving positive changes for the common good. They discussed the implications of citizens' non-participation in government, contemplating scenarios where neglect could lead to deteriorating community conditions. This discussion highlighted the importance of active involvement and empowered students to believe that they were capable of effecting change and contributing positively to society. The focus on advocacy and effecting positive change in Dimension 1 stimulated students to think about the changes they want to see in their school community. Students were excited to suggest ideas for improvement in their communities and discuss what they could do to stimulate these changes. Dimension 1 not only enhanced the students' understanding of their roles within the community but also encouraged them to see themselves as active participants capable of shaping a democratic society. Through these educational experiences, they gained a deeper appreciation of the decision-making processes and the formation of laws, empowering them with the knowledge and values necessary to contribute effectively to their communities.

Dimension 2: Applying Disciplinary Concepts and Tools

Dimension 2 utilized a combination of literature, multimedia resources, and peer teaching opportunities to effectively communicate complex concepts related to governance and the legislative process. One of the key activities in this section involved a thoughtful discussion on the book *The School With No Rules* (Moon, 2014). This narrative allowed students to explore a fictional setting where normal constraints were absent, prompting them to imagine a day at school without any rules. The book served as a powerful tool to illustrate the challenges that might arise in such an environment. Students enthusiastically engaged with the story, making comparisons between the disorder in the school and what might happen in a community lacking law. This discussion reinforced their understanding of the necessity of rules and laws, highlighting their roles in protecting rights and ensuring safety.

Further enhancing their grasp of the legislative process, the class watched the educational video "I'm Just a Bill" (Schoolhouse Rock, 1976/2014). This short film presents the legislative process more accessibly to the students, breaking down the complex journey of a bill becoming a law into a format that is both entertaining and easy to understand. Plus, it's just so catchy. The engaging and narrative-driven approach of "I'm Just a Bill" captured the students' attention and facilitated a deeper understanding of the legislative process, making an abstract concept more relatable and inviting.

We watched the entire three-minute video first, considering the question "What is a bill, and where does its process begin?" I wanted to emphasize the notion that bills start with an idea—that people, like us, can have an impact on the lawmaking process. After our initial viewing of the video, we discussed the importance of understanding how a bill becomes a law so that we can participate. I wanted to emphasize the journey a bill takes in becoming a law so that students were more familiar with the process as they continued through our legislative simulation. We watched the video a second time, considering the question "How does a bill become a law?" Students were asked to record notes during the second viewing, paying special attention to the different steps Bill takes in his journey to become a law. At the conclusion of the video, we discussed reasons why our character, Bill, might be seeming bored sitting on the steps of Capitol Hill; the role of Congress, committee, and the executive branch in the law-making process; and the specific steps in creating laws.

The students' reactions to the video were overwhelmingly positive. They found the song and animations engaging, and most were even singing along. Their thoughts before and after watching the video showed a shift in comprehension. Initially, students showed a lack of understanding about how laws are made, but after our discussion, students were able to discuss and order the steps of the legislative process. Overall, incorporating "I'm Just a Bill" into Dimension 2 had a significant impact on the students' learning. It made an abstract concept tangible and engaging, fostering a deeper understanding and sparking excitement about taking part in the legislative process in their school community. The combination of visual content, catchy music, and guided discussions helped students grasp the concept of how a bill becomes a law.

To continue, Dimension 2 incorporated a Jigsaw activity, where students were divided into small groups to explore different aspects of governance, focusing on the roles and responsibilities of the three branches of government—Legislative, Executive, and Judicial—particularly in the law-making process. Initially students were divided into small expert groups and assigned one of the branches of government from their classroom textbooks to study. Students then reorganized into new Jigsaw groups, each consisting of one or two members of the initial expert groups. In these new groups, students taught their peers about their expert topic. This peer-to-peer learning strategy not only increased engagement but also fostered a sense of accountability among the students. Observations during this activity showed heightened participation and collaboration, as students were excited to share their knowledge and learn from one another. The activities culminated in an evident increase in students' motivation to enact change within their school community. For example, students generated ideas for improving the breakfast program at the school, such as offering multiple lines for each grade level, expediting the process, and getting students to class on time. Additionally, students explored the possibility of new learning programs geared toward STEM fields, such as computer coding. Building on the foundational concepts of advocacy and civic participation introduced in Dimension 1, students felt empowered to suggest and advocate for positive changes in their environment.

Dimension 3: Evaluating Sources and Using Evidence

NCSS (2013) emphasizes that "Civics is the discipline of the social studies most directly concerned with the processes and rules by which groups of people make decisions ... and address public problems" (p. 34). In Dimension 3, students explored the tangible impact of civic engagement through hands-on activities that connected them directly with the legislative process. This phase of learning was introduced with an investigation of real-world applications of civics concepts, particularly highlighted by the study of Michigan Senate Bill 397 and a related article, "Mastodon Named State Fossil" (The University Record Archives, 2002).

The introduction of Senate Bill 397 provided an authentic example of how students can influence legislative outcomes. This lesson showed students the process by which a group of school children successfully proposed a bill to declare the Mastodon the state fossil of Michigan. Witnessing student success in making a legislative change significantly excited the students and instilled a sense of empowerment. This real-world example sparked a critical question and determination among the third-grade students: "How can I do that?"

Building on this momentum, students were guided through the application of surveying techniques to gather evidence and build support for their school improvement proposals generated in previous lessons. Students conducted surveys within their school community to understand public opinion on various issues they felt passionate about. The process taught them the importance of gathering empirical data to support their claims, a key step in effective advocacy. For example, students surveyed other classes' and teachers' opinions on new playground equipment (see Figure 4.1) and on the benefits of additional field trips at each grade level.

Moreover, the lessons emphasized the use of persuasive writing techniques. Students learned how to articulate their viewpoints compellingly, focusing on structure, clarity, and the power of well-supported arguments. This hands-on approach to learning about civics in Dimension 3 reinforced understanding of the legislative process and motivated students to consider how they could actively participate in shaping laws and policies in their communities.

House Bill No. 6

A **bill** is an idea for a new law, or a proposal for changing a law that is already in place. Your committee speaker will present your bill proposal to the class.

An act to Enhance Playground Safety and Equipment at our School

Title: What is the main goal of your proposal?

Observing the need for safe playground equipment, we propose Playground Safety and Equipment Enhancement at our school. The school soccer nets and jungle gym structure (blue bars) need to be replaced to increase student enjoyment at school. To increase fun for young students, a new slide will be purchased.

Preamble: Why is your bill necessary?

This law will require replacement of the old soccer field nets and the unsafe "blue bars" (jungle gym) with new playground equipment. The jungle gym will be safe for students to play on and the soccer nets will not break easily. Also, a new slide will be purchased for the younger students to play on.

Rule: What will the law explicitly say?

The new playground equipment we want to get will make playing outside safer. This means all of us can play without getting hurt. Right now, students are not even allowed to play on the blue bars because they are dangerous. Having new playground equipment will be exciting for all students, making us more motivated to play outside. This helps to keep us healthy and safe. Also, safety playground equipment will make playing outside more enjoyable for us.

We conducted a survey of 3rd, 4th and 5th graders to ask what changes they wanted to see on our playground. A majority of students asked for soccer nets that were not ripped and to be able to play on the blue bars that are off limits. We also interviewed first and second graders. Younger students said that the slides are not slippery anymore and they would like a new slide that they can have fun on. Teachers agree that the blue bars should be replaced so students can actually play on them.

We propose that some of the money we raise from our annual fundraiser be used to implement new playground equipment that will make playing outside more enjoyable and safe.

Purpose and Benefits: How will this bill make your school better? (remember to make reasonable proposals, and be persuasive and use strong supporting evidence to back up your claims?

Proposed by:

Figure 4.1 *Student Work Sample of a Final Bill Proposal*

Dimension 4: Communicating Conclusions and Taking Informed Action

Dimension 4 culminated in a hands-on simulation of the legislative process, which brought the concepts discussed in earlier IDM lessons to life. This stage was crucial not only in solidifying students' understanding of how government functions but also in empowering them to actively participate in democratic processes. Throughout Dimension 4, students were deeply involved in drafting, revising, and perfecting their own legislative bills. They took their practice and peer review sessions seriously, understanding the importance of crafting persuasive arguments that were well-supported with evidence. This careful preparation aimed to ensure their bills would stand up to scrutiny and achieve their intended goals. A significant component of this phase was the development of criteria for a "good bill." Students collaborated to define what made a bill effective, feasible, and persuasive. These criteria were then employed to evaluate each bill during simulated sessions of the House and Senate (see Figure 4.2 and Figure 4.3), where students had the opportunity to cast votes on the proposed legislation. This exercise not only enhanced their critical thinking and evaluation skills but also deepened their understanding of the qualities that contribute to successful legislative outcomes.

For example, during one conferencing session, I worked with a group of students drafting a bill to increase the number of field trips at each grade level from one trip each year to three. Students struggled with the idea of feasibility and were concerned about the cost of additional field trips and the lack of bus drivers in their school district, which limits the amount of drivers available for additional school trips. During our conference, we brainstormed ways to address these issues, investigating the cost of employing a private bussing company and the possibility of applying for grants or asking local businesses for support. As an illustration, in our community, the agricultural center offers multiple free educational programs targeted to each grade level and offers transportation grants to assist in the cost of transporting students to and from the facility.

In another instance, a group of students was constructing a bill to add outdoor learning spaces to their school campus, facing skepticism from their peers about the necessity of their idea, which arguably depleted its effectiveness. This led to a discussion in which students explored the benefits of outdoor learning experiences. The conversation shifted to place-based learning, where students examined alternative methods of outdoor learning that did not require the construction of new facilities.

When it came time to evaluate the bills in the simulated House and Senate sessions, students took their roles seriously, applying the criteria they had developed to assess effectiveness, feasibility, and persuasiveness. The room buzzed with anticipation as students monitored our electronic tally of votes closely (In our classroom, we utilized a Google Form for casting votes, which allowed us to project the responses for student viewing with incoming votes being tallied and displayed in real time). Waves of hooting and disappointment resounded through the room as more votes came in, altering the current standing of each bill.

The culmination of this IDM unit occurred in the school gym, transformed for the day into a bustling legislative chamber. Here, an "executive panel," composed of the school principal, curriculum director, and members of the Parent-Teacher Organization reviewed the students' bills, and the excitement in the air was palpable as one of the student-drafted bills passed. The cheers and elation that resonated throughout the gym were a testament to the students' investment and the

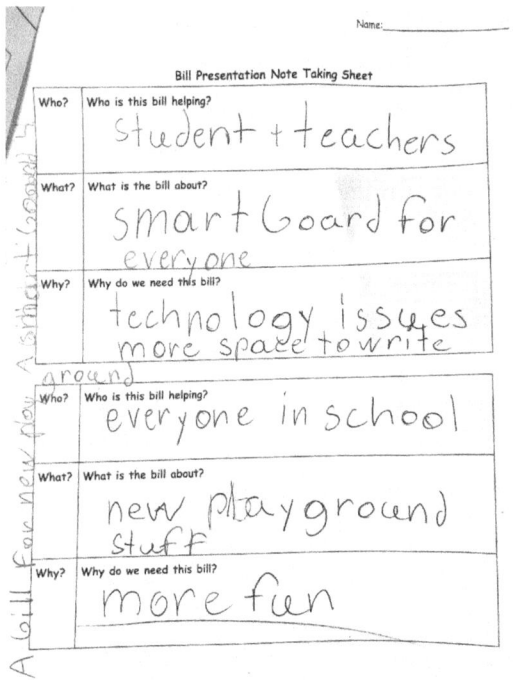

thrill of seeing their efforts result in meaningful and relevant outcomes. The pride that students exhibited was clear; they were proud not only of themselves but also of their classmates. This experience reinforced the relevance of civic education and its impact on their lives. It provided a concrete demonstration that their voices could be powerful and that they, even at a young age, could effectively contribute to their community and society.

Figure 4.2 *Student Work Sample of Bill Note Taking*

Figure 4.3 *Student Work Sample of Bill Effectiveness Critique*

Final Comments

Concluding this IDM unit on civic engagement in the legislative process, it was evident that the integration of film and the utilization of the C3 Inquiry Framework collectively fostered a transformative learning experience in the classroom. Through the use of film, students were not only engaged in understanding content but were also challenged to contemplate their roles as active citizens. The implementation of the C3 Inquiry Framework provided a structured approach for inquiry and informed action, enabling students to dive headfirst into civic concepts and develop essential skills for active participation in their communities. The emphasis on empowering students resulted in their observable shift from passive observers to proactive contributors in their communities. By recognizing their agency and fostering a sense of civic responsibility, students were empowered to advocate for change and make meaningful contributions to their school community.

While the lesson was an outstanding success, there is no perfect lesson. There are some adaptations that can be made to the lesson. One would be the use of different films. While "I'm Just a Bill" was a great hook for the lesson, there are other third-grade-level videos about the legislative process that could be used to help students visualize the process. Another would be to use other

Table 4.2 *Lessons Overview: Grade 3 Civics*

Dimension and Lesson	Description and Time Required
Dimension 1, Lesson 1 Exploring Community Roles and Civic Engagement	In the first lesson of Dimension 1, students are introduced to the compelling question for this unit, "How can we make a difference in our community?" Students will write an individual reflection to this prompt (5 minutes) followed by a Pair-and-Share discussion to expand on their ideas (5 minutes). The core activity involves teacher-directed instruction focusing on civic responsibility and common good (15 minutes) and a work session where students create mind maps linking various community roles to their contribution to the common good (15–20 minutes).
Dimension 1, Lesson 2 The Power of Civic Participation	The lesson begins with read-aloud of *The Voice That Won the Vote* by Elisa Boxer (2020), followed by a teacher-led discussion of critical themes (30 minutes). A Think-Pair-Share discussion prompts students to answer the questions "Why is it important to participate in our government?" and "What might happen if we don't?" to facilitate student writing (5 minutes). The lesson concludes with a writing task where students compose a short paragraph discussing their perspectives on the importance of civic participation, highlighting examples from the book (10–15 minutes).
Dimension 1, Lesson 3 Ideas for Improvement	In this lesson, students brainstorm potential improvements for their school community using a teacher-made graphic organizer (10 minutes). They engage in small group discussions to build on each other's ideas (5 minutes) and then use sticky notes to record the improvements they feel most passionate about (5 minutes). The lesson concludes with an exit ticket, prompting students to reflect on their initial responses to the compelling question "How can we make a difference in our community?" (10 minutes). A potential literature extension activity involves reading *If I Built a School* (Van Dusen, 2023) to stimulate creative thinking and generate ideas for school improvement (20 minutes).
Dimension 2, Lesson 1 What Are Laws, and Why Do We Have Them?	This lesson starts with responses to the question "What are laws, and why do we have them?" (5 minutes), followed by a Think-Pair-Share discussion (5 minutes). The class engages in a group read-aloud of *The School With No Rules* by Dr. Poppy Moon (2014; 25 minutes), aiming to help students grasp the significance of laws in familiar contexts. Finally, a brief review of the supporting question concludes the lesson, emphasizing that rules and laws maintain order, protect rights, and ensure fairness.
Dimension 2, Lesson 2 "I'm Just a Bill"	Students watch "I'm Just a Bill" (Schoolhouse Rock, 1976/2014) taking notes on key steps and terms in the legislative process (5 minutes). Students participate in a review of the steps and work in differentiated pairs to create flow charts mapping out the legislative process, possibly using premade templates (20–25 minutes). This activity may require access to the educational video for review. The lesson concludes with a brief discussion of the legislative process and displaying the flow charts on the class idea board for reference and reinforcement for future activities (10 minutes).
Dimension 2, Lesson 3 Branches of Government Jigsaw	Students use the Jigsaw teaching method to explore how the branches of government collaborate in the legislative process. They are divided into expert groups focusing on one branch—Legislative, Executive, or Judicial—and research their branch's roles and responsibilities using provided resources (15 minutes). Each group completes a graphic organizer detailing their branch's functions in the legislative process (5–10 minutes). After becoming experts, they teach each other about their branch in mixed groups each containing one or two students from the initial expert groups. (15 minutes). The Cult of Pedagogy provides a more detailed explanation of the Jigsaw teaching method (Gonzalez, 2015). Visual aids, structured discussions, and peer teaching foster collaboration. Finally, the importance of "checks and balances" is discussed (5 minutes).

Dimension 2, Lesson 4 It Starts With an Idea (Understanding the Legislative Process Through School Improvement)	To conclude Dimension 2, students engage in a legislative simulation activity, beginning with a review of "I'm Just a Bill" to reinforce understanding of the legislative process (5-6 minutes). The teacher introduces the simulation where students act as legislators to write and pass bills for school improvement (20 minutes). Revisiting the school improvement idea board, students combine ideas into broader themes and brainstorm feasible solutions (10 minutes). Finally, students complete an exit ticket reflecting on an improvement they would like to see in school and propose a rule to make it happen.
Dimension 3, Lesson 1 Investigating Legislative Advocacy	The bell ringer prompts students to consider essential characteristics for a successful bill (5-6 minutes). The teacher then introduces the first supporting question, framing the discussion around real-life examples of student impact on legislation, such as the naming of the Mastodon as the Michigan state fossil (20 minutes). Students analyze the steps taken by these student advocates, discussing their strategies and challenges (10 minutes). Next, students revisit the class idea board and school improvement suggestions, engaging in small group discussions to brainstorm advocacy steps for their desired changes and anticipate potential oppositions (10 minutes).
Dimension 3, Lesson 2 Community Voices	In this activity, students explore how they can identify areas of improvement within their community and gather evidence to support their ideas. Students become "the voice of the people" and employ various strategies for formulating investigations and gathering data and support for their arguments, such as using surveying methods, interest surveys, and student interviews. Students work collaboratively to manifest appropriate methods for data collection and evaluate their sources of evidence to ensure effectiveness (45 minutes). This lesson activity could extend two days.
Dimension 3, Lesson 3 Building Strong Arguments for School Improvement (lesson series)	In this lesson series, students use evidence to collaboratively create compelling arguments for improving their school. The teacher begins by explaining the structure of a bill and provides a bill proposal template to guide students through the writing process (15 minutes). Students integrate evidence from surveys, interviews, and student letters into their bills, refining their persuasive writing skills along the way (30-75 minutes). Students also create supporting multimedia materials, such as posters, to further persuade their peers and decision-makers (30 minutes). An exit ticket prompts students to reflect on their evolving understanding of what constitutes a "good" bill, documenting their learning journey (5 minutes).
Dimension 4, Lesson 1 Elements of Persuasion	In this lesson, students focus on effectively communicating and advocating for their proposals. They prepare and practice their presentations emphasizing evidence-based justification and persuasion (20 minutes). Peer review sessions provide opportunities for students to offer each other feedback for improvement (20 minutes). Students then revise their bills based on feedback and prepare final versions for the legislative simulation activity (15 minutes).
Dimension 4, Lesson 2 Final Decisions	Students generate criteria for evaluating bills (relevance, feasibility, impact) through guided brainstorming (15 minutes). Students participate in mock legislative sessions where students present their bills to both the House and the Senate before the bill advances to the executive panel (40 minutes). Students utilize their criteria for evaluation to cast votes in favor of bills to be passed (5 minutes).
Dimension 4, Lesson 3 Taking Informed Action	In this final lesson, students reflect on how understanding the legislative process empowers them to make a difference. They present their bills to the executive board, receiving feedback to refine their advocacy skills (20 minutes). Through reflection, they discuss the impact of their advocacy efforts and how they can apply their knowledge of advocacy and the legislative process in the future (20 minutes).

discussion-based strategies for this lesson. These could include the Circle of Knowledge and Gallery Walks (Roberts et al., 2022). Finally, it would be great to have parents and caregivers more involved from the beginning of the lesson. In the future, I would invite any parents or caregivers to take part to help their students in the development of the acts and laws that were developed for the school.

References

Anti-Defamation League. (2020, May 11). *Writing a bill*. www.adl.org/resources/lesson-plan/writing-bill

Bradford, M., Freeland, S., Kastl, E., Kooyer, J., McCauley, M., Raven, A., & Welch, S. (2016). *Michigan studies*. Michigan Open Book Project.

Boxer, E. (2020). *The voice that won the vote: How one woman's words made history* (V. Mildenberger, Illus.). Sleeping Bear Press.

Clark, C. (2024, February 28). *Persuasive writing for kids*. Speech and Language Kids. www.speechandlanguagekids.com/teach-persuasive-writing-children/

Gonzalez, J. [Cult of Pedagogy]. (2015, April 15). *The jigsaw method* [Video]. YouTube. www.youtube.com/watch?v=euhtXUgBEts

McConnell, D. B. (2009). *Meet Michigan*. Hillsdale Educational Publishers.

Moon, P. (2014). *The school with no rules*. YouthLight.

National Council for the Social Studies. (2013). *The college, career, and civic life (C3) framework for social studies state standards: Guidance for enhancing the rigor of K–12 civics, economics, geography, and history*.

Roberts, S. L., Wellenreiter, B. R., Ferreras-Stone, J., Strachan, S. L., & Palmer, K. L. (2022). *Teaching middle level social studies: A practical guide for 4th–8th grade* (3rd ed.). Information Age.

Schoolhouse Rock. (2014, August 18). *I'm just a bill* [Video]. YouTube. www.youtube.com/watch?v=SZ8psP4S6BQ (Original work published 1976)

State Fossil: Mastodon, S.B. 397 (Mich. 2002). www.legislature.mi.gov/documents/2001-2002/billanalysis/House/htm/2001-HLA-0397-a.htm

The University Record Archives. (2002, April 22). *Mastodon named state fossil*. https://record.umich.edu/articles/mastodon-named-state-fossil/

Van Dusen, C. (2023). *If I built a school*. Rocky Pond Books.

Yamada, K. (2014). *What do you do with an idea?* (M. Besom, Illus.). Compendium.

Chapter 5

Elementary Teacher's Experience With Using the C3 Dimensions With United States History and Film

Teaching Indigenous Resilience and Sovereignty Through Lacrosse History and Culture

Kate Van Haren

"What is that?"

"Isn't that the name of a town?"

"Oh, that's the game they play with sticks!"

These are just a few of the questions and statements that my fifth graders blurted out when I asked them about the game of lacrosse. It turns out that they knew very little. The student who confidently stated that it was a game played with sticks was actually thinking of field hockey. Although the game had not become popular in my small community yet, lacrosse is becoming more popular across the globe. This attention is likely spurred by lacrosse's induction as a new sport in the 2028 Olympic Games. As more and more students are exposed to the game, it is important to step back and consider its origins. Often called the "Creator's Game," lacrosse has been played by Indigenous peoples for thousands of years. Different Indigenous nations across what would become North America had different names for the game and different rules; although, it was a spiritual activity for many. It was also used as a way to settle disputes among different groups. This was one way to prevent widespread war and violence. Lacrosse's history involves a long colonial tradition of European settlers forgetting the deeply spiritual origins and claiming it as their own. In some cases, Indigenous peoples were denied the right to even play. Over the last few centuries, the game has become more associated with predominately white preparatory boarding schools than with its Indigenous origins (Downey, 2018).

In recent years, Indigenous communities like the Haudenosaunee Confederacy have used the game of lacrosse as a way to publicly advocate for their sovereignty. After years of advocacy efforts by the Haudenosaunee lacrosse players and community members, the Haudenosaunee Nationals are a recognized professional sports team of the World Lacrosse organization. The men's team gained their recognition in 1983, and the women's team was established in 2008 (Haudenosaunee

Nationals, n.d.-b). Because they are an independent nation, the Haudenosaunee team is separate from the United States team, and they often compete against each other. The Haudenosaunee, like other Indigenous nations, have continually resisted efforts to eliminate their culture and have not forgotten the cultural and spiritual significance of lacrosse. Their global recognition as an elite team allows them to teach others about their history as an independent nation and share their culture with an international audience. As the game of lacrosse grows in popularity, the success story of the Haudenosaunee Nationals presents an engaging opportunity to learn more about the histories of resilience and modern advocacy for sovereignty of Indigenous peoples across the United States.

Overview of the Lessons: How Do Indigenous Athletes, Like Those Who Play Lacrosse, Teach Others About the Resilience of Indigenous Cultures and Sovereignty?

The main films used in this lesson are *Spirit Game: Pride of a Nation* (Spirer & Baxter, 2017) and *Roots of Lacrosse* (World Wood Day, 2017). Both films feature Indigenous lacrosse players and Indigenous community members. *Spirit Game* follows the Haudenosaunee team as the Onondaga Nation hosted the 2015 World Indoor Lacrosse Championship. *Roots of Lacrosse* focuses on the historical significance of lacrosse and its spread across the United States. This film includes several speakers of the Oneida Nation in Wisconsin, which is one of the six nations of the Haudenosaunee Confederacy. In the 1800s, some members of the Oneida nation were forced to relocate to Wisconsin from their ancestral lands in New York, due to the newly established US government's policy of Indigenous removal and land dispossession.

This inquiry begins with students thinking about the importance and traditions of customs within their own communities. Through the lens of school sports, students were able to discuss how and why some traditions stayed the same and why some changed. This activity is designed to help students see that the game of lacrosse is more than just a fun activity in many Indigenous communities. The next two dimensions focus on the origins of lacrosse and the deep connection the Haudenosaunee people still have for the game. Students also explored how the Haudenosaunee use lacrosse to teach others about their cultures. After using the Haudenosaunee Nationals's story as a case study, students explored how lacrosse is important to the Ho-Chunk Nation, the original inhabitants of the land on which our school was built. Students explored how Indigenous athletes have a long history of competing in many different sports and use competition as a way to spread and teach their cultures to a wider community. Finally, students discussed their responsibilities in learning and sharing their knowledge of Indigenous peoples with their peers. The next learning activities focus on the origins of lacrosse and the deep connection the Haudenosaunee people still have for the game. (See Table 5.1 for an overview of the dimensions for this inquiry.)

Important note on terminology: In various clips, people will use the word "Iroquois," which has a complicated history. It is a term originally used by French settlers. For many years, the Haudenosaunee have advocated for the use of their original name. The lacrosse team was originally known as the "Iroquois Nationals," and the team officially changed its name in 2022 (Haudenosaunee Nationals, n.d.-a) after the release of both films. In previous classes, my students learned about the importance of names and efforts of Indigenous peoples to reclaim their names and languages. I explained to students that, although the films still used the term "Iroquois," we will use the name "Haudenosaunee," per the current wishes of the team.

Table 5.1 *C3 Framework Dimensions Overview: Grade 5 U.S. History*

C3 Framework Dimension and Standard(s)	Description and Resources
Dimension 1 D1.2.3-5. Identify disciplinary concepts and ideas associated with a compelling question that are open to different interpretations. D1.5.3-5. Determine the kinds or sources that will be helpful in answering compelling and supporting questions, taking into consideration the different opinions people have about how to answer questions.	In Dimension 1, students engage in discussions about key terminology, focusing on the complex meanings of "resilience" in the context of Indigenous communities and "sovereignty" as it relates to tribal self-governance. They then analyze their own family traditions and examine historical school sports photographs, comparing them to current practices. Through these activities, students draw connections between cultural continuity and the importance of traditions over time, preparing them to understand the significance of lacrosse to the Haudenosaunee people beyond its role as a sport. "Toward an anticolonial approach to civic education" (Sabzalian, 2019) *What does tribal sovereignty mean to American Indians and Alaska Natives* (Bureau of Indian Affairs, 2017)
Dimension 2 D2.His.1.3-5. Create and use a chronological sequence of related events to compare developments that happened at the same time. D2.His.2.3-5. Compare life in specific historical time periods to life today. D2.His.3.3-5. Generate questions about individuals and groups who have shaped significant historical changes and continuities. D2.His.4.3-5. Explain why individuals and groups during the same historical period differed in their perspectives. D2.His.5.3-5. Explain connections among historical contexts and people's perspectives at the time. D2.His.14.3-5. Explain probable causes and effects of events and developments. D2.His.16.3-5. Use evidence to develop a claim about the past.	In Dimension 2, students analyze film clips and use graphic organizers to gather information about the origins and significance of lacrosse, as well as the history and modern challenges of the Haudenosaunee Confederacy. Students examine issues of tribal sovereignty through the lens of the Haudenosaunee National team's passport controversy. Finally, they synthesize their learning by creating a conceptual statue design that reflects their understanding of lacrosse's cultural significance and modern interpretations. Lacrosse Player statue (Highsmith, 2016)
Dimension 3 D3.3.3-5. Identify evidence that draws information from multiple sources in response to compelling questions. D3.4.3-5. Use evidence to develop claims in response to compelling questions.	In Dimension 3, students analyze various sources, including film clips of traditional stick-making and contemporary game footage, to understand lacrosse's cultural and historical significance to the Haudenosaunee people. They engage in group discussions, relating generational practices to their own experiences, and use Venn diagrams to compare historical and modern lacrosse gameplay.
Dimension 4 D4.6.3-5. Draw on disciplinary concepts to explain the challenges people have faced and opportunities they have created in addressing local, regional, and global problems at various times and places. D4.7.3-5. Explain different strategies and approaches students and others could take in working alone and together to address local, regional, and global problems, and predict possible results of their actions.	In Dimension 4, students analyze current events, such as the Haudenosaunee's efforts to compete in the Olympics, and compare the significance of lacrosse for different Indigenous nations like the Ho-Chunk. They explore the broader impact of Indigenous athletes across various sports, creating trading cards to share this knowledge. Finally, students synthesize their learning by creating acrostic poems that reflect their understanding of lacrosse's cultural and historical importance to Indigenous peoples. North American Indigenous Athletic Hall of Fame, **https://naiahf.org/** "President Joe Biden and the White House support Indigenous lacrosse team for the 2028 Olympics" (Pells, 2023)

Dimension 1: Developing Questions and Planning Inquiries

This lesson started with students reviewing the compelling question, "How do Indigenous athletes, like those who play lacrosse, teach others about the resilience of Indigenous cultures and sovereignty?" Students were given the opportunity to discuss and ask questions about any terminology that was confusing. The questions at the beginning of this chapter were asked during this step. A Google image search and a brief discussion provided enough background to explain the basics of the game. None of the students knew about the Indigenous origins of lacrosse. In addition to "lacrosse," another word that tripped up some students was "resilience." This word is complex and can have multiple meanings depending on the context. The definition that I shared with the students was that *resilience* describes how Indigenous communities like the Haudenosaunee have survived and thrived despite hundreds of years of colonial efforts to take away their land and eliminate their cultures (Sabzalian, 2019).

I knew that "sovereignty" would also be a difficult term for students to understand. The United States Department of the Interior Bureau of Indian Affairs (2017) states that "tribal sovereignty ensures that any decisions about the tribes with regard to their property and citizens are made with their participation and consent" (para. 2). The concept of sovereignty had already been discussed in previous social studies lessons, but students needed more opportunities to learn about it. These opportunities are built into the inquiry activities.

After introducing and discussing important terminology, students brainstormed activities and traditions that were important to them. My students needed to understand that lacrosse was more than just a game to the Haudenosaunee. Although I hoped this realization would become more obvious as the inquiry progressed, I wanted my students to grapple with this idea from the very beginning of the inquiry. Students drew or wrote about their traditions and shared them with the class. Many students described family gatherings related to Christmas or other religious celebrations and events like Easter egg hunts that happened every year. Students stated that connecting with family was the important aspect of these events. I challenged students to think about how these traditions have changed over time. One of the mentioned changes included going out to eat instead of cooking a huge family meal at home. A student stated that nobody in the family had the time to cook that much anymore. Despite the changes, the student still looked forward to this event every year.

While the students in this particular class willingly engaged in this lesson, I was aware that not all students might have the same familial connections to traditions. The class also looked at various pictures from our school sports teams from previous decades. Fortunately, the school's social media page contained a Throwback Thursday collection of sports photographs spanning several decades of our school's athletic history. We examined four photographs, each featuring a different school sports team. By comparing and contrasting these photographs to today's sports events, students saw many changes but noted that school pride in our athletes remains the same. These two activities provided the opportunity for students to start making connections about the importance of traditions and cultures despite generational differences.

Dimension 2: Applying Disciplinary Concepts and Tools

The second dimension provided students with important content information about the game of lacrosse and the background of the Haudenosaunee people. The first supporting question introduced students to the origins of lacrosse. Students were given a graphic organizer to help answer the five basic questions of who, what, when, where, why, and how about the sport. I chose to use a section of the short clip, *Roots: Exploring the History of Lacrosse* (Premier Lacrosse League, 2020), because it provides a better description of the game than the two selected films. A group discussion at the end of the clip revealed that students were starting to understand that lacrosse was more than just a fun game for Indigenous players. At this point, students were still struggling to see how it could also be a spiritual practice. I assured students that this would become clearer as the inquiry continued.

The second supporting question focused on students understanding important background information about the Haudenosaunee people. I specifically chose not to spend too much time on the interesting but complicated histories of all six nations of the Haudenosaunee Confederacy. My students had already learned some of their history in previous classes. This inquiry focused more on how present-day Haudenosaunee people honor their history. It was easy for students to grasp that the Haudenosaunee Confederacy is made up of six different nations. Students were not surprised when interviewees in *Spirit Game* discussed how much of Haudenosaunee land had been taken away by European settlers. The second clip from *Spirit Game* for this supporting question focuses on how Nationals players refused to travel to the 2010 World Championships because they could not use their Haudenosaunee passports. They would have had to use United States passports because some countries refused to recognize their sovereignty and rights as an independent nation.

I debated showing students this clip because I thought the controversial topics might be too complicated for fifth graders. However, I was surprised how easily most students understood the Haudenosaunee perspective. I think students understood that passports are a symbol of an independent country. If you are a member of that country, of course, you would want to use that country's passport; although, some students did not understand why Haudenosaunee players would not just use their U.S. passports to follow their dreams, but they were beginning to understand the complications related to tribal sovereignty in modern times.

The third clip from *Spirit Game* describes how five brothers played together on the 2015 team. This family, who have played together since childhood, compared themselves to the animals who played in the first medicine game. After viewing these clips, students added more notes to their graphic organizers. During our group check-in, I was surprised by the different answers that students had written on their graphic organizers. It was clear that students understood the importance of lacrosse and grasped its spiritual importance. However, different students had focused on different material covered in the clips. The graphic organizers served as a great review for all the information covered thus far.

The final question of this lesson challenged students to use their new knowledge to create a statue honoring the people and traditions of lacrosse. This lesson was based on a statue that was built in the city of La Crosse, Wisconsin. The city was named La Crosse because French explorers witnessed different Indigenous groups playing the game (Childs, 2014). When I showed students a picture of the statue (Highsmith, 2016), they thought the statue needed more detail. I challenged students to create a statue that reflected their understanding of the game. Many students chose to include the animals from the original game in their images. Some students tried to interpret the concept of a medicine game by using modern medical symbols. The majority of statues focused on modern interpretations of the game with players in modern gear. I was comfortable moving on to the next dimension because I saw that students had grasped the basic concepts of the game, and we were trying to understand concepts like sovereignty and spirituality.

Dimension 3: Evaluating Sources and Using Evidence

In Dimension 3, students used interviews from players and those involved in the game to understand the cultural and historical significance that lacrosse plays in their communities. In the first lesson, students watched clips from *Roots of Lacrosse* of Haudenosaunee craftsmen making sticks using traditional methods. The craftsmen explained that making sticks helps them connect to their ancestors because they are engaging in a process that has existed for generations. They felt like the required hickory wood was a way to honor all the living creatures that provided essential materials for survival. Because this was a difficult abstract idea for students, the formative performance task for this supporting question was a group discussion. Students spoke of learning to hunt and cook from older family members. Centering the conversations around practices passed on from generations was a concept that students could understand. In the film clips, players describe how their sticks are among their most valuable possessions. One player describes how it is an extension of his being. Students were able to make a connection to important family heirlooms or objects that have important meanings and stories for them.

This understanding was essential when students attempted to answer the second supporting question. It is important to note that my students will never fully understand the spiritual significance of lacrosse. Like other Indigenous groups, Haudenosaunee ways of knowing are tied to deep understandings of cultural practices and belief systems that have existed for thousands of years. However, my students can understand the importance of these belief systems and learn to respect them. This is an important first step in students developing empathy and respect for other cultural practices. When students attempted to answer the question, "Why was the game of lacrosse important?" many of their answers appeared superficial and surface level. For example, students had a hard time articulating why it was considered a medicine game for reasons other than helping to heal players. However, they were willing to accept that lacrosse was more than just a game of fun. I could see the students' respect for Haudenosaunee beliefs starting to develop.

In the final steps of this dimension, students were asked to compare and contrast how lacrosse was played in the past with how it is played today. The clips from *Spirit Game* shown in this section were footage of the actual game being played. These clips were students' favorite sources of the entire inquiry. They cheered and booed for the Nationals as if they were watching live footage, not just portions of games from over a decade ago. Students were especially interested in the clip from the semifinal when the Haudenosaunee played the United States. This was a powerful visual of two different nations competing against each other. When asked to complete Venn diagrams (see Figure 5.1), students' understanding of how the game was played was evident. The majority of students focused on how lacrosse went from a regional activity to a sport played around the world. As mentioned in the previous activity, students had difficulty articulating exactly why the game remained culturally and spiritually important. However, they did recognize that the game was a similarity between past and present. Several students wanted to include the fact that the Haudenosaunee were the originators of the game, but the Venn diagram did not allow for them to add this fact.

Figure 5.1 *Students' Venn Diagrams of Past and Present Lacrosse*

Lacrosse in the Past	Similarities	Modern Day Lacrosse
Differences: 1. No team numbers 2. Small amount of spectators 3. Winged animals vs. land animals 4. Nets made with snew' 5. Traditional outfits	1. They play to have fun. 2. It is a way to honor their ancestors. 3. It is still a medicine. 4. They still work as a team. 5. Remember culture.	Differences: 1. Numbers on jerseys 2. Play in stadiums 3. Different human teams 4. Nets made with rope 5. Jerseys

Lacrosse in the Past	Similarities	Modern Day Lacrosse
Differences: 1. Never had a national anthem 2. Was used to solve problems 3. Indigenous people played 4. Made of hickory 5. Only men played	1. Played for their gods 2. Called a medicine game 3. Compare themselves to animals 4. Can be dangerous 5. Call it the Creator's Game	Differences: 1. National anthem is a prayer 2. Play in stadiums 3. Nations all over the world 4. Made of modern materials 5. Men and women play

Dimension 4: Communicating Conclusions and Taking Informed Action

Dimension 4 spotlights the profound role of sports in highlighting the cultural richness of local Indigenous communities. Through the lens of lacrosse, students explore how this tradition serves as more than just a game—it is a powerful avenue for Indigenous nations across the United States to assert sovereignty and proudly share their cultural legacy. Students should see sports as a platform for advocacy and cultural expression, deepening their appreciation for Indigenous contributions to society. Ultimately, this lesson empowers students to take informed action by educating others about the significance of Indigenous sports and culture.

The first supporting question asks students to explore how the Haudenosaunee continue to use their lacrosse team as a way to advocate for their sovereignty. Lacrosse will become an Olympic sport in 2028. The Haudenosaunee are actively advocating to compete in the Games as their own sovereign nation. Although they are recognized as an independent team in World Lacrosse, the International Olympics Committee (IOC) is a separate organization. The IOC's current position is that players must compete on the teams of nations that already have established teams, such as the United States and Canada. They stated that Haudenosaunee players will have to play on these teams. As of 2024, the Haudenosaunee Nationals were in the process of advocating for recognition. Senior White House Advisor Tom Perez stated, "I can't think of a more worthy candidate for inclusion than a confederation that literally invented the sport and has some of the most elite men and women in the sport in their nation" (Pells, 2023).

In addition to reading the article (Pells, 2023) as a group, students also viewed a clip from a local New York news station about the Nationals team and their Olympic dream (WGRZ-TV, 2022). This news clip was filmed almost 10 years after the 2015 World Cup footage covered in *Spirit Game* and features some of the same people. Students enjoyed seeing how some players had moved into new roles and hearing from new, younger players. This news clip and the article led to interesting discussion about how international sporting organization policies and Olympic eligibility regulations clashed with traditional concepts of tribal sovereignty that have existed for thousands of years. Due to the level of complexity of these issues, I used a class discussion to check for student understanding. I was pleasantly surprised that students demonstrated a clearer understanding of sovereignty after engaging in the previous dimension's activities.

Although students were still forming their own opinions about whether the Nationals should be able to compete under their own flag, they were able to seriously consider their perspective. When asked why then-President Biden decided to support the Haudenosaunee, one student stated, "Well, he must have learned about their history in school and agrees that they should be able to have their own team." The students and I then discussed why the Haudenosaunee asked the United States government for help. Student conversations focused on whether it was easier to teach others and change things when bigger groups of people became involved in projects.

The second video clip from *Roots of Lacrosse* revealed how a Wisconsin lacrosse player started a lacrosse club at California State University, Long Beach. The clip includes interviews with several Indigenous players. Although they are not Haudenosaunee, and their homelands and their ancestors may not have played the game of lacrosse, they understood its importance. My students related to the players who stated that the exercise made them feel more at peace and that competing in sport was an effective way for them to alleviate their anger.

The Haudenosaunee narrative of using the game to assert their tribal sovereignty, connect with their past, and share their culture with others are examples of Indigenous resilience. However, they are not the only Indigenous group to do so. Sabzalian (2019) states that creating partnerships and learning the histories of local Indigenous communities is an essential piece of teaching Indigenous histories. My school is located on the ancestral lands of the Ho-Chunk Nation. Throughout my teaching career, I have learned Ho-Chunk Nation history and discussed best teaching practices with Ho-Chunk educators and community members. The Ho-Chunk are from the Eastern Woodlands region of the United States and have a similar connection to lacrosse as the Haudenosaunee. After viewing a short film about Ho-Chunk lacrosse created by a Wisconsin-based television company (Discover Wisconsin, 2023), students identified similarities and differences between what the Haudenosaunee and the Ho-Chunk men discussed in their interviews. The most common similarity students cited was that both groups saw the game as a way to connect to their traditions. They were also invested in passing on this knowledge to future generations.

My students wondered why the Ho-Chunk did not have a professional lacrosse team. They were not content with my answer that the Ho-Chunk were a small community and did not have

Table 5.2 *Lessons Overview: Grade 5 U.S. History*

Dimension and Lesson	Description and Time Required
Dimension 1, Lesson 1 Introduction/Hook	This lesson begins with students reviewing the compelling question: "How do Indigenous athletes, like those who play lacrosse, teach others about the resilience of Indigenous cultures and sovereignty?" Students discuss and ask questions about unfamiliar terminology. A Google image search and brief discussion provide background on lacrosse. Students then brainstorm activities and traditions important to them, drawing or writing about these traditions and sharing with the class. The teacher emphasizes the importance of understanding that lacrosse is more than just a game to the Haudenosaunee. (15 minutes)
Dimension 1, Lesson 2 Personal Traditions and Culture	Students continue exploring personal traditions, sharing their drawings or writings with the class. Many describe family gatherings related to holidays or religious celebrations. Students are challenged to think about how these traditions have changed over time. The class discusses these changes and their implications. (15 minutes)
Dimension 1, Lesson 3 School Traditions and Change	The class examines pictures from the school's sports teams from previous decades, using the school's social media "Throwback Thursday" collection. Students compare and contrast these photographs with current sports events, noting changes while recognizing the continuity of school pride in athletes. This activity helps students make connections about the importance of traditions and cultures despite generational differences. (15 minutes)

Dimension 2, Lesson 1 Origins of Lacrosse	Students are given a graphic organizer to answer *who, what, where, when, why,* and *how* about lacrosse. The provided video clips will help them answer the questions. The class should briefly discuss the answers after they have a chance to answer the questions on their own. (15 minutes) Film Clips: *Roots: Exploring the History of Lacrosse*, 0:00–3:45 *Spirit of the Game: Pride of a Nation*, 2:45–4:00
Dimension 2, Lesson 2 Haudenosaunee People and Sovereignty	Students learn about the Haudenosaunee Confederacy and its six nations. They watch two short video clips: one about land taken by European settlers, and another about the Nationals players refusing to use U.S. passports for the 2010 World Championships. Students discuss the concept of sovereignty and add notes to their graphic organizers. (20 minutes) Film Clips: *Roots of Lacrosse*, 6:00–9:30 *Spirit of the Game* • 7:20–9:45 • 17:00–18:40
Dimension 2, Lesson 3 Modern Lacrosse and Cultural Significance	Students watch a clip from *Spirit Game* (17:00–18:40) about five brothers playing on the 2015 team. They complete their graphic organizers and participate in a brief group check-in. Students are then challenged to create a quick sketch or description of a statue honoring the people and traditions of lacrosse, based on a real statue in La Crosse, Wisconsin (Highsmith, 2016). (20 minutes; *Note*. Students may need more time to finish drawing.)
Dimension 3, Lesson 1 Traditional Stick-Making and Generational Connections	Students watch clips of Haudenosaunee craftsmen making sticks using traditional methods. They participate in a group discussion about practices passed down through generations, connecting it to their own experiences with family traditions. (15 minutes) Film Clips: *Roots of Lacrosse*, 0:00–5:45 *Spirit Game*, 22:00–24:50
Dimension 3, Lesson 2 Spiritual Significance of Lacrosse	Students explore the spiritual importance of lacrosse to the Haudenosaunee people by watching video clips of players describing their deep connection to the game. On the outline of a lacrosse stick, students will write down their current understandings and answers to the questions. (20 minutes) Film Clips: *Spirit Game* • 4:15–6:20 • 13:25–20:00 • 47:49–49:45 • 54:00–55:20 • 1:05:00–1:07:00 • 1:23:00–1:25:00
Dimension 3, Lesson 3 Comparing Past and Present Lacrosse	Students watch clips of modern lacrosse games, including footage of the Iroquois Nationals. They complete Venn diagrams comparing and contrasting how lacrosse was played in the past to how it is played today. (20 Minutes) Film Clips: *Spirit Game* • 13:25–17:00 • 54:00–55:20 • 59:00–1:02:00 • 1:03:40–1:05:20 • 1:13:00–1:19:00

Dimension 4, Lesson 1 Lacrosse and Haudenosaunee Sovereignty	Students read an article and watch a news clip about the Haudenosaunee Nationals' efforts to compete in the 2028 Olympics as a sovereign nation. They engage in a class discussion about the historical context of tribal sovereignty and its modern implications in sports. Students consider the historical relationship between the Haudenosaunee and the U.S. government, and how it influences current actions. (20 minutes) Sources: • *Roots of Lacrosse*, 14:35–18:45 • *Haudenosaunee Nationals Keep Olympic Dreams in Focus* (WGRZ-TV, 2022) • "President Joe Biden and the White House support Indigenous lacrosse team for the 2028 Olympics" (Pells, 2023)
Dimension 4, Lesson 2 Indigenous Representation in Sports	Students watch videos about lacrosse's role in different Indigenous communities, including the Ho-Chunk. They compare and contrast the historical and cultural significance of lacrosse for various Indigenous groups. Students then research and create trading cards for Indigenous athletes from various sports, exploring how these individuals have shaped historical narratives and cultural representation. (20 minutes) Film Clip: *Ho-Chunk lacrosse: Discovering the ancient Native American sport*
Dimension 4, Lesson 3: Reflection and Acrostic Poem	Students reflect on their learning throughout the inquiry, considering how historical perspectives on Indigenous sports and culture have evolved. They create acrostic poems using an important word associated with lacrosse, addressing the compelling question about how Indigenous athletes teach others about the resilience of Indigenous cultures and sovereignty over time. (25 minutes)

the same resources as the Haudenosaunee. Students wanted to know if and where Ho-Chunk athletes competed. In order to answer their questions, I did my own research. I learned that the North American Indigenous Games are held every four years. In addition to lacrosse, Wisconsin Indigenous athletes compete in a variety of sports including golf, swimming, and wrestling (Pells, 2023). When I shared this information with students, they were interested in knowing if Indigenous athletes compete in professional sports that are not traditionally considered Indigenous activities. Fortunately, the North American Indigenous Athletics Hall of Fame is a useful resource (**www.naiahf.org**). The website provides brief, easy-to-read biographies of influential athletes. This activity allowed students to see the diversity of Indigenous nations within the United States, and students created trading cards to share with their peers.

As opposed to the confused questions I received at the beginning of the lesson, students now were uttering statements like,

> "Lacrosse was created by Indigenous People."
>
> "Indigenous people today have the same religious beliefs that they've had for thousands of years."
>
> "We talked about sovereignty before, but I think I understand that it's really important now."

Originally, I planned to have students complete a writing activity as part of their summative assessment. It was clear that students were reasoning through complex ideas and thoughts. I determined that a full essay would be difficult for students to complete. Students had been willing to share and discuss their thought processes throughout the inquiry. Trying to make students articulate their developing understanding in complete and structured sentences might have limited their ability to fully express the complex ideas they were exploring. At that stage in their writing development, students could more effectively demonstrate their understanding through discussion and creative expression. Instead, I put the compelling question on the board and challenged them to think of an important word they associated with the lacrosse. I had students write acrostic poems answering the compelling question (see Figure 5.2). I was pleased to see that students were able to understand the historical and cultural importance for both the past and present Ho-Chunk people. Although there is no specific mention of the Ho-Chunk in the poems, students stated that the Haudenosaunee experience with lacrosse could describe the Ho-Chunk experience as well.

Figure 5.2 *Students' Acrostic Poems*

Gathering Family	**P**repare for fun	**S**eeking the win!
Obtain the ball	**R**eunite Culture	**P**reparing for the Game!
Add respect for creators	**A**ccept defeat, keep trying	**I**magine your ancestors beside you!
Love each other	**C**reate peace among nations	**R**un down the field to score!
Share your lifestyle	**T**ry hard and connect	**I**mmerse yourself in the game!
	Improvise Skills	**T**hink about your ancestors and tell their story!
	Care about your culture	
	Enjoy the game	

Final Comments

When crafting this Indigenous Discourse Module, I recognized the importance of fostering inquiry skills even among elementary students. By providing them with age-appropriate materials and guiding questions, I aimed to cultivate their curiosity and critical thinking from an early age. Utilizing films and examples like lacrosse helped make complex historical concepts accessible and engaging for young learners. Despite the limited selection of documentary film options, I meticulously curated clips that not only addressed our guiding questions but also resonated with the students by connecting past struggles to present-day realities in ways they could comprehend. Witnessing the students' enthusiasm and their ability to surpass my expectations throughout the lesson affirmed the value of nurturing inquiry skills at every stage of education.

References

Bureau of Indian Affairs. (2017, August 19). *What does tribal sovereignty mean to American Indians and Alaska Natives?* **www.bia.gov/faqs/what-does-tribal-sovereignty-mean-american-indians-and-alaska-natives**

Childs, A. (2014, December 11). *La Crosse, Wisconsin: How a city got its name.* Lacrosse All Stars. **https://laxallstars.com/la-crosse-wisconsin/**

Discover Wisconsin. (2023, February 5). Ho-Chunk lacrosse: *Discovering the ancient Native American sport* [Video]. YouTube. **www.youtube.com/watch?v=tY6sTejFBZg&ab_channel=DiscoverWisconsin**

Downey, A. (2018). *The Creator's game: Lacrosse, identity, and Indigenous nationhood.* University of British Columbia Press.

Haudenosaunee Nationals (n.d.-a). *About Haudenosaunee Nationals Lacrosse.* **https://haudenosauneenationals.com/pages/about-haudenosaunee-nationals-lacrosse**

Haudenosaunee Nationals. (n.d.-b). *Our history.* **https://haudenosauneenationals.com/pages/our-history**

Highsmith, C. M. (2016) *Statue in downtown La Crosse, Wisconsin of two Winnebago Tribe members playing lacrosse, the game that the tribe invented and after which the city on the Mississippi River is named* [Photograph]. Library of Congress. **www.loc.gov/item/2016631276/**

Pells, E. (2023, December 6) President Joe Biden and the White House support Indigenous lacrosse team for the 2028 Olympics. *AP News.* **https://apnews.com/article/lacrosse-olympics-biden-haudenosaunee-8ebf449d752db21b807ceee9c174b937**

Premier Lacrosse League. (2020, November 24). *Roots: Exploring the history of lacrosse.* [Video]. YouTube. **www.youtube.com/watch?v=JxM5mcuCR8M**

Sabzalian, L. (2019). The tensions between Indigenous sovereignty and multicultural citizenship education: Toward an anticolonial approach to civic education. *Theory & Research in Social Education, 47* (3), 311–346. **https://doi.org/10.1080/00933104.2019.1639572.**

Spirer, P., & Baxter, P. (Directors). (2017). *Spirit game: Pride of a nation* [Film]. One Bowl Productions.

WGRZ-TV. (2022, January 20). *Haudenosaunee Nationals keep Olympic dreams in focus.* [Video]. YouTube. **www.youtube.com/watch?v=sMFxV4NIaVQ&ab_channel=WGRZ-TV**

World Wood Day. (2017, October 26). *Roots of lacrosse by IWCS* [Video]. YouTube. **https://youtu.be/GCyv_4TYf2Q?si=xZQV7CimOI3KpXAF**

Chapter 6

Secondary Teachers' Experience With Using the C3 Dimensions With World History and Film

The Silk Road and the 21st Century: Co-Teaching Ancient China as a Map to the Present

Starlynn R. Nance and Taylor Hawes-Guldenpfennig

As the compelling question—"Does China make the world flat?"—is posted for the first time, the students just stare at the screen, tilting their heads to one side before a number of whispers arise from the silence stating, "The world is round," and "This is a dumb question." Although it is not true in a literal sense, the compelling question gives the students pause. Throughout the unit, students gain more content knowledge, and the strict interpretation of that "dumb" question softens. The students begin to interpret the compelling question differently, and their answers begin to be more fluid and less rigid. This gives the students an environment for thinking, writing, and reading as they develop confidence to create a claim based on evidence instead of just shuffling through a chapter to find a correct answer. Because the purpose of social studies is to "help students examine vast human experiences ... and [also examine] the past [to] participate in the present" (National Council for the Social Studies [NCSS], n.d.), teachers can prepare C3 inquiry units to switch from a teacher-centered format to an inquiry-based, student-centered classroom experience to accomplish this purpose. This unit follows the C3 Framework, using content and disciplinary literacies, historical thinking skills, authentic assessments, and film (in the form of a documentary) that align to the rationales for teaching social studies. Does China make the world flat? Let's find out.

Overview of the Lessons: Does China Make the World Flat?

The goal of this C3 inquiry unit is to teach Ancient China by incorporating three themes from the National Council for the Social Studies *National Curriculum Standards for Social Studies*: Time, Continuity, and Change; Production, Distribution, and Consumption; and Global Connections (NCSS, 2010). These are implemented into all four dimensions of the middle school Silk Road unit. The students will focus on globalization throughout the unit, which develops understanding of the Silk Road and its value through trade routes and in Ancient China (see Figure 6.1). The unit introduces the students to concepts like resources, economic decision-making, cultural diffusion, and the costs that are taken for economic growth. These themes interconnect in the four dimensions and develop critical thinking, allowing students to connect the past to the present. In addition, students will gain knowledge about globalization and global connections realizing positive and/or negative outcomes of each. Focusing on the C3 standards for the sixth through eighth grade, students will be asked to use analysis and inference as they break down the primary and secondary sources and other historical events. Students will look at the content from an ancient perspective but also in "a broader historical context" (NCSS, 2013, D2.His.1.6–8) by using critical literacy to question the author for bias or a different perspective.

Figure 6.1 *Bulletin Board*

Although some teachers know about the C3 Framework, implementing it may look impossible with required state and district standards and/or testing. However, this chapter is an example of how the C3 Framework fits into the required curriculum, giving the students a richer context and bringing ancient history to the present. As seen in Table 6.1, this unit will focus on globalization starting with Dimension 1 and hook the students' interest from the beginning of the first lesson. They will use historical thinking skills including sourcing, analyzing, contextualizing, and corroborating to analyze primary and secondary sources, to begin asking questions, and to be introduced to the compelling question. Dimension 2 includes teaching content where teachers create lessons pertaining to required standards or objectives. Teachers can use different instructional strategies and assessments for students to gain the background knowledge before beginning Dimension 3. Our next dimension will require students to analyze primary and secondary sources that connect to the background information. This will allow the students to develop a claim to answer the compelling question in paragraph form. Dimension 4 uses the past and connects it to the present, engaging students to compare and contrast the effects of globalization to the world they live in. Critical analysis is used to develop a plan of action and to implement that plan to conclude the unit. (See Appendix for a reference list of strategies used in this inquiry.)

Table 6.1 *C3 Framework Dimensions Overview: Middle School World History*

C3 Framework Dimension and Standard(s)	Description
Dimension 1 D1.1.6-8. Explain how a question represents key ideas in the field.	In Dimension 1, the students will complete the hook activity (analyzing pictures of art and Teacher Talk) where they will start to get interested in Ancient China. They will be introduced to the compelling question, "Does China make the world flat?"
Dimension 2 D2.His.1.6-8. Analyze connections among events and developments in broader historical contexts.	In Dimension 2, the students will engage with three supporting questions with formative performance tasks that includes geography, dynasties, and cultural diffusion.
Dimension 3 D3.1.6-8. Gather relevant information from multiple sources while using the origin, authority, structure, context, and corroborative value of the sources to guide the selection.	In Dimension 3, the students will investigate primary and secondary sources to verify content learned in Dimension 2. The supporting questions and formative tasks use historical thinking skills to bring the past to the present by learning about labor markets, ethical and moral issues, and policies that influence trade.
Dimension 4 D4.7.6-8. Assess their individual and collective capacities to take action to address local, regional, and global problems, taking into account a range of possible levers of power, strategies, and potential outcomes.	In Dimension 4, students take learning into their own hands by using knowledge from Dimensions 1–3 and by solving a student-driven issue concerning their community.

Dimension 1: Developing Questions and Planning Inquiries

In Dimension 1, the students were exposed to the hook during the staging of the compelling question exercise. On the board in a slideshow presentation were three images that depict or represent the Silk Road. Under the pictures was one statement, "Source the pictures above," but as many students pointed out, there were no sources on the pictures. Since there were no formal names, dates, or identifying markers, students needed to infer each source from background knowledge. Students filled out the teacher-made graphic organizer (individually) and analyzed the pictures. The students then decided on a term, from prior knowledge, that the three pictures of art represented. The students were quiet when they were completing the assignment, but some looked around as if they were stumped. As the students completed this activity, they formed a Think-Pair-Share (TPS) group and discussed their three terms and the reasons they thought the terms represented the pictures on the slides. As the teachers walked around the classroom, both stopped to conference with the groups. The groups were successfully answering content questions correctly and using terminology from previous chapters like "civilization," "trade," "religion," and "economy."

As they finished the TPS, I got the students' attention to participate in a whole class Teacher Talk where students shared out their words from their groups. Each group shared three words they decided on from their discussion with each other. I wrote those words on the board and put checkmarks next to the words that were duplicated. I asked the students to create a Mind Map (I modeled how to create one on the board.). I gave the following directions: "Using the terms we have collected (for example, "trade," "money," "religion"), list the words that seem to be most important from our list." I asked the students to share out, whittling down the list, and then asked, "Are any other words coming to mind as we are thinking aloud during the activity?" A student raised his hand and said, "China and the Silk Road." All the students were interested in this revelation and started to nod in agreement. I asked, "What is one word that represents all three pictures?" and the overwhelming majority of students answered "trade". I then asked the students, "If you think this could be China and the Silk Road, and your one word is 'trade,' can you think about any other words that also describe trade moving in different areas, such as other countries or territories?" This took several rounds of Teacher Talk and Quality Questioning, but the students did get to "globalization," and I continued the Teacher Talk, asking the students to define that term and explain how it affects trade in ancient times and today. After the students gave me their answers, I made sure to correct and redirect those whose answers were not on topic and eventually posted the definition of "globalization" on the board. I asked the students to write it at the bottom of their Mind Map.

I continued, "From today's class and new knowledge you have gained, answer the Exit Ticket compelling question, 'Does China make the world flat?'" This baffled the students, and some had a visceral response (e.g., "This is dumb," "The world is round," "This doesn't make sense," rolling of eyes), but I simply reminded them to put their answer on their paper and turn it in as their Exit Ticket. The Exit Ticket was graded with feedback in the form of guiding questions and handed back to the students the next day. They would be able to use this on their final authentic assessment.

Dimension 2: Applying Disciplinary Concepts and Tools

In Dimension 2, the students are introduced to three supporting questions that build background knowledge of the Silk Road as dictated by the grade-level standards. The students engaged in map activities, a Gallery Walk, and textbook content-focused Centers that concentrate on geography, history, and economics of Ancient China.

Dimension 2: Supporting Question 1

The first supporting question—"Did the physical geography of Ancient China present ancient people with challenges?"—gives the students a visual to think about the geography of Ancient China and how the Silk Road formed. From the district-approved textbook or other content used in class, the students answered this question by analyzing the features that characterize Ancient China. Students became familiar with neighboring countries, cities, deserts, mountain ranges, and bodies of water. In groups or as a whole class, the students plotted the important features on the map of Ancient China. It is important to add questions to the map activity or place questions on a slideshow presentation so students can begin to think about how geography would influence ancient people and movement.

It is recommended to have the students in groups (Centers or Literature Circles) plotting neighboring countries then answering questions about what they are plotting and how they can answer the supporting question. For example, I asked a group of students working on the map, "What is your first impression of Ancient China?" Most of the students answered about the size and realized its place in the world. One student asked if it looks the same then as it does now. I simply asked, "Does it?" One student in the group pointed to the map on the wall and began to compare and contrast from the ancient map they were using. They decided it is a little different, and I asked them the supporting question and told them to have an answer and evidence to their answer when I came back around to the group. I conferenced with each group as they moved through the Centers and then called the class together. I simply asked the supporting question, and each group discussed their answers and gave evidence from the map to back up their answers.

Dimension 2: Supporting Question 2

The second supporting question begins a study into the dynasties of Ancient China with a focus on the relationship with the Silk Road. With a teacher-developed graphic organizer and Gallery Walk, the students experienced each of the major dynasties. After completing the Gallery Walk and finishing their graphic organizer, the students answered the supporting question as a teacher-facilitated Teacher Talk. I asked the students what accomplishments they felt *prohibited* the Silk Road, pausing as they highlighted the answers on the graphic organizer. I asked the students what accomplishments they felt *encouraged* the Silk Road, pausing as they circled the answers on the graphic organizer. I then gave directions to successfully participate in the Teacher Talk, using two sentence stems so they would identify the dynasty and back up their claim with evidence (from the Gallery Walk and textbook). I modeled for the students how to use the two sentence stems: "___ dynasty prohibited the Silk Road by [add your evidence to complete the sentence]" and "___ dynasty encouraged the Silk Road by [add your evidence to complete the sentence]." Students answered each sentence stem as I used the Cold Calling technique and asked other students to agree or disagree with a student's claim (sentence stem). The next student would agree or disagree and have to back up their answer with more evidence gathered from the Gallery Walk. It took the students some time to get into a rhythm of responding to their classmates, but after a few minutes, more students grew confident in sharing their claims and dialoging their answers. This strategy teaches the students to dialogue and not debate.

Dimension 2: Supporting Question 3

I posed the questions from supporting question 3, "What was the purpose of the Silk Road?" and "Did it cause cultural diffusion to take place?" I kept the same style of dialogue talk as the strategy, having the students turn the questions into the stem and then answering the questions. I had other students react and add to the answers, either agreeing are disagreeing with evidence. At first, the answers were very superficial and at the lower, or knowledge, level of Bloom's Taxonomy, but as I began to ask follow-up Quality Questions using higher level Bloom's (or Depth of Knowledge [DOK]), the student answers began to have more depth and analysis. By having the students think about the supporting questions, the students engaged in annotating a chapter of the text and answering the supporting questions. The students worked together through their annotations to create the Mind Map to use on the authentic assessment. The students worked efficiently with very little questions. The students seemed to be nervous about the answers, so I used the class time to monitor answers and made sure they were getting correct information from the text to place on their Mind Map. I also gave hints about content missing from the Mind Map and where to find it in the chapter. At the end, I reminded them that the authentic assessment (P.E.E.L.) would be assigned soon. I had the students participate in a Four Corners Exit Ticket to get them thinking about using the content from the dimensions to answer the question, "Does China make the world flat?" Teachers can find the full Exit Ticket in the IDM blueprint in Chapter 9.

Dimension 3: Evaluating Sources and Using Evidence

Dimension 3 is focused on using historical skills to analyze sources that help answer the supporting and compelling questions. Using sources allows the students to practice skills used by historians to develop claims or counterclaims while connecting the past to the present.

The teacher will use lessons published by the Council for Economic Education (CEE; Wight & Morton, 2007); full written directions can be found in the IDM blueprint and inquiry in Chapter 9. Moving the students from the ancient to the present, students completed the supporting questions by using primary and secondary sources, including a documentary. The students focused on using different types of historical skills, such as close reading, annotation, reading, contextualization, corroboration, and sourcing. As I started to focus the students on the first supporting question and handed out the documents, it was very important to model the skills using the Read Aloud and Think Aloud strategies. The first supporting question is a great example to model the skills so, as the lesson progresses, the skills are easier for the students. After modeling for the students Close Read with Metacognitive Markers, I started the Teacher Talk with the students. I restated the supporting question and asked about the symbols (used in the annotation) as conversation starters. I asked the students to start with the circles. Most of the circles included the concepts "arbitrary," "equilibrium," and "collusion." I told the students it is important to know what words mean so they can understand what is being taught, especially if the subject is new to them. I asked the class if anyone knew what the chosen word meant, and some students would guess while others would share the correct answer. I instructed the students to write the correct definition in the outer edge of the document. I chose a student to conduct a Read Aloud from the section the word came from and used Teacher Talk to gauge understanding of the section. I repeated this with all the symbols and was confident the students were grasping the new concepts. I asked them to compare Ancient China with our new information about trade. They were able to use the new concepts and compare them with our content of Ancient China in a Teacher Talk session. One student said that shipping things to different countries from China could be considered a new Silk Road: "Airplanes could be the new camels." The students did an excellent job of using all Metacognitive Markers with the documents and answering the questions at the end of the activity. The students did not have any issues with writing complete paragraphs/answers using the evidence from the document and showing understanding of the concepts.

Using documents from the CEE, the students continued learning about trade and sweatshops using the Jigsaw instructional strategy. The supporting question engaged the students in ethical and moral issues by using different approaches to analyze these issues. Students were placed in their first group to become the expert, and then they were placed in the second, or share-out, group to become a teacher and learner. The whole class Teacher Talk would be a formative assessment or a check for understanding to clear up any misinformation or guide the students to a deeper meaning of content. The students really liked this lesson because they had more autonomy to express themselves in each group and preferred using the different approaches as a lens to see ethical and moral issues in different ways.

After the students have a firm grasp of the content, supporting question 3 asked the students to evaluate the three policy options dealing with the sweatshops. As a facilitator, the teacher modeled for the students what "evaluate" means and how to successfully answer an evaluation question. The students engaged in analyzing a documentary using focus clips. This documentary, *China Blue* (Peled, 2007), was filmed in China and follows a young girl in a sweatshop and her experiences of living and working in those conditions. The students watched the entire documentary in class as a primary source, which can be used as evidence in the authentic assessment.

During these lessons, students were more independent in answering the three supporting questions, and I reminded the students to use the supporting questions as sentence stems when discussing in their groups. I heard a variety of conversations and answers about the documentary. Overall, the response to the documentary ranged from apathy to concern. Some students were very disconnected from Jasmine Li's life in the sweatshop and were not connecting the documentary with content learned in the unit. For example, some students were concerned about her well-being but did not see the connection to globalization. One student stated, "at least she has a job," while another student pointed out that, in the United States, she would not be working but attending school. I asked the students what the age difference is from the girl in the documentary to themselves, and they realized she was only one to two years older. This impromptu conversation allowed me to ask follow-up questions that linked the students back to the pictures from the hook (Staging the Compelling Question) and supporting questions posed in Dimensions 1 and 2. From this conversation, I focused the students on the documents used in this dimension and other concepts in Dimensions 1 and 2. In groups, throughout this dimension (Cooperative, Jigsaw, and TPS groups), students engaged in looking more closely at the evidence (see Figure 6.2), including the film clips, to answer the supporting questions, and they also developed a claim for the compelling question, "Does China make the world flat?"

Figure 6.2 *Solutions on the Board*

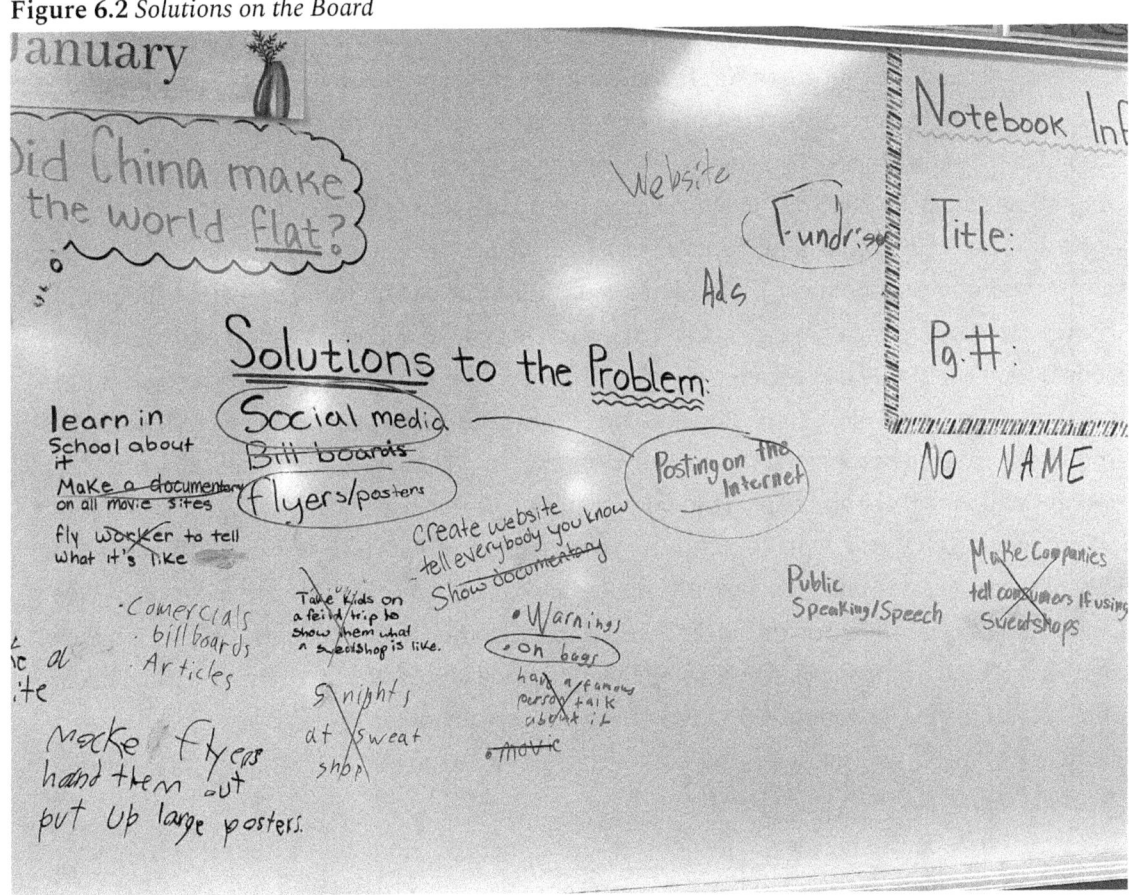

Dimension 4: Communicating Conclusions and Taking Informed Action

Dimension 4 is divided into two parts. The first part is for students to individually answer the compelling question in a first draft using the P.E.E.L. method. (The middle school students from this class were taught how to complete a P.E.E.L. paragraph at the beginning of the school year during the Skills Unit. If you have not taught the P.E.E.L. method to the students, I recommend adding a day of instruction to do so.) Students could use their notes and documents from all three dimensions to develop a claim and complete the essay. The students had one 50-minute class period to work on this while the teacher moved to each student and conferenced with them about their P.E.E.L. draft. Students will need to complete the draft and bring it to class the next day to use in their groups.

The purpose of the second part of Dimension 4 is to communicate conclusions and implement action. On the second day of Dimension 4, I simply asked, "From the Ancient China content to the content used from the 2005 documentary, do you see any issues that relate to our community?" I wrote all ideas on the board, and the students narrowed down the ideas to one that was appropriate for the classroom environment. The students in one class decided that they saw a lot of people throw stuff away instead of fixing it. I asked the students how this idea fits with the concept of globalization and stated that the group had to fill five minutes with a discussion. The conversation was a great exchange where some students used the new concepts from economics and examples from the sweatshop documentary to back up their claims. Unless the students speaking had misinformation or there was a lull in the conversation, I did not intervene.

The second question I asked the class was, "What is the solution and how can we, third hour, fix it?" The students listed many examples, including one student who suggested that our class go to China. All ideas were listed on the board as equal to each other. Some students had very grandiose ideas, but after the students had exhausted their ideas, we went through each of them individually after I explained the limitations we had as a class (e.g., we cannot leave the classroom, we have no money to spend, we cannot interrupt other classes, etc.). Using those limitations, the students decided which ideas to cross off (see Figure 6.2).

I asked the students how they could find out about what their community (the school) knows about trash and globalization. Students' rudimentary answers were to ask others. I helped the students find tools to quantify their answers in a form of a survey. Each student was tasked to give (and collect) the survey to five people in the community. The students brought the answers back the next day, and they used the raw data to analyze the answers, find themes, and come up with a solution. Remembering our limitations, the students landed on a public service announcement (PSA). I asked the students what that means. Many shared out, then I asked, "How can we find out?" One student said, "Google it." I reminded them that they needed a valid website that answered their question. After they wrote a definition and explanation, with a reference, on the board for the class, the students were given time to look at PSAs on different topics online or share out any they remembered in their own life. One student reminded the class of the buzzing on the radio about weather or the loud siren for a tornado warning for the town once a month, and then asked if that was a PSA. The students looked at me, and I said, "I don't know. What tools in the classroom do you

Table 6.2 *Lessons Overview: Middle School World History*

Dimension and Lesson	Description and Time Required
Dimension 1 Staging the Question	This first lesson is the hook and introduction to the compelling question. The students engage in a graphic organizer, Think-Pair-Share, Teacher Talk, and a Mind Map to determine one word to describe the activity with the pictures of art from the Silk Road. Dimension 1 should take one to two days to complete, if the district is on a traditional schedule, or one day on a block schedule.
Dimension 2 Supporting Question 1 Does the physical geography of Ancient China present ancient people with challenges?	The students will engage in a map exercise to analyze physical features that characterize Ancient China. Using the featured source, students will learn about neighboring countries, cities, deserts, mountain ranges, and bodies of water. This lesson in Dimension 2 will take one day to complete on a traditional schedule or half a day on a block schedule.
Dimension 2 Supporting Question 2 How does the accomplishments of the different dynasties prohibit or encourage the Silk Road?	The students will engage in a Graphic Organizer, Gallery Walk, and Teacher Talk to learn about each dynasty and the relationship to the Silk Road. Completing the Gallery Walk will assist the students in answering the supporting question and gathering evidence to answer the compelling question. This lesson in Dimension 2 will take two days on a traditional schedule or one day on a block schedule.
Dimension 2 Supporting Question 3 What was the purpose of the Silk Road, and did it cause cultural diffusion to take place?	The students will engage in close reading and annotating the Silk Road chapter from the district-approved textbook. Students will focus on cultural diffusion when learning about the Silk Road. Students will answer the supporting question using a Mind Map and Centers. This lesson in Dimension 2 will take two days on a traditional schedule or one day on a block schedule.
Dimension 3 Supporting Questions 1. Can you identify the causes of sweatshops and distinguish between two main types of labor markets (regarding sweatshops)? 2. Describe three ethical approaches that are used to analyze moral problems and apply the three ethical approaches to sweatshops. 3. Evaluate three policy options for dealing with sweatshops.	Dimension 3 allows the students to use historical thinking skills to bring concepts of trade and globalization to the present. Students can compare and contrast the Silk Road with trade in China. The lessons are taken from the Council for Economic Education (Wight & Morton, 2007) and supplemented with the documentary *China Blue* (Peled, 2007). The students learn about sweatshops, different types of labor, ethical approaches to labor, and moral problems with labor. Using the primary and secondary sources, students evaluate policies dealing with sweatshops. Using the documentary as a first-hand account and all other content from Dimensions 1–3, the students will be prepared to answer the compelling question. This lesson in Dimension 3 will take four days on a traditional schedule or two to three days on a block schedule.
Dimension 4 Supporting Questions 1. Using our new information, do you see an issue in our community that is similar to the content from our unit? 2. Now that the class has chosen [issue], what is this class going to do about it? 3. Now that the class has the solution, what does implementation look like?	Dimension 4 is student centered and inquiry based. The teachers will use the supporting questions to move the inquiry forward so students can decide on an issue from the community that reflects the content learned in the unit. The teacher is just the facilitator and does not tell the students what issue to choose nor how to solve it. See the full IDM inquiry in Chapter 9 for details. This lesson in Dimension 2 will take three to four days on a traditional schedule or two to three days on a block schedule.

have to find out if that is a PSA?" Students brainstormed in their group and researched the answer. After the students felt confident with their research about what a PSA is and why it is used, I asked the students how they were going to use the PSA as a solution to the initial problem of trash and its relation to globalization. The students researched this problem for several days without my input, reading about solutions from other areas, reading about laws from the community, and calling offices to find information. After they completed their research, they developed a PSA in the form of a morning announcement (It was their responsibility to get it approved and to select one class representative to read it) and a class X (formally Twitter) account that was run by the teacher and approved by the principal. Students wrote and sent the text to the teacher via email to post on the account. These posts included information about how to reduce trash, informational statistics, and tagged free-trade stores or companies that did not use sweatshops. I had zero input in Dimension 4 and was a facilitator, only asking questions to prompt deeper thinking.

The evaluation for this unit was to finish the P.E.E.L. draft students wrote at the beginning of Dimension 4 by adding a section about communicating their findings and implementing their action plan to the problem associated with the historical content. The students completed their essay and brought it to class where they shared their essays with the class in a short presentation for the final evaluation to the unit.

Final Comments
Tips and Tricks

Beginning with the staging the question (or hook) lesson, I was a facilitator and did not offer any answers or correct way to think or answer until the end when we define "globalization." I had prepared Quality Questions prior to the class and used those to not only help the students stay on task but also think deeper about analyzing the pictures, thinking about historical terms, and using prior knowledge from the class. It is very important to use the techniques of Quality Questioning and the proximity technique during the staging/hook. I did not stay in one spot in the classroom and always asked questions to help the students think deeper about the pictures. In one TPS group, I listened to their discussion and asked, "Are there any other words that we have used in past units or on the walls you could discuss?" Students began to check out the bulletin boards, word wall, and posters that would aid them in developing their list. I always listened to the conversation first and then built on their thought process with a question or statement. Most questions I had prepared, but some were on the spot. I always used Bloom's Taxonomy verbs, so the students had some action behind the questioning. Using DOK questioning would also work really well during this lesson/unit.

The content in Dimension 2 is from the state and/or district standards, so it was important to get it all in. My Dimension 2 is representative of the grade-level standards we created from the state standards because we are required to give the same unit evaluation in a multiple-choice format. It was a good idea to give this common assessment at the end of Dimension 2 so I could collect data and be ready for the common assessment data team meetings. Also, in Dimension 2, I used different types of talk. Teacher Talk is for content knowledge, and the questions I asked were based more in knowledge and comprehension to check for understanding of the supporting questions, which were our objectives for the content. This type of talk allowed me to have oral formative assessments and to reteach the objectives as necessary at that moment. Dialogue and discussion were different types of talk used throughout the unit. Dialogue is talk between the students and can occur at any level of Bloom's Taxonomy, though it usually includes more analysis of the content, while discussion occurs at the higher levels of Bloom's Taxonomy and involves evaluation and synthesis. Dialogue and discussion can be guided by the teacher to teach these styles of talk, but they are student-centered and require the student to use evidence and critical thinking to get to the answers.

Dimension 3 requires students to become more independent learners while the teacher becomes the background facilitator. This dimension focuses on primary (and some secondary) sources, so students use historical thinking skills. I recommend teaching the students the skills cards from the Digital Inquiry Group (n.d.) at the beginning of the year in a skills unit or prior to this unit. The students need to be told that they are now historians and that the teacher is the facilitator then list the roles on the board. This will help students to become more independent in their learning; the goal is to use their skills and tools without the teacher being the center of learning. This is easier said than done, but having C3 inquiry units as the curriculum will reinforce skills and independence throughout the year. If you are new to being a facilitator of learning, it is very hard, especially if your primary mode of instruction is lecture. Personally, we do not believe in the effectiveness of lecture, especially at this age level, and instead use many instructional strategies splattered throughout the lesson in a day in Teacher Talk. Inquiry is not the teacher telling the students what their ending action is or giving examples of what to do. Inquiry is the students finding out for themselves, and in our experience, failure is the best teacher. You, as the facilitator, ask questions to help the students think deeper and never give answers.

Dimension 4 is a complete student-centered activity. They will individually write their draft essay answering the compelling question and are guided through communicating their conclusions and taking informed action. The key is to guide and be full of questions to facilitate different issues that come up in Dimension 4. One suggestion is to define "community" so that the students know what population they are working with. In our experience, as part of the communicating conclusions, principals have allowed students to speak at morning announcements and have approved student-made posters to hang in the halls throughout the school, a teacher-made and teacher-run X (formerly Twitter) account for the project, and posts on the school website. The students have had to get permission to do these activities, so it is part of communicating conclusions. The problem and action plans are created by the students, so if you teach six world history classes a day, you will have six different problems and action plans. This is how students learn to solve real-world problems and learn that there is not one way to do it. They will learn to use history, research, and critical thinking to be a part of the solution, no matter the limitations.

An Enhancement From Taylor

This enhancement lesson seeks to provide students another tangible connection between the Silk Road and modern globalization. To begin, I had students identify where their tennis shoes were made. This can be done by checking the tag contained within their shoes relatively easily during class. Additionally, students could check the tag on their t-shirts to provide more variety in their responses, since many students wear the same brand of shoes. I had students share out with a partner and then as a whole group the locations on their shoes. This can be done visually as a class using a word cloud generator, writing on the whiteboard, or even pinning on a digital map via resources such as Padlet. I then facilitated a whole group discussion, asking questions such as "Describe what you see" and "What does this tell us about globalization?" Students should be able to make connections between the variety of locations (predominantly in countries located in Asia or South America) and that of previously learned content about sweatshops, globalization, and the Silk Road.

After completing the introductory activity, I divided students either into pairs or small groups and gave every student a copy of the article, "The Real Cost of Fast Fashion" (Anastasia, 2017). Students can read the article in pairs, or as a small group, annotating with their Metacognitive Markers. After completing their annotations, I directed students' attention to the posters hanging up around the room. I informed students that we now are going to complete a Graffiti Wall activity (see Figure 6.3). This means that students go around the room to each poster and answer whatever question or prompt is present at that station. (Example responses or sentence stems can be provided on each poster to guide students.) After each group had the opportunity to share out on all posters, I provided students time to conduct a Gallery Walk around the room to review others' responses. Graffiti Wall topics could include but are not limited to the causes for the rise of fast fashion, factors that led to fast fashion becoming a three-billion-dollar industry, effects of fast fashion on workers and on the environment, as well as connections between fast fashion and the Silk Road. After reviewing the Graffiti Wall, students created a Frayer Model definition of "fast fashion" using what they learned from the article. During group work time, I rotated around the room, assessing student work and conferencing with groups to ensure they were on task and generating quality ideas.

Figure 6.3 *Fast Fashion Pictures*

Once all groups completed their Graffiti Wall and Frayer Model definition, I facilitated a whole class discussion, allowing students to ask questions or provide additional insights. I asked students questions such as, "What are the main ideas discussed in the article regarding the impacts of fast fashion?" "How does globalization contribute to the rise of fast fashion?" "What are some of the environmental and social costs mentioned in the article?" and "How does the concept of the Silk Road relate to globalization and trade, and how might it be contrasted with modern global supply chains in the context of fast fashion?" I asked students to summarize what they had learned about the costs of fast fashion and its connections to globalization and historical trade routes. We then discussed potential solutions or actions individuals could take to address the negative impacts of fast fashion. These discussions brought up ideas such as shopping at thrift stores rather than buying new or boycotting major brands that neglect their workers or the environment and buying from small businesses instead. Students even made connections to the documentary viewed previously in class regarding sweatshops.

As an Exit Ticket, I had students write a short reflection on what they found most surprising or concerning about the article and how it has influenced their views on consumer choices. These responses were collected on a sticky note and then posted to the door of the classroom on their way out of the room. While not necessary, this engaging enhancement provides students with valuable opportunities to discover meaningful connections between historical trade routes, contemporary global supply chains, and their own consumer choices.

References

Anastasia, L. (2017, September 4). The real cost of cheap fashion. *The New York Times Upfront.* **https://upfront.scholastic.com/pages/archives/articles/the-real-cost-of-cheap-fashion.html?language=english#1070L**

Digital Inquiry Group (n.d.) *Reading like a historian.* **https://inquirygroup.org/history-lessons**

National Council for the Social Studies. (n.d.). *Definition of social studies.* **www.socialstudies.org/about/definition-social-studies**

National Council for the Social Studies. (2010). *National curriculum standards for social studies: A framework for teaching, learning, and assessment.*

National Council for the Social Studies. (2013). *The college, career, and civic life (C3) framework for social studies state standards: Guidance for enhancing the rigor of K–12 civics, economics, geography, and history.*

Peled, M. (Director). (2007). *China blue* [Film]. Teddy Bear Films.

Wight, J. B., & Morton, J. S. (2007). What should we do about sweatshops? In *Teaching the ethical foundations of economics.* National Council on Economic Education.

Appendix
Reference List for Strategies Used

Adams, N. E. (2015, July). Bloom's taxonomy of cognitive learning objectives. *Journal of the Medical Library Association, 103* (3). 152–153. **https://doi.org/10.3163%2F1536-5050.103.3.010**

Allyn, P. (2019, March 7). *Let's commit to celebrating the read-aloud year-round.* National Council of Teachers of English. **https://ncte.org/blog/2019/03/celebrating-the-read-aloud/**

Camel and Rider. [Terracotta sculpture]. (618–906). Middlebury College Museum of Art Visual Descriptions Highlights Tour. **https://sites.middlebury.edu/museumvisualdescriptions/camel-and-rider/**

Dorr, H. (2023). *How to set up learning centers: A comprehensive guide for teachers.* TeachStarter. **www.teachstarter.com/us/blog/how-to-set-up-learning-centers-classroom/**

Francis, E. M. (2017, May 9). *What is depth of knowledge?* ASCD Blog. **www.ascd.org/blogs/what-exactly-is-depth-of-knowledge-hint-its-not-a-wheel**

Gregory, G. H., & Chapman, C. (2012). *Differentiated instructional strategies: One size doesn't fit all* (3rd ed.). Corwin.

Gonzalez, J. (2015, April 15). *4 things you don't know about the jigsaw method.* Cult of Pedagogy. **www.cultofpedagogy.com/jigsaw-teaching-strategy/**

Henry, L. A. (n.d.). *Building reading comprehension through think-alouds.* ReadWriteThink. **www.readwritethink.org/classroom-resources/lesson-plans/building-reading-comprehension-through**

History.com Editors. (2023, June 6). *Silk road.* **www.history.com/topics/ancient-middle-east/silk-road**

Johnson, R. T., & Johnson, D. W. (1994). An overview of cooperative learning. In J. Thousand, R. A. Villa, & A. I. Nevid (Eds.), *Creativity and collaborative learning: A practical guide to empowering students and teachers* (pp. 31–44). Brookes Press.

Lambert, K. (2012, April). *Tools for formative assessment techniques to check understanding and processing activities.* **https://www.utwente.nl/en/examination/faq-testing-assessment/60formativeassessment.pdf**

Pei, S. (2017, June 1). *History of art on silk road revealed by cultural exchange.* Chinese Social Sciences Today. **www.csstoday.com/Item/4490.aspx**

Silver, R. G. (2012). *First graphic organizers: Reading.* Scholastic.

Smith, J. [Jwyks]. (2016, January). *Strategy #1—The graffiti wall (Engagement strategies series).* Musings from the Middle School. **https://musingsfromthemiddleschool.org/2016/01/strategy-1-the-graffiti-wall-engagement-strategies-series.html**

Teaching Tolerance (n.d.). *Strategy: Thinking Notes.* **https://www.learningforjustice.org/sites/default/files/general/Thinking%20Notes.pdf**

The University of Adelaide (n.d.). *Mind mapping.* Writing Centre Learning Guide. **www.adelaide.edu.au/writingcentre/resources/writing-resources#preparing-to-write**

Wisconsin Department of Public Instruction (n.d). *Frayer Model 6–12*. **https://dpi.wi.gov/reading/literacy-practices-bank**

Zakaria, R. (2022, May 17). *How to Use PEEL writing in your assignments*. ICS Learn. **www.icslearn.co.uk/blog/study-advice/how-to-use-peel-writing-in-your-assignments**

Chapter 7

Secondary Teacher's Experience With Using the C3 Dimensions With Economics and Film

Exploring the Economic Dynamics of Home Fronts During WWII: An Inquiry Into Resources and Effective Propaganda

Cameron Pack

As the bell rings, tenth-grade students enter their world history classroom and settle into their seats. On the smart screen, they are greeted with an image of the Michelin Man and three thought-provoking questions: (a) Who is this mascot? (b) Does he have any connection to food? and (c) Did he play a role in World War II? Drawn in, the students ponder the questions, glancing at the compelling question on the whiteboard, which reads, "Can the home front determine a war?" Normally, the compelling question provides a hint for the bell ringer activity, but today, the students are left to rely solely on former knowledge and critical thinking skills. The students began to talk to their neighbors, and a common theme emerged: "What does this marshmallow man have to do with a home front?" Other groups focused solely on the bell ringer and answered the first two questions with their partner but did not manage to answer the third correctly. The best educated guess was from a group that stated, "The tire company provided the tires for all allies." Watching the students engage in their groups reminded me of the purpose of social studies, which is "using an inquiry-based approach [to] help students examine vast human experiences through the generation of questions, collection and analysis of evidence from credible sources ... and the application of social studies knowledge and disciplinary skills" (National Council for the Social Studies [NCSS], 2023). As my students answer and ask questions, searching prior knowledge to answer the questions, the group discussions fostered a microcommunity where they practice skills essential for future participation in local, national, and global civic life (NCSS, 2023). Throughout this inquiry, students will explore content, develop historical thinking skills, and undergo authentic assessments that align with the core principles of teaching social studies.

Overview of the Lesson:
Can the Home Front Determine a War?

This C3 inquiry aims to lead tenth-grade students to critically think about the home fronts of World War II and to answer the compelling question. The question was designed for students to think more holistically about the war rather than just military battles and leaders. This inquiry integrates the Economic Decision-Making and Global Interconnections from the NCSS *National Curriculum Standards for Social Studies* (2010). These standards are woven into all aspects of the home front inquiry, introducing students to concepts such as human capital, physical capital, natural resources, and economic decision-making during wartime. The standards are found in NCSS C3 Framework as "D2.Eco.6.9-12. Generate possible explanations for a government role in markets when market inefficiencies exist" and "D2.Eco.7.9-12. Use benefits and costs to evaluate the effectiveness of government policies to improve market outcomes" (NCSS, 2013, p. 37). The interconnected themes span across the four dimensions of the inquiry, encouraging critical thinking about historical connections and their relevance to the present day. Students will have the opportunity to analyze and compare conflicts worldwide, drawing parallels between current global scenarios and historical home front experiences from the Allied and Axis powers during World War II. This inquiry also demonstrates the processes of Dimensions 2 and 3 as students hone their analytical skills by dissecting primary sources, secondary sources, and historical events. They will explore learned content from the inquiry and examine a 20th-century event by employing critical literacy to identify bias, perspective, and more.

Based on my experiences, C3 or inquiry-based learning is an excellent way of getting students involved in the learning process, integrating these approaches may pose challenges due to state/district standards or testing requirements. It necessitates the application of critical thinking skills by students to address historical problems, thereby equipping them to tackle contemporary challenges. However, this C3 inquiry is designed to seamlessly align with the mandated curriculum, enriching students' historical knowledge by immersing them in the realities of World War II and demonstrating its relevance to the present.

Within this inquiry, students will delve into the economics of the home front, beginning with Dimension 1 with an engaging hook to captivate their interest. (See Table 7.1 and Table 7.2 for an overview, and see Chapter 9 for the full IDM inquiry.) Students will apply historical thinking skills such as sourcing, analyzing, contextualizing, and corroborating as they examine primary and secondary sources, leading them to formulate their own questions and explore the compelling question. Moving into Dimension 2, teachers will deliver content aligned with required standards and objectives, utilizing various instructional strategies and assessments to ensure students grasp the foundational knowledge essential for Dimension 3. Here, students will analyze mostly primary sources in connection to the background information, crafting a well-supported claim or counterclaim to address the compelling question in written form. In addition, Dimension 3 connects the content further by introducing Allied and Axis films used as propaganda on the home fronts. Students have no prior knowledge concerning the films, so they corroborate with their peers to determine a connection to the home front and the reasons why this connection matters. Dimension 4 bridges the past to the present by tasking students with applying their newfound knowledge to effect positive change within their school community. Through critical analysis, students will devise a plan of action and implement it, culminating the inquiry with a transformative learning experience.

Table 7.1 *C3 Framework Dimensions Overview: High School World History*

C3 Framework Dimension and Standard(s)	Description and Resources
Dimension 1 D1.3.9-12. Explain points of agreement and disagreement experts have about interpretations and applications of disciplinary concepts and ideas associated with a supporting question.	In Dimension 1, the students will complete the hook activity where they will determine how the Michelin Man helped during World War II and start to get interested in the home fronts of World War II. This will be their introduction to the compelling question, "Can the home front determine a war?" *Why a Tire Company Gives Out Food's Most Famous Award* (Miller, 2024)
Dimension 2 D2.Eco.13.9-12. Explain why advancements in technology and investments in capital goods and human capital increase economic growth and standards of living.	In Dimension 2, the students will engage in a lesson that clarifies the terminology that they will need in Dimension 3, it will also clarify how these terms are related to the compelling question.
Dimension 3 D3.1.9-12. Gather relevant information from multiple sources representing a wide range of views while using the origin, authority, structure, context, and corroborative value of the sources to guide the selection.	In Dimension 3, the students will investigate primary sources, primarily from the UK and Germany, to gain an understanding of the various home fronts of World War II and how they affected the success or failure of the war. These lessons will be four to five days. *World War 2 – The Home Front* (2015) Nazi posters (Bytwerk, 2023) *The WWII Home Front in Japan* (Hicks, 2003) National Archives lesson plans (2021) "The Stomach for the Fight" (Pine, 2023) *Mein Leben für Irland* (1941)
Dimension 4 D4.8.9-12. Apply a range of deliberative and democratic strategies and procedures to make decisions and take action in their classrooms, schools, and out-of-school civic contexts.	In Dimension 4, students will determine a problem in their school and use what they have learned from the past (in the previous dimensions) to create something to address a problem at their school happening in the present.

Table 7.2 *Lessons Overview: High School World History*

Dimension and Lesson	Description and Time Required
Dimension 1, Lesson 1 The Michelin Man	This first lesson is the hook. Conduct a teacher talk and collect predictions from the questions posted (10 minutes), watch the YouTube video, "Why a Tire Company Gives Out Food's Most Famous Award" (Miller, 2024; 15 minutes), and conduct a Think-Pair-Share formative assessment (10 minutes). As an exit ticket, the students will define "capital" and then list as many forms of capital as they can (10 minutes).
Dimension 2, Lesson 1 Four Economic Terms	Students will divide into four separate groups to create Frayer Models for one of the following terms: "human capital," "physical capital," "natural resources," and "home front" (20 minutes). Create a Jigsaw expert group and then have expert students teach the class (15 minutes). Conduct a Teacher Talk as a class and correct any information where there was confusion, and conduct a class discussion about the correlation between the terms.
Dimension 3, Lesson 1 UK Propaganda	Students will divide into Cooperative Groups and complete a Gallery Walk with the UK propaganda posters placed around the classroom (30 minutes). Use Teacher Talk to clarify and discuss the propaganda (15 minutes).
Dimension 3, Lesson 2 German Propaganda	With German propaganda on the smart board, have students guess what the behavior the propaganda is trying to influence by writing their answers on individual white boards. The winning group receives points (40 minutes). Discuss answers at the end with a Teacher Talk (5 minutes).
Dimension 3, Lesson 3 Nazi's Influence Ireland	Students will watch parts of *Mien Leben für Irland* (00:00:04–00:04:30) and complete a Think-Pair-Share over what they have watched. Then watch another clip (01:15:39–01:17:15) with another Think-Pair-Share activity (35 minutes). Facilitate a Teacher Talk about the different ways propaganda can be used and how individuals, businesses, and society can be affected by propaganda (10 minutes).
Dimension 3, Lesson 4 Propaganda and the War	Students will conduct an e-Gallery Walk, answering questions on a teacher-made source guide based on propaganda used in WWII by Germany, UK, and Japan (35 minutes). Teacher Talk will be used to clarify and answer any questions the students still have (10 minutes).
Dimension 4, Lesson 1 Brainstorm School Problems	Students will use this time to brainstorm issues found in their school and ways they may bring awareness to this issue by using knowledge they have gained about the home front and propaganda (45 minutes).
Dimension 4, Lesson 2 Taking Action	Students create a plan and take action to bring awareness to their chosen school issue (2–4 days).

Dimension 1: Developing Questions and Planning Inquiries

In Dimension 1, I needed to motivate the students to be interested in the topic and teach them to develop questions of their own about the topics. This skill would follow the students through the dimensions, especially Dimension 4. The students began Dimension 1 by trying to answer the Michelin Man Bell Ringer questions as described at the beginning of this chapter. After allowing the students to gather their thoughts and discuss quietly, I began calling on students to answer who the Michelin Man was. Some of the students I called on first had silly answers, such as, "Is that the marshmallow guy?" or "Isn't he from Ghostbusters?" Eventually a student stated, "He is the mascot for a tire company." I replied to the student, "Does he have anything to do with food?" The students started attempting to answer how a tire company and food could possibly be related and eventually made the connection to Michelin Stars. I reply with more Quality Questions like, "Is this tire company the same company that hands out the most prestigious culinary award in the world?" and "Why would they do that?" These additional questions went unanswered. Giving students time to ponder, I asked the last Bell Ringer question. Even though the connection between food and the tire company was clear, both my regular and advanced classes both responded with simple answers. This formative Teacher Talk assessed what the students knew and what they could guess from prior knowledge and their collaborative learning groups. Students would be using content and inquiry to learn these important answers (see Figure 7.1).

Figure 7.1 *Michelin Man Bell Ringer Bulletin Board*

After the Bell Ringer, we watched the YouTube video "Why a Tire Company Gives Out Food's Most Famous Award," by Tasting History with Max Miller (2024). While delivering a recipe for a Michelin Star-level chicken dish from the 1930s, Miller also explains how a tire company got involved in rating restaurants. Essentially, it was done to convince car owners to drive more so that they would buy more tires. Although Miller is a YouTube influencer and *not* a historian, he explains, using primary and secondary sources, that during World War II, both the Axis and Allied powers used the maps found in the Michelin guides. These maps were the most accurate maps of French cities available at the time for each side to get their hands on. At this point, one student mentions that it was clever for a tire company to give out maps to encourage people to travel (though not connecting that when people drive more, they need more tires). More students shared what stood out to them in the video, and students began to correctly answer the questions posed in the Bell Ringer. Initially, I felt apprehensive about presenting this video to a couple of my classes that necessitate continuous engagement to maintain effective classroom management, but each class found the video enjoyable and entertaining, adding that, in their opinion, the chicken needed more seasoning. The students watched the video, completed notes, and then successfully answered all content-focused questions about the tire company. The students then completed a Think-Pair-Share activity answering, "What was the Michelin company's most important contribution to the war effort?" As I walked around the room and the students discussed the question, they easily came up with the answer that the tire company's development of maps of France was their most important contribution. The students were unwittingly making the connection of a company seemingly unrelated to the military or war influencing a violent conflict on a global stage. To end Dimension 1, the students demonstrated their new knowledge by clearly defining "capital" (remind them that it is an economic term and not a geographic term). From their definition, the Exit Ticket asked the students to list the type of capital that is available to governments. Some student answers were "money, the military, gold, buildings, and roads." From the Teacher Talk, some students connected the term to the economics of the war. This Exit Ticket assessed if students could start to connect economic concepts with historical events, which would begin Dimension 2 the next day.

Dimension 2: Applying Disciplinary Concepts and Tools

The next class lesson will involve the students applying disciplinary concepts and tools about the economics of the home front in times of war. Students will use the Frayer Model activity to learn the economic terms focused on the home front (see Figure 7.2). The graphic organizer is a piece of paper split into four parts: definition, characteristics, examples, and non-examples. The goal is for students to gain a deeper understanding of an economic concept from Dimension 2. (If a teacher has not used a Frayer Model in prior lessons, it is recommended to model it.) After modeling the Frayer Model or stating directions, I asked the supporting question, "How did capital and resources work with a country at war?" Most students show some slight confusion at the question, and I try to gauge the room on how much background information is known through the class after completing Dimension 1. I then ask, "What is capital?" As the students think about their answers from the Exit Ticket the class prior, I split the class into four groups, one group per vocabulary term: "human capital," "physical capital," "human resources," and "home front." Each group worked together to fill out their Frayer Model using the 1-1 technology available. I set a ten-minute timer for the groups to complete the Frayer Model. I moved around the room to clarify any confusion by answering questions or asking questions to focus the topic. Once their Frayer Models are completed, create one expert group by selecting a student from each group. These students will take turns completing their particular Frayer Model on the whiteboard. The goal is for the other three groups to learn the concept and complete a new Frayer Model. Students should have four completed Frayer Models after the expert group completes the teaching assignment.

Figure 7.2 *Frayer Models on Bulletin Board*

After the fourth rotation, students have learned from each other and not through teacher lecture. The students take their regular seats, and the teacher begins a whole class Teacher Talk. The students spent time noting the difference between human capital and physical capital using the content of the Frayer Models during the Teacher Talk. For example, one student noted how human capital is a person's life and time, while physical capital is what people spend their lives and time trying to attain. After much back and forth among the students, with very little teacher interruption, I asked the class to list examples of resources that are used to produce goods and services. After the Frayer Model activity, students gained confidence of content and quickly shouted out, "water, oil, iron, and wood." Some students even argued that time was a resource used to produce goods and services. As an Exit Ticket, the class answered in P.E.E.L. format (for further information on the P.E.E.L format, see the explanation in the IDM in Chapter 9), "Why are human capital, physical capital, and natural resources important to a country?"

Dimension 3: Evaluating Sources and Using Evidence

Dimension 3 took five days to complete during which students spent time gathering, evaluating, and using evidence to support their claim or counterclaim for answering the compelling question. The first two days of this three-day dimension involves answering the supporting question, "After entering the war, what happened to the goods and services of a country?"

The bell ringer began with a scenario. I explained that World War III has broken out and all the men in the US between the ages of 18–41 have been drafted. Enemy forces are conducting air raids on big cities by dropping bombs on them. I ask aloud, "What should be done with the children?" and "What should be the role of women in this situation?" This bell ringer does several things. Firstly, it allows students to imagine what would happen if all the young adult males were to disappear, while bombs were being indiscriminately dropped from the sky. Many students brought up two current events—the crisis in Israel and Palestine and the crisis in Ukraine and Russia—to the scenario in their discussions. The students voiced what that might look like if something similar were to happen in America. The students also discussed what would happen if the United States were invaded by an outside power. One student stated his family would just "move to the country," while another stated that they "would go and fight." As I let the students share, a wide range of ideas surfaced including, building bunkers in the city or exiling everyone until the war is over. However, the conclusion was a "dystopian situation like the *Hunger Games* "; the children should be sent from the cities, and the women should take over the roles of working in the factories. I asked about the *Chronicles of Narnia*, and many of the students audibly said "Oh," understanding that they have seen a children's movie that portrays that children were sent away to the countryside. I then began a Teacher Talk about the realities of the United Kingdom and Germany during World War II. This included air raids, the threat of invasion, children being sent away to the countryside with distant relatives or volunteers, and women taking over traditional roles of men in the workforce.

The first activity follows the Teacher Talk and includes United Kingdom home front sources, which are posted around the classroom. I divided the class into seven small groups, each with a source guide which included three to four questions about each source. The students then began the Gallery Walk (see Figure 7.3; A full explanation is in the IDM in Chapter 9) and rotate around to each source, answering the questions found on the source guide. At the end of the class period, after each student has finished with their guide, a Teacher Talk will be conducted about the propaganda posters. This Teacher Talk included whole class explanations from the students. One student did not understand why the United Kingdom had to use propaganda when there was an existential threat like the Nazis. Another student interjected and said, "People don't always do what is in their best interest." Another noted that "maybe some people were doing what they needed to do to be successful in the war, but some others just needed an extra push." During this Teacher Talk, I limited how much I spoke, and instead, allowed the students the freedom to talk through possible answers to the compelling question, allowing them to use their critical thinking skills to determine possible reasons for why propaganda had to be used then and is still used today.

Figure 7.3 *Gallery Walk Examples on Bulletin Board*

The next class period started with the supporting question about how Nazi Germany's home front possibly looked different from the United Kingdom's: "How did economic decisions affect the well-being of individuals, businesses, and society during WWII in Germany and the United Kingdom?" Most of the students voted "different" because of Hitler. Their discussion gave an idea of a caricature of Hitler being cartoonishly evil so the home front must be just as dark and evil as well. One student imagined a lot of dark imagery and skulls in the home front propaganda, including slave labor in the factories. Each class period, I asked the students to explain why they believed Nazi Germany's propaganda would look different than the United Kingdom's. I got a variety of answers ranging from "Nazis are just the bad guys, so of course, it has to look different" to some insightful economic conversation about the difference between the UK being an island and Germany being landlocked. This interaction engaged the students in both Allied and Axis powers' home fronts during WWII. For the next activity, I passed out mini-whiteboards and markers to each student in my class. On the smartboard, I showed one of eight different Nazi home front propaganda posters and had the students analyze and interpret the source. With each source, I gave the students two minutes to formulate a guess about the poster's source and place it on their whiteboard. The students held up their answers and were given points for correct answers. This motivated the students through competition for bragging rights to have thoughtful answers and kept the entire class engaged.

By the end of the lesson, I again asked the class if the United Kingdom's home front looked different from Nazi Germany's home front, and the answers in the classes were now more similar than when I originally asked the question. With that realization, I asked the class if they could make any generalizations about the home fronts based on the answers from the Teacher Talk. One student pointed out that, of course, there were fewer supplies because all the "stuff" was going to soldiers at war, and that women had to take over the jobs men traditionally held.

On the last day of Dimension 3, we watched film clips from *Mein Leben für Irland*. Based on the title, this film seems to be about the classic struggle of impoverished Irish citizens against a cruel English government. However, from the very beginning, these notions are cast aside when the title is shown in German, and the actors all are speaking German, and the release date for the film was in

1941. With all of these factors, this film becomes something much more than a tale of classic Irish resistance, but one of effective Nazi propaganda that uses history as a weapon.

The first clip from the film (00:00:04–00:04:30) shows a British constable and soldiers coming to collect rent money from an Irishman for his home, but the Irishman claims to have bought the home outright. The constable disagrees, and in an ensuing argument, a child is hurt. Have the students conduct a Think-Pair-Share activity about what they believe is going on. Most students could not understand why the Irish and English people were speaking in German. When the class shared out, most students came to the conclusion that the British were the antagonists in the film; therefore, the Germans made this film to make the British look bad. Some commented about the "Robin Hood vibe" to the film.

The next clip (01:15:39–01:17:15) depicts a school graduation, where the British principal is discussing how to be a good citizen. This event is interrupted by gunfire, and one of the main characters steps out of line and burns an English flag. The class completed another Think-Pair-Share to discuss what they believe is going on. They discussed concepts such as rebellion, anger, and frustration. After the conversations, the students concluded "that the Germans were trying to convince the Irish to rebel against the English."

The e-Gallery Walk began with a multiple-choice source guide leading the students through three different websites that detail three very different home fronts during WWII. As my students moved through these different websites, I made sure I was available to answer any questions. Most of the questions were about the Japanese home front, which was an additional Axis example.

Once the students completed the e-Gallery Walk, they wrote a P.E.E.L. paragraph answering the question, "Can a home front determine a war?" (see Figure 7.4). By this time, most of the students agreed that a home front can absolutely determine whether a war is successful or not based on what is happening behind the frontlines. One student compared the success of the U.S. home front during WWII with the failures of the U.S. home front during the Vietnam War. The student stated in their P.E.E.L. answer that the home front is essential in influencing the outcome of any war. They used prior knowledge of the Vietnam War as an example, stating that it was a failure of both the home front and propaganda on the part of the United States. They went on to state that during World War II, civilians supported the war due to effective propaganda, and the war was successful because of this. They concluded that because Vietnam was a failure as a war and as a propaganda campaign, there is a strong case to be made that a home front can decide a war. This P.E.E.L. answer displays a student connecting something he learned from a previous history class to the current history class, and being able to compare and contrast historical events based on their success or failure is an invaluable skill.

Figure 7.4 *Exit Ticket on Bulletin Board*

Dimension 4: Communicating Conclusions and Taking Informed Action

Dimension 4 is the action step of C3 inquiry experience. It is where the students take what they have learned, connect it to the past, and act on an issue in their present. In this inquiry, the students have learned a significant amount about the UK and Germany's home front and the propaganda these two countries used during World War II. If the students imagined that the high school was their home front, what are the problems their home front faces? How could the students influence their peers to fix said problems?

At the beginning of Dimension 4, the students listed problems in the school that they would like to bring awareness to. Through this line of questioning, students brainstormed some serious answers but also some ridiculous answers. Once the students started thinking about what they could change in the school, I began a Teacher Talk discussing how we can use the skills we have learned over the inquiry to bring awareness to these problems and make a positive change. The students discussed this back and forth for a while but relatively quickly reached the conclusion that they could address some of the issues in their lives through home front propaganda. One student commented that convincing students to walk faster in the hallway should be easier than convincing mothers to leave their children in the countryside. I had to agree with that student's astute observation.

I handed out the rubric, objective, directions, and tasks to the students, stating that they were to "create a project to bring awareness to a problem in the high school environment and propose solutions based on lessons learned from the home front lesson." Students could select any problem; the only limitations were that they had to adhere to the policies of the school. Over the next two class periods, students had time to brainstorm and create projects to make positive changes at school. Their actions included a podcast promoting female sports, a commercial suggesting no more homework, and a poster about the school's replacing the iconic "Tiger Head" in front of the school with a metal sign. This activity helped students to apply learned content and skills in order to be involved in issues related to school life and to care about it as their community.

Final Comments

This inquiry delves into the World War II home front experience in the United Kingdom and Germany through an economic lens. These experiences are divided into four dimensions of student learning. Students analyze primary and secondary sources, enhance critical thinking skills, and draw connections between historical events and modern-day implications.

During Dimension 1, what worked best was the YouTube video and how it linked a food video with history, and the exit ticket of listing capital being the only thing that was iffy with this lesson. I only say this because the students didn't truly understand the connection until the next day. If I were to change something from this dimension, I would add a question about capital to the bell ringer so the students can gain some knowledge of the word before the lesson begins. The students seemed to have really enjoyed this lesson, especially the bell ringer and the video. The advanced class, as usual, stayed engaged throughout, and were able to have deeper conversations about the content, with them even diverging into a conversation about how it would look in the current political climate if a tire company's maps were being used in the Israel-Palestine crisis. My regular education students always like answering questions related to mascots, especially ones they have seen before, and/or recognize. The video is very engaging, moving from cooking a chicken recipe, but slipping in expertly delivered history lessons. It really seemed to keep the attention of even my most lackadaisical students. One student even mentioned that they were going to try and cook the chicken recipe shown in the video. What my students least enjoyed was listing the capital, but the exit ticket directly relates with the next lesson, and therefore, though they may be confused how it related at the time, it will all connect the following day.

Overall, my students seemed to really enjoy Dimension 3. They did voice some boredom of walking around the room and seeing the different propaganda posters, because it was something that they were used to, however, their answers about what the propaganda posters were trying to incite and persuade the population to do were well thought out. The students loved the experience of using the whiteboards in a game-like setting to guess the German propaganda posters' purpose. They were laughing, not on their phones, and chatting with each other about what the German propaganda could possibly mean. They even came up with their own team names and were cheering every time they got one right. Finally, the e-Gallery Walk was a nice change of space and allowed the students to use their inquiry skills to find some answers on their own in a controlled environment.

Dimension 4 seemed to go as well as it could with some mishaps from myself. The students will need additional motivation to get started, because being creative with little stipulations can be hard for some people, try not to give them any direct ideas, but more concepts, like although I asked in the bell ringer what issues there are in school, I didn't put any stipulations on it other than to follow school policy. If a student was stumped, I simply asked if they liked everything in the school, which of course they did not. Once they found something they didn't like, finding a medium to express themselves usually went relatively easy. One student, who struggles with behaviors pretty consistently, made a podcast that surprised me about how the school lunches needed to be of higher quality, and I don't know if she did it on purpose, but it sounded like a 1940s radio commercial. They will have a plethora of issues with the schools but may need just some ideas on how to bring awareness to these issues, but with some guidance, meaning allowing student discussion among themselves, getting examples from peers, they will be able to do it on their own. Many students leaned towards doing posters like the propaganda posters they had seen in the inquiry, but several used this as an opportunity to show their creativity using different mediums, such as podcasts, Canva digital posters, commercial videos, and overall, it really came out well in the end.

Finally, I had issues letting go of the reins, meaning that I have had students struggle in the past with an immense amount of freedom, and so to avoid that, I gave more stipulations than was necessary in a true inquiry. In the future, I would just have the students think about issues in their community or school and completely come up with everything else on their own with me only providing materials and support. I think the reason I felt nervous about letting go of the reins was that I had a product in my head I wanted them to strive for, and therefore, gave them more direction than was probably necessary for Dimension 4. However, they still were connecting the past to the present, by using propaganda they had seen in the 1940s to address issues on their version of a home front. This just was not as prevalent as it could have been.

There are several tips for other teachers who may attempt this inquiry, firstly, to enhance student engagement, consider incorporating interactive activities such as Gallery Walks and gamification. Teachers should attempt to provide clear explanations of key concepts and definitions that can help scaffold learning for students. Foster critical thinking skills by asking probing questions during discussions and analysis of sources. Lastly, allow students the freedom to brainstorm actionable solutions to address local school issues, fostering a sense of civic responsibility among them, and don't be afraid to let go of the reins and have the students do the work.

References

Bytwerk, R. (2023, August 2). *Nazi posters: 1939-1945*. German Propaganda Archive. **https://research.calvin.edu/german-propaganda-archive/posters3.htm**

Hicks, S. (2003, March 20). *Simon Partner: The WW II home front in Japan*. Duke Today. **https://today.duke.edu/2003/03/japan_lecture0321.html**

IMDb.com. (1941, February 17). *Mein Leben für Irland*. IMDb. **https://www.imdb.com/title/tt0033895/**

Kimmich, M. W. (Director). (1941). *Mein leben für Irland* [Film]. Tobis Film. Internet Archive. **https://archive.org/details/1941-Mein-Leben-fuer-Irland**.

Miller, M. [Tasting History with Max Miller] (2024, February 20). *Why a tire company gives out food's most famous award* [Video]. YouTube. www.youtube.com/watch?v=-Y_TWPbmiRE&t=934s

The National Archives. (2021, September 2). *The home front*. www.nationalarchives.gov.uk/education/resources/home-front/

National Council for the Social Studies. (2023, November 8). *New definition of social studies approved*. **www.socialstudies.org/media-information/definition-social-studies-nov2023**

Pine, L. (2022, October 27). *The stomach for the fight: The food policies used by the Nazis to maintain control in the Third Reich*. HistoryExtra. **www.historyextra.com/period/second-world-war/nazi-germany-food-policies-second-world-war-shortages-propaganda-black-market-ersatz-hunger-plan/** (Reprinted from "The stomach for the fight: The food policies used by the Nazis to maintain control in the Third Reich," 2022, *BBC History Magazine, 23*[10], 58–64)

Swan, K., Lee, J., & Grant, S. G. (2018). *Inquiry design model: Building inquiries in social studies*. National Council for the Social Studies; C3 Teachers.

World War 2—The home front. (2015). Home Front History. **www.homefronthistory.com/the-home-front**

Chapter 8

Secondary Teacher's Experience With Using the C3 Dimensions With Social Science Integration and Film

Teaching Students to See the World Through Another's Eyes: An Online Course

Taylor Hawes-Guldenpfennig

In their final reflection for Sociology II, one student shared a profound insight into the importance of empathy and understanding in the study of others' experiences. They wrote, "Seeing the world through others' eyes does not mean knowing exactly what they went through, but instead understanding them. It's knowing you may not know what they truly went through, but I can understand that it was difficult, demeaning, and undeserving." This student could have been talking about any number of historical events, cultures, or identities. However, these comments were written during a sociology lesson where students interpreted the impact that inequality has on cultures, groups, and identities. Additionally, students had to analyze why distribution of power and inequality can result in conflict. By the end of the unit, students had to propose and evaluate possible alternative responses to inequality. Specifically, this unit looked at these sociological terms through the lens of residential schools' impact on the Indigenous peoples in Canada. This unit reflects the goals of the National Council for Social Studies (NCSS) by helping students develop the consciousness and skills needed to identify sources of inequality and to address possible solutions for the future.

According to the American Sociological Association (2024), *sociology* can be defined as the study of social life, social change, and the social causes and consequences of human behavior. In this way, the content contained within a sociology course can be broad and extremely diverse. The opportunity to bring in both current events and past historical experiences is what makes the subject unique. Sociology is a science, and as such, utilizes research methods to allow sociologists the chance to investigate the world around them. Sociological inquiry seeks to understand the world by identifying meanings that people and cultures attribute to certain behaviors, objects, and experiences (NCSS, 2013, pp. 74–75). It utilizes the scientific method, is based on critical thinking, and requires students to examine how they are influenced by their social positions. In this way, students learn how to effectively participate in a diverse and multicultural society and develop a sense of personal and social responsibility (NCSS, 2013, pp. 74–75).

Sociology can help students to understand their own as well as others' social problems. Certain people who may identify with a group can provide or reject opportunities for power. These same groups can reinforce social stratifications. As a result, conflicts can arise as competition for valued resources or diminished access to resources (e.g., education, healthcare, employment, food) leads to one group holding power over another.

The lessons presented in this chapter address NCSS C3 Framework standards for students in grades 9–12. Throughout the unit, students will examine conflict, power, and identity as it relates to the experiences Indigenous peoples had in Canada throughout history. Students will compare and contrast primary and secondary sources with a documentary film, *We Were Children* (Wolochatiuk, 2012), to further students' analysis of the compelling question.

Sociology II is an elective class which is taught asynchronously. Each Sunday night, students could view the folders for the upcoming week and had a full seven days to complete all assignments at their own pace. This course is self-guided, with film clips and varying degrees of interaction with the instructor through discussion boards, feedback on assignments, and video lectures. However, students were provided a weekly pacing guide, as well as one workday per week to get caught up on assignments. The complete Inquiry Design Model (IDM) inquiry can be found in Chapter 9.

Students may be familiar with the experiences of Indigenous peoples in the United States from their history courses but have not analyzed the root cause of these experiences nor the impact this treatment has had on the culture and identity of Indigenous peoples over the course of hundreds of years.

Canada's history offers students a unique opportunity for learning, as their residential schools and policies against Indigenous peoples persisted until 1997 when the last residential school closed. The Canadian government has since sought to repair the injuries caused by policies forced upon the Indigenous peoples in Canada and to include these nations in reparations, curriculum writing, and other reconciliations (Austen, 2023). However, students will learn that the mistreatment of Indigenous peoples does not only pertain to the nations in North America. There are hundreds of nations around the world who were treated in a similar way by their local governments (Amnesty International, n.d.). In this way, it helps students to see the world through others' eyes, to increase their understanding of group dynamics, and to develop tolerance of differences.

Table 8.1 *C3 Framework Dimensions Overview: Grade 12 Sociology*

C3 Framework Dimension and Standard(s)	Description and Resources
Dimension 1 **D1.1.9-12.** Explain how a question reflects an enduring issue in the field.	In Dimension 1, students will complete an introductory "hook" activity to pique their interest about the topic of culture as it relates to our world and society. After completing this activity, they will be introduced to the compelling question for this C3 inquiry unit, "Can you see the world through others' eyes?" *"Let It Go" from Frozen according to Google Translate* (Reese, 2014)
Dimension 2 **D2.Soc.15.9-12.** Identify common patterns of social inequality. **D2.Soc.16.9-12.** Interpret the effects of inequality on groups and individuals. **D2.Soc.17.9-12.** Analyze why the distribution of power and inequalities can result in conflict. **D2.Soc.18.9-12.** Propose and evaluate alternative responses to inequality.	In Dimension 2, the students will engage in five digital lessons that teach the content for the unit. The students will discuss their new knowledge by answering the compelling question via discussion posts, online activities, or other forms of digital engagement. *British Columbia in a Global Context* (Geography Open Textbook Collective, 2014)
Dimension 3 **D3.1.9-12.** Gather relevant information from multiple sources representing a wide range of views while using the origin, authority, structure, context, and corroborative value of the sources to guide the selection.	In Dimension 3, the students will investigate and analyze a variety of primary and secondary sources to verify content learned in Dimension 2. Students will be completing research into the topic to reinforce what they have learned so far. These lessons will be three "days" but can be self-paced as students need in the online format. *Truth and Reconciliation Lesson Plan* (Royal BC Museum, n.d.) *We Were Children* (Wolocahatiuk, 2012) *Residential Schools lesson plan* (Law Lessons, n.d.)
Dimension 4 **D4.1.9-12.** Construct arguments using precise and knowledgeable claims, with evidence from multiple sources, while acknowledging counterclaims and evidentiary weaknesses. **D4.7.9-12.** Assess options for individual and collective action to address local, regional, and global problems by engaging in self-reflection, strategy identification, and complex causal reasoning.	In Dimension 4, students will propose and evaluate an alternate response to inequality. They then will develop a plan of action where they describe possible solutions to this problem via a summative writing assessment.

Dimension 1: Developing Questions and Planning Inquiries

In Dimension 1, students completed a discussion board post regarding the importance of translation and communication via the district-provided learning management system. Students watch a video of a singer who performs a version of Disney's hit song "Let It Go" after it has been run through Google Translate into various languages then finally back into English. Similar to the game of telephone, the end result is song lyrics that look nothing like the original. After viewing the video, students answered the following questions:

- If no written alphabet existed in the English language, how would you text?
- How do you communicate as a community with no letters?
- Explain how proper translation and understanding is vital in avoiding confusion and

cultural misunderstandings.

The goal of this activity is to get students thinking about the importance of communication and language to cultural identity. One function of these questions is to set the stage for an inquiry focused on critical social issues like power, scarce resources, conflict, stratification, and identity through surfacing these issues inductively and in a personally meaningful and relatively safe way. Being able to understand one another is key to informing the way we may treat people who are different from ourselves.

Many students landed on the idea of communicating via emojis. However, it was important to ask students in return, "Do emojis ever get misinterpreted?" Students then had to develop another way of communicating that would guarantee no room for error, which was impossible to find. After allowing time for discussion, the teacher presented students with the unit's overarching compelling question: "Can you see the world through others' eyes?" The teacher then provided a brief introduction to the unit regarding the topic of study and significance of the subject to sociology.

Dimension 2: Applying Disciplinary Concepts and Tools

Dimension 2 in this unit focuses on the historical roots of conflict and inequality through the lens of Indigenous nations. Students begin by identifying and defining key concepts related to the unit of study. Students were told that these terms would be referenced throughout the unit, so it was extremely important to learn their definitions, characteristics, and examples so that they could better understand the unit content as a whole.

These terms included the following:
- scarce resources
- conflict
- identity
- social stratification
- inequality (as it relates to power)

Students kept track of their definitions by creating a set of five Frayer Model graphic organizers (see Figure 8.1). Each student was provided with instructional videos created by the instructor for each of the key concepts. While viewing, students filled in Cornell Notes with important information they learned about each term. After viewing the video, students were asked to complete a Frayer Model for each vocabulary word. Then, students sought to make a connection between these terms (that seemingly related to economics) to their sociology coursework.

Examples of student definitions include the following:
- **scarce resources:** Scarce resources are things that are generally low in supply and high in demand. It can be physical objects or work.
- **conflict:** Conflict is what makes us unique. If we all had the same opinions, there

would be no individuality.

- **identity:** We can take on multiple identities depending on things like where we go and who we are with.
- **stratification:** This is the system in which society categorizes people.
- **inequality:** The uneven distribution of objects, treatments, and socialization.

For this activity, students struggled with making the connections between sociology and economics. Some students left this portion of the assignment blank. Others emailed that they did not understand what to do for this section. If students were unfamiliar with economics topics prior to taking the course, they were less likely to see the relationship and connectivity. However, some students did make the connections between the two subjects. One student stated, "All of these relate to sociology because they all relate back to how we interact with each other. Our identity changes with other people, and we also may treat others differently because of who they are because of equality."

Figure 8.1 *Sample Frayer Model*

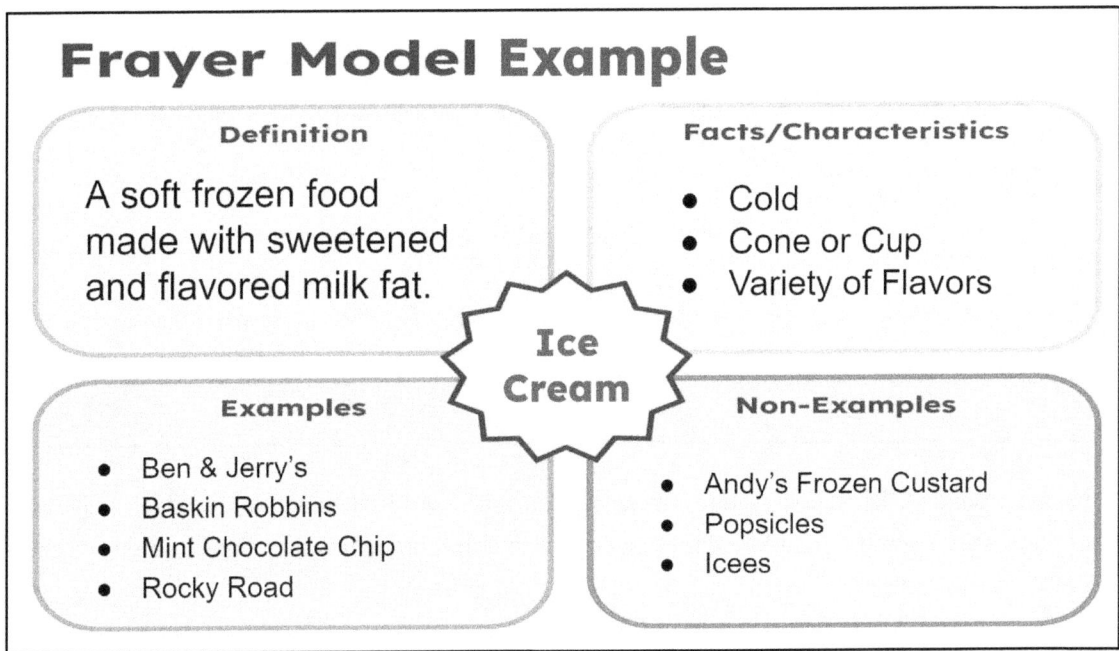

The following day, during the introductory activity, students were asked to generate a definition for "culture" utilizing an image of an iceberg covered in different identifying traits or characteristics (see Figure 8.2). Some were above the water line, and others fell below. After viewing the image, students were able to create their own definition and answer a set of processing questions to be able to connect culture and identity to the experience of being a cultural outsider or insider. These discussion posts were well developed. One student stated:

Culture is the beliefs and ideals that connect you with others around you. The traits that fall in the hidden depths are those you must use to connect with others. Using things like nonverbal communication, eye contact, and body language make us connect with those around us. We don't see the hidden depths of those around us which can lead us to making jump decisions about them that aren't really true. People outside the culture may not know the true meaning of why they do the things they do, and only seeing the physical acts and not the meaning behind them can cause wrong opinions. I don't feel I have a strong cultural background. I feel as though I've been an insider inside the Christian community because even though I am not religious some of my family are. I have felt like an outsider when around people of other religions, I do not follow or have knowledge about it.

The visual provided to students resonated with them, and their analysis was in depth.

Figure 8.2 *Iceberg Activity Discussion Board Prompt*

Culture is like an iceberg. Sometimes certain aspects of our culture are above the waterline and can be seen easily (i.e., food, clothing). Other culture traits fall below the water and cannot be seen so easily (i.e., religion). Visible aspects are obvious to people outside one's culture, while invisible aspects are hidden to people outside the cultural group.

Answer the discussion board questions below.
1. Write a definition for **culture**.
2. Discuss how traits that fall in the "hidden depths" matter in forming and maintaining relationships.
3. How do traits in the "hidden depths" impact perception and stereotypes?
4. If much of one's culture is invisible what are the **implications** for cultural outsiders?
5. Describe your cultural experiences. When have you been a cultural outsider? When have you been an insider?

Implications = the possible consequences, effects, or outcomes that may result from a particular action, decision, event, or situation.

Once the groundwork had been laid for keywords contained within the unit. Students were given the opportunity to record their initial thoughts regarding the compelling question. Students wrote initial statements like,

> You cannot see the world through someone else's eyes in a way that is beneficial to those around you. There are experiences and opinions that one cannot feel or have due to where/how they were raised. It is not possible to fully understand someone, as each person is unique and has their own thoughts, feelings, experiences, and perspectives.

These responses can be collected in the form of whole class discussion, discussion board posts, or other data collection such as Padlet, Curipod, and other resources.

With the necessary sociological terms defined, the teacher is now able to have students identify how inequalities in society can ultimately generate conflict. Students were asked to analyze a set of

United Nations data regarding inequalities in the world (i.e., education, poverty, gender, etc.). After doing so, the teacher prompted students to refer back to their findings, asking further questions to identify student learning: "Look at your Frayer Models. How can you describe the data using the terms 'stratification,' 'scarce resources,' and 'identity'? What do these numbers say? What does that tell us about inequality? How can these inequalities result in conflict?" By setting the stage for how scarce resources and other inequalities exist around the world, students are able to identify ways that this inherent competition can lead to conflicts.

Students who had completed their Frayer Models previously with quality and detailed information did very well with this analysis assignment. However, students who did not complete their prior assignment, or did so with minimal effort, had minimal information to work with on their data analysis assignment.

It is important that students understand how Indigenous nations existed in many places prior to their "discovery" by Europeans, each with their own unique cultural identity, and how this "discovery" impacted the nations specifically. This was done by viewing a video defining the term "settler colonialism." This gives students the origins of inequality and the foundation for future governmental policies. They then moved into a more focused discussion regarding the government-sponsored removal of Indigenous nations as expansion increased, resulting in more and more conflict and the ultimate creation of residential schools, whose main goal was to strip these peoples of their so-called "savage" culture.

Dimension 3: Evaluating Sources and Using Evidence

In this stage of the unit, students are asked to broaden their understanding through a more global study of inequality and conflict. Students began by conducting a case study of Indigenous peoples in Canada. This was done via analysis of primary and secondary sources regarding the policies, experiences, and impact on those who lived in residential schools. At this point in the unit, students were asked to view a clip from the documentary *We Were Children* (Wolochatiuk, 2012) to compare and contrast these eyewitness accounts to what they learned previously from the primary and secondary sources.

In this documentary film, the profound impact of the Canadian government's residential school system is conveyed through the eyes of two children who were forced to face hardships beyond their years. As young children, Lyna and Glen were taken from their homes and placed into church-run boarding schools where they suffered years of physical, sexual, and emotional abuse, the effects of which persist in their adult lives (Wolochatiuk, 2012).

However, the mistreatment of Indigenous peoples is not unique to North America. The teacher asked students to independently research another Indigenous nations' experiences from around the world. Students were asked to avoid North American nations; however, Indigenous peoples in any other country or continent were fair game. The teacher provided a list and sign-up sheet where students could choose a nation or submit their own for review and research. Students chose nations such as the Sámi, Aboriginal Australians, the Adivasi peoples, the Taíno or Arawak peoples, Polynesians, Mayans, and the Bhil people.

Students were tasked with signing up for their chosen research topic via websites like SignUpGenius to ensure that a variety of nations were represented. This was done on a first-come-first-served basis; however, students were allowed to submit an alternative nation for study. There were no students who chose their own nation. No more than two students were allowed per group to allow for increased variety. There were, however, still students who did not sign up and researched nations within the United States like the Cherokee, which was not allowed on this particular assignment.

Once students had independently researched their chosen Indigenous people or culture, they were given a chance to share their findings with the class. The teacher asked students virtually to connect their findings to the key concepts from the very beginning of the unit and to make connections between the experiences of their chosen Indigenous people and that of those in Canada. What is the same? What is different? How was the culture and identity of this group of people affected by their experiences? This activity allows students to see the lasting impact that historical policies toward Indigenous nations has had on whole communities, which is still affecting them to this day. Most students quickly realized that this idea of removal, restriction, or mistreatment of people is not exclusively American. The discussion was rich, with students making connections to experiences around the world and across the historical narrative.

One student who researched the Aboriginal Australians stated:

> I think this is a very similar process to the Indigenous people of Canada as once settlers moved in, the Indigenous were forced off their land and forced to assimilate to their way of life. The people of Canada were put into schools, similar to the reserves the Aboriginals were put into. I think both [Indigenous peoples] faced lots of abuse over the years for simply just existing, and both need proper apologies. They both were issued formal apologies by their country's leader, but both apologies were deemed insincere and not enough. The attempts to memorialize and remember the past have also fallen short. For example, in October 2023 Prime Minister of Australia Anthony Albanese staged a referendum to try and get the Aboriginal and Torres Strait people a voice within the government, but the vote fell short. I think the idea was a step in the right direction and I am very disappointed to hear it did not pass. I think all countries, including Canada, should enforce this rule and get more diversity within their government, especially from the groups they had once tried to abolish.

Once these connections have been made, students are given the opportunity to summarize their thinking by answering the compelling question in a P.E.E.L. paragraph format (see Figure 8.3; University of Hull, 2023).

Figure 8.3 *P.E.E.L. Paragraph Instructions*

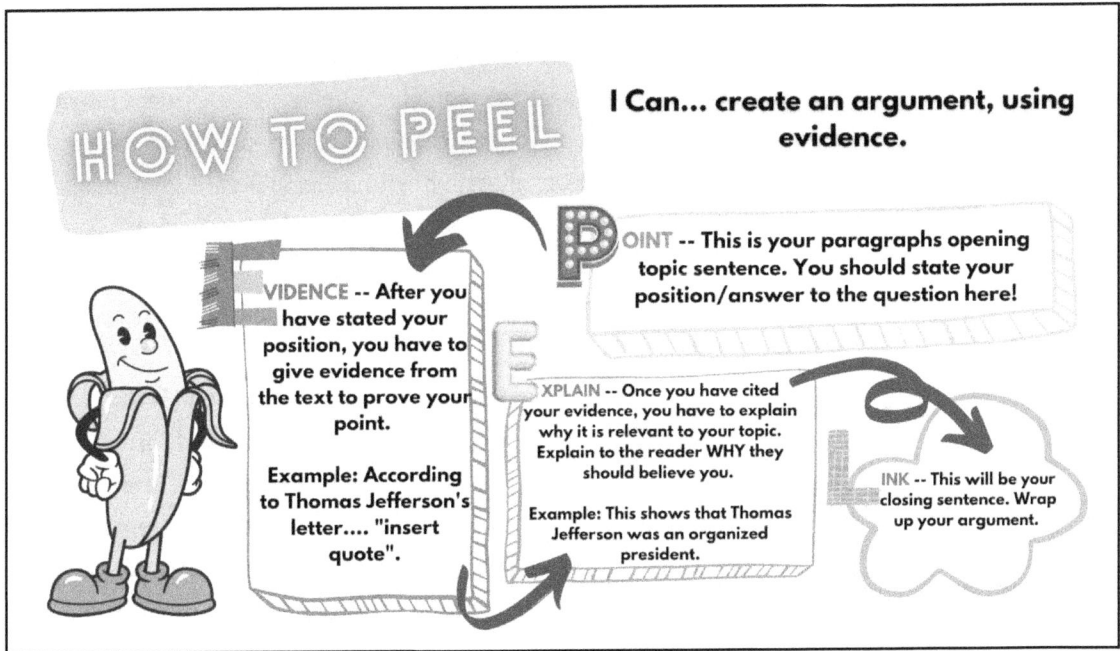

Some students were able to make quality connections between what they had learned and what they see within their community. There were a variety of responses and positions both for and against the compelling question. Students created responses such as the following:

> I believe that it's possible to see the world through others' eyes to an extent, and only if you are truly open to seeing more than just what you would like to see. Seeing the world in others' eyes exactly the way they do is impossible, but understanding their history and the challenges they face is a close second. You have to be willing to understand, and willing to know that while you may not understand, you can still try. Listening to what others have to say is the first step to seeing through their eyes and putting yourself in their shoes.

Others took the question literally, stating that looking into someone's eyes can tell you their emotional state.

Dimension 4: Communicating Conclusions and Taking Informed Action

This portion of the unit seeks to have students think critically about all they have learned throughout the study of inequality and the impact it has on cultures throughout history. After analyzing primary and secondary sources regarding residential schools, as well as making connections to other Indigenous experiences on a global scale, students were asked to identify and propose possible solutions to inequality (see Figure 8.4). This was done utilizing a written essay format. Students were provided a grading rubric and framework that asked them to answer the prompt: "Propose and evaluate alternative responses to inequality." Their responses were to use the five key concepts from the beginning of the unit and specific examples to support their findings. This culminating activity is a perfect time to ask questions that help synthesize their new knowledge and demonstrate a broader and more integrated civic and ethical understanding.

Figure 8.4 *Summative Assessment*

Final Comments

This unit was a wonderfully comprehensive set of lessons that students successfully demonstrated their learning through different assignments and discussions. However, their motivation to do well or to provide in-depth analysis was not always there.

An example on how to complete the Frayer Model was provided (using the term "ice cream") which guided students through what was expected for their definitions. This went well, but students did not understand what to do within the note taking or connections portion of the activity, especially if they were not used to taking Cornell Notes, and emailed to ask further questions. When needed, the teacher would schedule virtual meetings to help guide students through the assignment. Additionally, feedback was provided on the assignments themselves for future use. These two tasks could be separated more easily with synchronous instruction, allowing for whole group discussion. Additionally, teachers could allow students to work in pairs more easily during face-to-face classwork.

After viewing all the discussion board posts, teachers can use the students' reaction to this line of questioning as an opportunity to connect these current problems to a historical root. Students began a broader study of imperialism, colonialism, and exploration that led to contact with Indigenous peoples.

Table 8.2 *Lessons Overview: Grade 12 Sociology*

Dimension and Lesson	Description and Time Required
Dimension 1, Lesson 1 Introduction/Hook	This first lesson is the "hook" into our inquiry unit. Students will be completing a digital discussion board utilizing the district's chosen learning management system. Students will create their original post answering the discussion questions (5–7 minutes*). Then, students will respond to at least one other classmate within the discussion board (5–7 minutes). Once students have posted, the teacher will interact with all posts, posing questions for further discussion (25 minutes). Students are required to respond to the teacher with new information (10 minutes). Discussion Board Questions: • If no written alphabet existed in the English language, how would you text? • How do you communicate as a community with no letters? • Explain how proper translation and understanding is vital in avoiding confusion and cultural misunderstandings. *This online course was asynchronous, and assignments were due weekly. Time stamps are provided for potential use in synchronous learning environments.

Dimension 2, Lesson 1
Defining Key Terms
	This second lesson will begin the portion of the unit that will cover content objectives. To begin, the teacher will share unit objectives with students (3 minutes). After, the teacher will introduce the compelling question for the unit, "Can you see the world through others' eyes?" (2 minutes). For asynchronous learning, this will be done via video instruction.
	    Students will then complete a digital assignment utilizing Frayer Models to define the following key terms necessary for understanding unit content: "scarce resources," "conflict," "identity," "stratification," "inequality" (15 minutes).
	    After defining each term, they will view an instructional video where the teacher will review important information for each term, ensuring that students have correct responses. During these videos, students will complete a notes section of their assignment so that they can remain engaged during the instructional videos (25 minutes).
	For the "exit ticket" students will complete a discussion board with their initial answer to the compelling question, "Can you see the world through others' eyes?" Students should use the vocabulary terms as well as their notes from the instructional videos to formulate their responses (5–7 minutes).
	Unit Objectives:
	• *Identify* common patterns of social inequality.
	• *Interpret* the effects of inequality on groups and individuals.
	• *Analyze* why the distribution of power and inequalities can result in conflict.
	• *Propose and evaluate* alternative responses to inequality.

Dimension 2, Lesson 2 Defining Culture	On day two of Dimension 2, students will complete a "bell ringer" introductory activity. In this activity, students will analyze an image of an iceberg. They will utilize this image of the iceberg to write their own definition for the term "culture" (12 minutes). Students will complete this activity via a discussion board. After their discussion board, students will have a digital assignment analyzing data regarding social inequalities in our society. Students will have to answer questions like: What do these numbers say? What does that tell us about inequality? Why can these inequalities (e.g., oil, land, water, resources) result in conflict? Students will complete this analysis, referring back to their Frayer Models from the day before to complete their responses (35 minutes). Discussion Board Questions: • Write a definition for the term "culture" using the image provided. • How does this relate to identity? • Describe things that are important in shaping your cultural identity. What would it feel like if these things were taken away from you?
Dimension 2, Lesson 3 Conflict Throughout History **Lesson Standards** **D2.Soc.15.9-12.** Identify common patterns of social inequality. **D2.Soc.16.9-12.** Interpret the effects of inequality on groups and individuals. **D2.Soc.17.9-12.** Analyze why the distribution of power and inequalities can result in conflict.	To begin lesson three of Dimension 2, students will begin by analyzing the roots of imperialism. First students view a video that defines the term "imperialism." They then will analyze the impact imperialism had on Indigenous peoples in Africa, after the Berlin Conference. Students should be familiar with this topic from previous history courses. Students view a set of secondary sources (e.g., maps, videos, and political cartoons) related to imperialism in Africa. Students are asked to state what each of these sources reminds them of. They then must formulate their own definitions. At the end of Dimension 2, an assessment over the topic of imperialism will be provided to students. This will be a six-question review of information covered in Dimension 2 (45 minutes).
Dimension 2, Lesson 4 Indian Removal Act (1830) **Lesson Standards** **D2.Soc.15.9-12.** Identify common patterns of social inequality. **D2.Soc.16.9-12.** Interpret the effects of inequality on groups and individuals. **D2.Soc.17.9-12.** Analyze why the distribution of power and inequalities can result in conflict.	For Lesson 4 of Dimension 2, students begin by viewing a video that defines the term "settler colonialism" and the ways it impacted Indigenous nations in the United States during Westward Expansion. They then analyze primary and secondary sources by moving through seven stations regarding the Indian Removal Act (1830) in the United States (45 minutes). This can be done with a digital Gallery Walk or with physical stations in a classroom setting.

Dimension 2, Lesson 5
Summarizing Your Learning
 	
Lesson Standards
D2.Soc.15.9-12. Identify common patterns of social inequality.
D2.Soc.16.9-12. Interpret the effects of inequality on groups and individuals.
D2.Soc.17.9-12. Analyze why the distribution of power and inequalities can result in conflict.
	For the fifth lesson of Dimension 2, students will summarize their findings from previous class periods in a discussion board. This could also be done in a more informal whole group discussion. Additional time to complete the stations or other activities has also been built into the beginning of class (45 minutes).
	Discussion Board Questions:
	• Reflection: After reading through the documents, please reflect on the arguments for and against the Indian Removal Act.
	    o What were the arguments for and against Indian Removal?
	    o Provide *at least* two reasons for, and two reasons against.
	• Based on the video *What is settler colonialism?* how does the United States treatment of Indigenous persons relate to colonialism/imperialism?
	• What does it mean to remove a people? Can you think of any other examples throughout history or current events?

Dimension 3, Lesson 1 Case Study: Indigenous Peoples in Canada **Lesson Standards** D3.1.9-12. Gather relevant information from multiple sources representing a wide range of views while using the origin, authority, structure, context, and corroborative value of the sources to guide the selection.	To begin Dimension 3, Lesson 1, students will be completing a digital activity, analyzing a variety of sources (both primary and secondary) regarding Indigenous boarding schools in Canada, the Canadian response, reparations, and official apologies. During this time, students should also view the clips from the documentary, *We Were Children* (Wolochatiuk, 2012), to corroborate what they learned in the sourcing activity. This can be done in a variety of ways, including a digital self-paced assignment, partner work, stations/Gallery Walk, etc. (45 minutes). Film Clips: • 0:00–5:00 • 5:00–14:00 • 15:00–17:35

Dimension 3, Lesson 2 Compare and Contrast Experiences **Lesson Standards** **D3.1.9-12.** Gather relevant information from multiple sources representing a wide range of views while using the origin, authority, structure, context, and corroborative value of the sources to guide the selection.	For Dimension 3, Lesson 2, students will be comparing the experiences of other Indigenous peoples around the world to those that they learned about previously in Canada. Students will be encouraged to think globally, as they cannot select Indigenous nations from the United States or Canada. These can be, but are not limited to, Indigenous peoples in Australia, New Zealand, Pacific Islands, Sweden, India, Jamaica, Caribbean Islands, or South America. Students will be researching an Indigenous nation of their choosing. The teacher should ensure a variety of Indigenous peoples are chosen, so students must sign up for a nation, thus eliminating that option for other students (3 minutes). In an asynchronous classroom, this can be done via a sign-up website, a Google Doc, email chain, or video meeting as a class. Students will conduct their research individually, ultimately posting their research findings in a class-wide discussion board (20 minutes). Students will be required to respond to at least one other classmate (5–7 minutes). The teacher will respond to each student with questions to further discussion (10 minutes). Students will be required to respond to the teacher directly with their learning (5–7 minutes). Discussion Board Questions: <ul><li>According to your research, what inequality did you find?</li><li>What stratification issue was there?</li><li>What conflict was there?</li><li>How did this conflict impact your chosen group's identity?</li><li>Compare and contrast your group's experiences with that of Indigenous people in Canada. What is the same? What is different? Why do you think this is?</li></ul>
Dimension 3, Lesson 3 Answering the Compelling Question **Lesson Standards** **D3.4.9-12.** Refine claims and counterclaims attending to precision, significance, and knowledge conveyed through the claim while pointing out the strengths and limitations of both.	To finish out Dimension 3, Lesson 3, students will complete a digital assignment or written response answering the compelling question "Can you see the world through others' eyes?" This will follow the P.E.E.L. paragraph format (point, evidence, explain, link). Students will utilize information learned throughout the unit so far. Their responses should be well developed with specific evidence from previously completed activities (45 minutes).
Dimension 4, Lesson 1 Taking Action **Lesson Standards** **D2.Soc.18.9-12.** Propose and evaluate alternative responses to inequality. **D4.1.9-12.** Construct arguments using precise and knowledgeable claims, with evidence from multiple sources, while acknowledging counterclaims and evidentiary weaknesses.	In Dimension 4, Lesson 1, students will complete their inquiry unit and demonstrate their knowledge through a summative assessment. For this activity, students will write an essay response addressing a problem they see within their community. Students should propose a solution to a problem that they identify regarding inequality in our society. This written response will be completed as a digital assignment with a rubric provided by the teacher (45 minutes).

Note. This was an asynchronous course where students worked independently with minimal guidance, so timing adjustments can be made as the teacher sees fit for synchronous pacing guides or face-to-face learning.

Teachers should ensure they outline a clear rubric with expectations regarding this assignment. Leaving it open ended led some students to provide minimal analysis, and some did not provide examples from the unit. Others clearly used generative artificial intelligence to write their responses. By having these clear expectations outlined as part of the assignment via a grading rubric, student responses may have been better developed and provided more in-depth analysis than those who participated in this unit originally.

While students had a clearly outlined rubric and several class periods to write out their essays, many students did not properly address the question. For these essay responses, students were asked to propose and evaluate potential solutions to inequality. Most of the class chose to analyze their selected Indigenous nation as well as the impact of inequality on Indigenous peoples throughout history. However, they did not propose any true *solutions*. Statements like, "I will first talk about the history of the Aboriginal People and the inequality they faced, then the impact this had and how situations like this can be resolved" were common. They simply stated that there are inequalities and that these exist because of differences in beliefs, ethnicity, or other factors. Students may have briefly addressed inequality and posed general solutions such as the following response:

> Apologies don't matter when the actions don't show it. To fight for inequality means to fight for the people who may not be able to fight for themselves. It means to use your privilege and fight to implement things such as equal opportunities, both economic and social.

This flaw could be alleviated in synchronous courses by having individual student check-ins to ensure they are on the right track with their writing. Additionally, teachers could have students brainstorm ideas first in pairs or a whole group discussion, prior to outlining their personal thoughts in their own individual essays.

Additionally, there were obstacles throughout simply due to the asynchronous nature of the course. Students are not required to meet with the teacher and have minimal contact outside of posting in discussion boards or emailing when they have questions (which very few do). The course is primarily filled with students in their final semester of senior year who often exhibited signs of distraction, and their responses and the quality of their work occasionally reflected this shift in focus. If this unit were taught in person, there would be less opportunity for students to ignore expectations or to utilize artificial intelligence when generating their responses to assignments. There would also be more chances for the teacher to allow for group work or whole group discussion to build on each other's learning.

Oftentimes, sociology courses tend to focus on modern-day issues, without necessarily looking to the root cause within a nation's history. Around the world, residential schools sought to forcibly fracture Indigenous cultures. The results of these are still being felt today across Indigenous communities as surviving nations' members grapple with the human rights violations and historical trauma that has been suffered by entire communities.

As Sierra (2023) states,

> The reality is that governments and churches used residential schools to systematically separate, abuse, and indoctrinate Indigenous children. Even today, society at large—and, more importantly, the impacted Indigenous communities—struggles to comprehend an arrangement designed to scrub away culture. (para. 2)

This unit forces students to look at the ripple effect history has and to identify ways to prevent making the same mistakes in the future.

While they can never undo the mistakes of our past, students, after completing this unit, will have the skills necessary to create a brighter future where identities and cultures are celebrated, protected, and preserved. They simply have to do it by looking through another's eyes.

References

American Sociological Association. (2024). *Careers in sociology.* www.asanet.org/careers-in-sociology/

Amnesty International. (n.d.). *Indigenous peoples' rights.* www.amnesty.org/en/what-we-do/indigenous-peoples/

Austen, I. (2023, January 21). Canada settles $2 billion suit over "cultural genocide" at residential schools. *The New York Times.* www.nytimes.com/2023/01/21/canada-indigenous-settlement.html

Geography Open Textbook Collective. (2014). *British Columbia in a global context.* BCcampus. http://opentextbc.ca/geography/

Law Lessons. (n.d.). *Residential Schools.* https://lawlessons.ca/curriculum/grade-9/residential-schools

National Council for the Social Studies. (2013). *The college, career, and civic life (C3) framework for social studies state standards: Guidance for enhancing the rigor of K-12 civics, economics, geography, and history.*

Reese, M. K. [Twisted Translations]. (2014). *"Let it go" from Frozen according to Google Translate (Parody)* [Video]. YouTube. www.youtube.com/watch?v=2bVAoVlFYf0

Royal BC Museum. (n.d.). *Residential schools and reconciliation.* https://learning.royalbcmuseum.bc.ca/pathways/residential-schools-reconciliation/

Sierra, A (2023). *The history and impact of residential schools.* PBS. www.pbs.org/articles/the-history-and-impact-of-residential-schools

University of Hull. (2023, November 3). *Grammar resource: Paragraph structure.* University of Hull Library SkillGuides. https://libguides.hull.ac.uk/grammar/paragraphs

Wolochatiuk, T. (Director). (2012). *We were children* [Film]. Eagle Vision; eOne Television; National Film Board of Canada.

Chapter 9

Ready-Made Lessons for Elementary and Secondary Teachers

Introduction

The following Inquiry Design Models (IDMs) are teacher developed, classroom ready, and correspond to chapters three through eight. As mentioned in earlier chapters, the goal for the C3 inquiries was to highlight Dimension 2 and incorporate film to enhance elementary and secondary students' experience of learning social studies. The IDM blueprints follow the order of chapters 3–8. For an optimal teaching experience, we recommend reading the chapters first to gain insight, learn the framework, take into account teacher tips, and read about the students' experiences during the inquiries.

SEAN BOYLE AND LORI BOYLE

Elementary Geography

How did geography contribute to the differences in early American colonies?

Supporting Questions Dimension 2
1. What were major physical geographical features of the 13 colonies?
2. How did the climate in the colonies contribute to regional growth?
3. What major Native American groups lived in areas attempted to be colonized by England?

Supporting Questions Dimension 3
1. What are some positive and negative consequences of European and Native American relationships during colonization?
2. What were major industries in the three colonial regions, and how did those industries help shape the colonies?
3. How did geographical features (e.g., Hudson River, Chesapeake Bay, Appalachian Mountains) influence colony locations?

Supporting Questions Dimension 4
1. Using what we have learned, what physical geographical features are needed to start a new settlement?
2. Using what we have learned, in addition to physical features, describe other factors that play a part in choosing the location of a new settlement?
3. Using what we have learned, where would you establish a settlement that would be successful?

Elementary Geography

	How did geography contribute to the differences in early American colonies?
Standards and Content	**C3 Standards:** D2.Geo.6.3-5. Describe how environmental and cultural characteristics influence population distribution in specific places or regions. **NCSS Themes:** ❸ People, Places, and Environments ❺ Individuals, Groups, and Institutions ❾ Global Connections
Staging the Compelling Question	**Dimension 1:** Introduce the compelling question by having the students play a simulation game (www.misocialstudies.org/locationsimulations.html) to determine where they would place a settlement. As geographical features and clues are revealed, have students turn and talk with others in their group about new clues, where to place a settlement, and why. After table talk, the teacher will facilitate a full class discussion asking tables for their decision and explanation of the settlement site.

Dimension 2

Supporting Question 1	Supporting Question 2	Supporting Question 3
What were major physical geographical features of the 13 colonies?	How did the climate in the colonies contribute to regional growth?	What major Native American nations lived in areas attempted to be colonized by England?
Formative Performance Task	**Formative Performance Task**	**Formative Performance Task**
Analyze the physical features that characterize the 13 original colonies, focusing on mountain ranges and bodies of water.	Formulate a response, in groups, to questions posed by the teacher about how different climates would affect colonization.	Create a Venn diagram to compare and contrast different Native American cultures.
Featured Sources	**Featured Sources**	**Featured Sources**
Source A: Map of physical features of 13 colonies	**Source A:** *Colonial America: 3 Regions of Colonies* (Video) **Source B:** Blank map of 13 colonies for students to label	**Source A:** Map of Native American nations and their locations **Source B:** *Comparing the Lives of Native Peoples* (Video)

Dimension 3

Bell Ringer:
Quick Write (students will write a 2-3 sentence response): Describe how climate influenced the formation of colonies.

Supporting Question 1	Supporting Question 2	Supporting Question 3
What are some positive and negative consequences of European and Native American relationships during colonization?	What were major industries in the three colonial regions, and how did those industries help shape the colonies?	How did geographical features (e.g., Hudson River, Chesapeake Bay, Appalachian Mountains) influence colony locations?

Formative Performance Task	Formative Performance Task	Formative Performance Task
Create T-chart and list positive and negative consequences of European and Native American relationships.	Complete a teacher-created mini quiz about industries in the colonies	Answer questions about how colonial regions were influenced by major physical geographical features. Create an edible map of the United States.
Featured Sources	**Featured Sources**	**Featured Sources**
Source A: Teacher-made slideshow	Source A: Teacher-made slideshow Source B: *Comparing New England, Middle, and the Southern British colonies* (Video; pause to discuss each region)	Source A: Map of physical features of 13 colonies Source B: The Edible United States Source C: Teacher-made slideshow

Dimension 4

Supporting Question 1	Supporting Question 2	Supporting Question 3
Using what we have learned, what physical geographical features are needed to start a new settlement?	Using what we have learned, in addition to physical features, describe other factors that play a part in choosing the location of a new settlement.	Using what we have learned, where would you establish a settlement that would be successful?
Formative Performance Task	**Formative Performance Task**	**Formative Performance Task**
Make a list of important geographical features in groups and then share with the class.	Play the simulation game again. Discuss how their decisions have changed since the first time playing and why.	See summative task.
Featured Sources	**Featured Sources**	**Featured Sources**
No sources	Source A: Simulation game	Source A: Teacher-made slideshow detailing four needed parts of a map (title, compass, key or legend, scale)

Summative Performance Task	*How did geography contribute to the difference in early American colonies?* Construct an argument by creating a map of where you would locate a new settlement including a scale, key, compass, and title. Focus solely on surrounding areas, not what would be included inside the settlement. On the back of the map, write four to five sentences explaining your location and why you settled there.

Overview

Inquiry Description

This inquiry leads students through an investigation of the early American colonization period. It focuses on the geography (physical, cultural, climate) and the effects of the geography on the colonization of North America. Students will engage maps and video to examine and analyze the locations of English colonies in North America. An extension lesson could use an AI tool (recommended tool: **www.magicschool.ai/**) to have an academic conversation with colonists about their lives and struggles in early America. The students will create a map exhibiting the location of a new settlement and its surrounding geographical features. Students will go through all four dimensions of C3 Framework.

This inquiry is expected to take four to five days with 55-minute class periods. The inquiry time frame could expand if teachers think their students need additional instructional experiences (e.g., supporting questions, formative performance tasks, featured sources, writing, watching documentary clips). Teachers are encouraged to adapt the inquiry to meet the needs and interests of their students. This inquiry lends itself to AI, differentiation, and modeling of historical thinking skills while assisting students in reading and viewing the variety of sources.

Structure of the Inquiry

Dimension 1: The "hook" activity and introduction to the compelling question
Dimension 2: Content (using C3 Framework, NCSS Themes, state/district curriculum)
Dimension 3: Primary, secondary, and documentary sources to evaluate
Dimension 4: Action plan and implementation with authentic assessment

Dimension 1

Staging the Compelling Question

Go to the Michigan Social Studies Hub webpage for location simulation activities and begin the settlement location simulator "Where should we locate our colonial town?"

Teachers may implement this task with the following procedures:
- Have students in small groups discuss each new geographical feature that is revealed and how that would help them choose the best location for their settlement. Give about one minute for discussion.
- After small group discussion, have a teacher-facilitated whole class discussion, as the teacher will call on small groups to explain their answers.

Source: Michigan Department of Education. (n.d.). *Where should we locate our...?* www.misocialstudies.org/locationsimulations.html

Dimension 2

Supporting Question 1

The first supporting question is "What were major physical geographical features of the 13 colonies?"

The formative task is to analyze the physical features that characterize the 13 original colonies focusing on mountain ranges and bodies of water.

Teachers may implement this task with the following procedures:
- After allowing students several minutes to examine the map (Source A), have a whole class discussion to analyze geographical findings.
- The teacher will have the same map on the projector screen, asking specific questions and explaining details about key geography of the region.

The following source was selected to complete the tasks:

- **Source A:** Map of physical features of 13 colonies. Use map titled *Appalachian Mountains* from Britannica. (n.d.). *Appalachian Mountains: Media*. www.britannica.com/place/Appalachian-Mountains/images-videos
- *Note.* The teacher can use maps from an alternative online source if needed.

Supporting Question 2

The second supporting question is "How did the climate in the colonies contribute to regional growth?"

The formative task is as follows: Groups will have mini whiteboards at their table. As a group, they will formulate a response to questions posed by the teacher about how different climates would affect colonization.

Teachers may implement this task with the following procedures:
- Teacher will distribute a blank colony map (Source B) to each student, explaining that throughout the video, there will be times to complete certain sections of the map.
- Teacher will play the video (Source A), pausing when needed to allow students to complete tasks.
- Once the video is complete, the teacher will distribute a mini whiteboard and marker to each student. The teacher will then ask teacher-generated questions about the video and the climate and characteristics of each region in the 13 colonies.

The following sources were selected to complete the tasks:
- **Source A:** Miacademy Learning Channel. (2024, December 6). *Colonial America: 3 regions of colonies - U.S. history for kids* [Video]. YouTube. www.youtube.com/watch?v=7PXnraFcTnM (Play the entire video, pausing to allow students to complete tasks as directed.)
- **Source B:** Blank map of 13 colonies for students to label from Education.com. (n.d.). *The thirteen colonies*. www.education.com/worksheet/article/13-colonies/

Supporting Question 3

The third supporting question is "What major Native American nations lived in areas attempted to be colonized by England?"

The formative task is as follows: Students will create a Venn diagram to compare and contrast different Native American cultures.

Teachers may implement this task with the following procedures:
- The teacher will distribute a blank Venn diagram and one Native American map (Source A) to each student.
- Prior to playing the video, the teacher will facilitate class discussion. The teacher will ask probing questions such as "How are people different?" and "How do those differences affect places like this class, your neighborhood, your city, the state of Michigan?"
- After asking some probing questions, the teacher will play the video (Source B), stopping as the teacher sees fit to explain information seen in the video.
- Once the video is complete, the teacher will review the map of Native American nations with the students, focusing mainly on the nations located in the original 13 colonies.
- In small groups, the teacher will allow 10-15 minutes for students to discuss and complete Venn diagrams comparing and contrasting Wampanoag and Powhatan nations. The students are encouraged to use the video that was played or any online sources they find to help them complete the diagram.
- After 15 minutes, the teacher will facilitate a full class discussion on the findings in each group's diagram.

The following sources were selected to complete the tasks:
- **Source A:** Smithsonian National Museum of the American Indian. (2018). *Northern Plains treaties: Is a treaty intended to be forever?* Native Knowledge 360° https://americanindian.si.edu/nk360/plains-treaties (Scroll down and click *Map: World Views*
  Note. The teacher can use maps from an alternative online source if needed.)
- **Source B:** Harmony Square—Educational Videos and Activities. (2019, October 9). *Comparing the lives of Native Peoples: Learn about the history and culture of Native Peoples* [Video]. YouTube. www.youtube.com/watch?v=NErXRVfm1uU (Play the entire video.)

Dimension 3

Supporting Question 1

Bell Ringer:
- On the projector screen, the teacher will type a Quick Write prompt: Describe how climate played a part in forming the 13 colonies.
- The teacher will allow four to five minutes for the students to type a two- to three-sentence response in their Quick Write journal.

The first supporting question is "What are some positive and negative consequences of European and Native American relationships during colonization?"

The formative task is as follows: Students will create a T-chart and list positive and negative consequences of European and Native American relationships

Teachers may implement this task with the following procedures:
- When the students enter the class, the teacher will have the Quick Write on the projector screen and allow the students four to five minutes to complete their journal entry. The teacher will then ask one or two students to share their answers and facilitate a discussion based on the answers.
- The teacher will use a self-made slideshow presentation (Source A) to teach students about the relationship between the early colonists and the Native Americans. As the teacher progresses through the slideshow, be sure to ask questions such as "How would this make them feel?" or "Would this make setting up a colony easy or difficult?"
- Once the slideshow is complete, the teacher will help the students create a T-chart and allow small group discussions for 8-10 minutes about the positive and negative consequences of the relationships between early colonists and the Native Americans.
- After about 10 minutes, the teacher will facilitate a whole class discussion about the group answers.

The following source was selected to complete the task:
Source A: A teacher-created slideshow, including slides about food, Columbian Exchange, and diseases

Supporting Question 2

The second supporting question is "What were major industries in the three colonial regions, and how did those industries help shape the colonies?"

The formative task is a teacher-created mini quiz about industries in the colonies.

Teachers may implement this task with the following procedures:
- The teacher will use a self-created slideshow (Source A) to introduce the students to the different industries and to which regions those industries belonged. The slideshow also needs to include information about how those industries created differences in wants and needs between the colonies.
- After the slideshow, the teacher will start the video (Source B) at 1:15 and let the video play until 3:19, pausing it there. The teacher will facilitate a discussion and ask questions relevant to that section of the video.
- After the discussion, the teacher will restart the video at 5:27 and play until 7:02.
- Once again, the teacher will facilitate a discussion and ask questions relevant to that section of the video.
- After the discussion, the teacher will restart the video at 8:49 and play until 9:42.
- Then the teacher will facilitate a discussion and ask questions relevant to that section of the video.
- Following the third section of the video and the discussion of that section, the teacher will hand out the teacher-created mini quiz to the students.

The following sources were selected to complete the tasks:
- **Source A**: Teacher-developed slideshow
- **Source B**: Civics Review. (2022, November 9). *Comparing New England, Middle, and the Southern British colonies* [Video]. YouTube. www.youtube.com/watch?v=D_MUtWssRJE

Supporting Question 3

The third supporting question is "How did geographical features (e.g., Hudson River, Chesapeake Bay, Appalachian Mountains) influence colony locations?"

The formative task is as follows: The teacher will say a major physical geographical feature of colonies and/or ask questions about how colonial regions were influenced by geography and have students respond with which colonial region(s) exhibit that type of geography. Students will also create an edible map of the United States.

Teachers may implement this task with the following procedures:
- First, the teacher will facilitate discussion in the whole class using a self-made slideshow presentation (Source C) detailing the physical geographical features of the 13 colonies. The teacher will ask questions to class such as "How would this affect settlements?" or "Why would this be important to the colonists?"
- Following the slideshow, the teacher will distribute one map to each student detailing the physical geographical features of the 13 colonies (Source A). Give the students a few minutes in small groups to discuss what they see on the maps and then have a whole class discussion about their findings.
- After the whole class discussion, the teacher will have a list of physical geographical questions that relate to the colonies. The teacher will take about five to six minutes to ask the questions, get correct responses from students, and briefly explain the answers so all students can understand.
- The students will create an edible physical features map of the United States (see Source B).

The following sources were selected to complete the tasks:
- **Source A:** Britannica. (n.d.). Appalachian Mountains: Media. www.britannica.com/place/Appalachian-Mountains/images-videos (Use map titled *Appalachian Mountains*.)
- **Source B:** A. W. Creations. (2019). Social studies lesson plan: The edible United States. Teachers Pay Teachers. www.teacherspayteachers.com/Product/Social-Studies-Lesson-Plan-The-Edible-United-States-4339694
- **Source C:** Teacher-developed slideshow (*Note*: The teacher can use maps from an online source if needed.)

Dimension 4

Overview

In Dimension 4, students will use what they have learned and apply it. The supporting questions will no longer be to inquire about basic or background information but rather to expand the students' thinking about the geography of the colonies. In this section, the students will be asked to think back upon what they have learned and to begin to apply it to the creation of what will be the summative assessment: a regional map of where they would choose to settle a colony. By using the information they have learned, students will be able to apply their knowledge in detail and give explanations for their decisions on location based on climate, geography, native inhabitants, etc. Prior to the summative assessment, the teacher will play the simulation game once again with the students, having them use the information they have learned in the lesson to better help them choose a location for a successful settlement.

Supporting Question 1

The first supporting question is "Using what we have learned, what physical geographical features are needed to start a new settlement?"

The formative task is as follows: Students will make a list of important geographical features in their group and then share with the class.

Supporting Question 2

The second supporting question is "Using what we have learned, in addition to physical features, describe other factors that play a part in choosing the location of a new settlement."

The formative task is as follows:

Teachers may implement this task with the following procedures:
- Play the simulation game again.
- Discuss with students how their decisions have changed since the first time playing and why.

The following source was selected to complete the task:
Source A: Simulation game, "Where should we locate our colonial town?" Michigan Social Studies Hub (www.misocialstudies.org/locationsimulations.html)

Supporting Question 3

The third supporting question is "Using what we have learned, where would you establish a settlement that would be successful?"

The formative task is the summative task.

The following sources were selected to complete the task:
Source A: Teacher-developed slideshow detailing four needed parts of a map (title, compass, key or legend, scale)

Summative Performance Task

Students will create a map on construction paper using crayons, markers, and colored pencils of where they would locate a new settlement including a scale, key, compass, and title. Students need to focus solely on surrounding areas, climate, native inhabitants, and geographical features, not what would be included inside their settlement.

As the teacher walks through class, be sure to talk with students asking them about where their water sources are, food sources, land formations, and climate. Remind the students about their scale and how far things are away since this is a map during a time period before trains, planes, and automobiles.

On the back of their map, students will write four to five sentences explaining their location and the reasons they settled there.

References

A. W. Creations. (2019). *Social studies lesson plan: The edible United States.* Teachers Pay Teachers. **www.teacherspayteachers.com/Product/Social-Studies-Lesson-Plan-The-Edible-United-States-4339694**

Britannica. (n.d.). *Appalachian Mountains: Media.* **www.britannica.com/place/Appalachian-Mountains/images-videos**

C3 Teachers. (2021, September 16). *Inquiry design model.* **https://c3teachers.org/idm/**

Civics Review. (2022, November 9). *Comparing New England, Middle, and the Southern British colonies* [Video]. YouTube. **www.youtube.com/watch?v=D_MUtWssRJE**

Education.com. (2020). The thirteen colonies. **www.education.com/worksheet/article/13-colonies/**

Harmony Square—Educational Videos and Activities. (2019, October 9). *Comparing the lives of Native Peoples: Learn about the history and culture of Native Peoples* [Video]. YouTube. **www.youtube.com/watch?v=NErXRVfm1uU**

Miacademy Learning Channel. (2022, September 18). *Colonial America: 3 regions of colonies - U.S. history for kids* [Video]. YouTube. **www.youtube.com/watch?v=frfPhtzKuSk&t=3s**

Michigan Department of Education. (n.d.). *Where should we locate our...?* **www.misocialstudies.org/locationsimulations.html**

National Council for the Social Studies. (2013). *The college, career, and civic life (C3) framework for social studies state standards: Guidance for enhancing the rigor of K–12 civics, economics, geography, and history.*

Smithsonian National Museum of the American Indian. (2018). *Northern Plains treaties: Is a treaty intended to be forever?* Native Knowledge 360° **https://americanindian.si.edu/nk360/plains-treaties**

Samantha Faivor

Grade 3 Civics

How can we make a difference in our community?

Supporting Questions Dimension 1
1. What are different ways people can help improve their community?
2. Why is it important for people to participate in their community government?
3. What ideas do we have that could help make our school community better?

Supporting Questions Dimension 2
1. What are laws, and why do we have them?
2. What are the steps in the legislative process?
3. How do the different branches of government work together to create laws and govern?
4. What role do citizens play in the legislative process, and how can understanding the legislative process help us to advocate for changes in our community?

Supporting Questions Dimension 3
1. How can we make a real difference in our community through the legislative process?
2. How do we identify areas for improvement within our school community and gather evidence to support these ideas?
3. How can we use this evidence to create strong arguments (bills) for improving our school?

Supporting Questions Dimension 4
1. How can we effectively communicate and advocate for our proposals to ensure they make a positive impact on our school community?
2. What factors should we consider when deciding whether to support or oppose a bill?
3. How does understanding the legislative process and actively using our voices empower us to make a difference in our community?

Grade 3 Civics

	How can we make a difference in our community?
Standards and Content	**C3 Standards:** D2.Civ.2.3-5. Explain how a democracy relies on people's responsible participation, and draw implications for how individuals should participate. D2.Civ.4.3-5. Explain how groups of people make rules to create responsibilities and protect freedoms. D2.Civ.7.3-5. Apply civic virtues and democratic principles in school settings. **NCSS Theme:** ⑩ Civic Ideals and Practices
Staging the Compelling Question	**Dimension 1:** Respond to the compelling question, "How can we, as students, actively participate in making a difference in our community?" by completing a Quick Write individually. Discuss your ideas with a partner using the Think-Pair-Share strategy, then share insights with the larger group. Document initial thoughts to capture your current understanding of community involvement. Revisit the compelling question after exploring. Record your revised thoughts and new ideas using a T-chart: initial ideas in the "What I Thought" column and updated insights in the "What I Think Now" column.

Dimension 1

Supporting Question 1	Supporting Question 2	Supporting Question 3
What are different ways people can help improve their community?	Why is it important for people to participate in their community government?	What ideas do we have that could help make our school community better?
Formative Performance Task	**Formative Performance Task**	**Formative Performance Task**
Analyze different roles that community members can play in improving their communities. Create a visual mind map linking community roles to the actions they take to improve the community. Answer: How does each role contribute to the common good?	Evaluate the impact of civic participation and advocacy on community government. Write a short paragraph discussing why students think it is important to participate in government. Answer: Why does having a say in government matter, and what can happen if people choose not to participate?	Brainstorm possible proposal ideas for school improvement.
Featured Sources	**Featured Sources**	**Featured Sources**
Source A: Teacher-developed example of a mind map **Source B (supplemental):** Teacher-developed vocabulary presentation on "community," "civic participation," and "common good"	**Source A:** *The Voice That Won the Vote* by Elisa Boxer, illustrated by Vivien Mildenberger	**Source A:** Teacher-developed school improvement brainstorming graphic organizer

Exit Ticket Suggestion:
Revisit your responses to the compelling question. Reflect on your initial thoughts and whether your views have changed based on what you have learned and discussed.

Dimension 2

Supporting Question 1	Supporting Question 2	Supporting Question 3	Supporting Question 4
What are laws, and why do we have them?	What are the steps in the legislative process?	How do the different branches of government work together to create laws and govern?	What role do citizens play in the legislative process, and how can understanding the legislative process help us to advocate for changes in our community?
Formative Performance Task	**Formative Performance Task**	**Formative Performance Task**	**Formative Performance Task**
Discuss the nature of laws and their importance in society.	Watch "I'm Just a Bill" from *Schoolhouse Rock* and map out the legislative process.	Explore the roles and interactions of the three branches of government in the legislative process.	Identify specific problem areas within your assigned school improvement categories and begin brainstorming potential solutions to these problems.
Featured Sources	**Featured Sources**	**Featured Sources**	**Featured Sources**
Source A: *The School with No Rules* by Dr. Poppy Moon	**Source A:** *Schoolhouse Rock*, "I'm Just a Bill"	**Source A:** District-approved grade 3 Social Studies textbook **Source B:** Teacher-developed Jigsaw organizer	**Source A:** *Schoolhouse Rock*, "I'm Just a Bill" **Source B:** Teacher-made presentation of legislative simulation **Source C:** School improvement ideas generated to answer Dimension 1 SQ 3. Supplemental: *What Do You Do With an Idea?* by Kobi Yamada

Exit Ticket Suggestion:
Answer the prompt, "Identify one improvement you would like to see in our school. Provide two ideas for making that improvement happen."

Dimension 3

Bell Ringer:
"What are the important characteristics of a good bill?" Write down at least three qualities you think every bill should have to be successful. You will revisit your intuition reflections to this question at the conclusion of Dimension 3.

Supporting Question 1	Supporting Question 2	Supporting Question 3
How can we make a real difference in our community through the legislative process?	How do we identify areas for improvement within our school community and gather evidence to support these ideas?	How can we use this evidence to create strong arguments (bills) for improving our school?

Formative Performance Task	Formative Performance Task	Formative Performance Task
Discuss and analyze the role of students in the legislative process through a real-life example.	Conduct an investigation and gather data to identify improvement areas within the school community.	Develop bills for school improvement based on collected evidence.
Featured Sources	**Featured Sources** Student Generated	**Featured Sources** Student Generated
Source A: Michigan Senate Bill 397 Source B: *Mastodon Named State Fossil* (article)	Source A: Student surveys, interviews with community members, and/or student letters	Source A: Teacher-developed bill proposal writing organizer and template Source B: Student-collected data and evidence

Exit Ticket Suggestion: Revisit your initial response to the question "What are the important characteristics of a good bill?" Reflect on your initial thoughts and whether your views have changed based on what you have learned and discussed. Document your revised thoughts and ideas you have developed.

Dimension 4

Supporting Question 1	Supporting Question 2	Supporting Question 3
How can we effectively communicate and advocate for our proposals to ensure they make a positive impact on our school community?	What factors should we consider when deciding whether to support or oppose a bill?	How does understanding the legislative process and actively using our voices empower us to make a difference in our community?
Formative Performance Task	**Formative Performance Task**	**Formative Performance Task**
Present proposed bills to classmates, practicing advocacy and communication skills. Provide feedback, to others, on bill practicality, persuasion effectiveness and utilization of evidence. Amend bill proposals based on feedback and prepare a final version for the legislative simulation activity.	Generate criteria for evaluating bills and conduct votes on whether to pass them.	Present approved bills to a school/district professional for final approval. Reflect on the legislative simulation experience.
Featured Sources	**Featured Sources** Student Created	**Featured Sources**
Source A: Teacher-developed effective advocacy and communication guide	Source A: Student-generated criteria rubric for evaluating bill proposals	Any sources from Dimensions 1–4

Summative Performance Task	**ARGUMENT** *How can we make a difference in our community?* Use content from Dimensions 1–3 to construct arguments for proposed school improvements, using evidence gathered from their assessments of school needs and community interest.
	EXTENSION Invite a local government official to discuss the impact of community involvement and the legislative process or take a field trip to the state's capital to explore the center of state government operations.
Taking Informed Action	**UNDERSTAND** Identify community needs within the school that can be addressed and explore how civic mechanisms can be leveraged to initiate changes, connecting to learning about the legislative process.
	ASSESS Evaluate the potential impacts and benefits of proposed improvement bills, considering feedback from peers and outcomes of implementing change.
	ACT Present bills to an "executive board" of school professionals, advocating effectively for necessary changes within the community.

Overview

Inquiry Description

This inquiry leads students through an exploration of civic engagement and the legislative process, focusing on how students can actively participate and make impactful changes within their community. Utilizing a comprehensive understanding of government functions and advocacy, students will investigate the role of citizens in shaping public policy and governance. This lesson incorporates a practical simulation of the legislative process where students draft, debate, and vote on school improvement bills, learning to advocate effectively for community changes.

This inquiry was originally intended for integrated learning spanning all content areas for five school days. The lessons lend themselves to cross-curricular learning experiences utilizing persuasive writing, literature studies, data analysis, and civic learning; it is estimated to take 15–18 days with 50-minute class periods. This inquiry lends itself to collaboration, discussion and debate, active learning, civic engagement, and ongoing reflection and should be adapted to meet the needs and interests of students.

Structure of the Inquiry

Dimension 1: Introduction to the compelling question and activities that stimulate thinking about civic participation
Dimension 2: Civics content (using C3 Framework, NCSS Themes, state/district curriculum)
Dimension 3: Using primary, secondary, and student-obtained sources to formulate arguments based in evidence (constructing bill proposals for school improvement)
Dimension 4: Taking informed action through formal presentation of school improvement proposals.

Dimension 1

Staging the Compelling Question

Start the unit by posing the compelling question to the class, "How can we make a difference in our community?" Allow students to reflect and write initial responses. Employ the Think-Pair-Share discussion strategy and have students discuss their ideas for making a difference in their community. Once students have had an opportunity to share their initial thoughts, collect their responses. After conducting the activities for Dimension 1, revisit the compelling question. Ask students to reflect on their initial thoughts and whether their views have changed based on what they have learned and discussed. Have students document their revised thoughts and ideas they have developed. To facilitate this reflection, teachers can utilize a T-chart. In the "What I Thought" column, students record their initial ideas and wonderings. In the "What I Think Now" column, they document their new understanding and thoughts after learning about advocacy and the common good.

Supporting Question 1

The first supporting question is "What are the different ways people can help improve their community?"

The formative task is as follows:
- Students will analyze different roles that community members can play in improving their communities and create a visual mind map linking community roles such as volunteers, local government officials, first responders, educators, and healthcare workers to the actions they take to improve the community (running educational programs, participating in local decision-making, protecting others, etc.) focusing on how these roles contribute to the common good. This mind map will answer the supporting question, depicting how different people can contribute positively to their community.
- Start by introducing the concept of a community and discuss the different people or groups of people that make up a community (such as educators, first responders, students, civilians, etc.) Explain that each of these roles contributes to making the community better in various ways. Show a teacher-developed example of a mind map to demonstrate how to visually organize these ideas. Then have students brainstorm specific actions these community members might take. Provide students with templates and assist them in creating their own mind maps, illustrating how these roles contribute to the common good and how multiple groups of people may share the same contributions.

Teachers may implement this task with the following procedures:
- Conduct a brief discussion about "community" "civic participation," and "common good."
- Lead students in brainstorming specific actions that different community members take to contribute to the common good. Discuss the different people or groups of people that make up a community (e.g., educators, first responders, students, civilians, etc.). Explain that each of these roles contributes to making the community better in various ways.
- Show a teacher-developed example of a mind map to demonstrate how to visually organize these ideas. Then have students brainstorm specific actions these community members might take. Provide students with paper or templates and assist them in creating their own mind maps, illustrating how these roles contribute to the common good and how multiple groups of people may share the same contributions.
- Divide students into small groups and provide them with large sheets of paper and markers. Encourage students to think about and represent different sectors of community improvement and the ways they are connected.

The following scaffolds and other materials may be used to support students as they work with sources:
- The teacher can use cooperative grouping, premade templates for the community role maps, and lists of roles and examples of their contributions to support students and to prompt thinking.
- The teacher can utilize this activity to assess student understanding of how individuals contribute to a community in various ways.

The following sources were selected to provide a comprehensive understanding of community dynamics and the impact of individual contributions. This will provide students with foundational knowledge of civic participation to build upon in later lessons.

- **Source A:** Teacher-developed example of a mind map
- **Source B (supplemental):** Teacher-developed vocabulary presentation on "community," "civic participation," and "common good"

Supporting Question 2

The second supporting question is "Why is it important for people to participate in their community government?"

The formative task is as follows:
- Students will read *The Voice That Won the Vote* (Source A) and engage in a guided discussion of the significance of using their voice to participate in government.
- Discuss the broader implications of the story by asking questions like "Why is it important for everyone to have a say in their government?" and "What might happen if we don't participate in our government?"
- Bridge the historical context of the book with current examples of how voices are still being used for advocacy and change in government. Consider local bond proposals, campaign volunteering, climate change initiatives, Social Justice Movements, or community led initiatives to emphasize advocacy in modern government.

Teachers may implement this task with the following procedures:
- Introduce *The Voice That Won the Vote* (Source A) and discuss its context and relevance to modern civic participation.
- Relate the story to contemporary examples where civic engagement has led to change in community policies.
- Ask students to write a paragraph about the importance of participation in community government using examples from the book and discussion.

The following scaffolds and other materials may be used to support students as they work with sources: The teacher can use discussion guides for *The Voice That Won the Vote*, Think-Pair-Share discussion strategies, and writing prompts to help students formulate reflections on civic participation.

The following source was selected to illustrate the significance of civic engagement and advocacy:
Source A: Boxer, E. (2020). *The voice that won the vote: How one woman's words made history* (V. Mildenberger, Illus.). Sleeping Bear Press.

Supporting Question 3

The third supporting question is "What ideas do we have that could help make our school community better?"

The formative task is as follows:
- Students will actively evaluate their school community using a teacher-developed graphic organizer. Students will individually work to generate two lists: "What I Like About My School" and "What Could Make My School Better?"
- Students will then meet with small groups to discuss their ideas.
- Encourage students to add to or modify the items on their lists.
- To answer the third supporting question, give each student a sticky note or two and place their top two school improvement ideas on the front board.

Teachers may implement this task with the following procedures:
- Distribute graphic organizers for students to list what they like about their school and what could be better.
- Facilitate small group discussions to refine ideas and encourage peer feedback.
- Guide students in selecting the ideas they feel most strongly about for the class idea board. Provide each student with a sticky note or two to record their ideas and post to the class school improvement idea board.

The following scaffolds and other materials may be used to support students as they work with sources: The teacher can use cooperative grouping, graphic organizers to structure idea generation, and teacher conferences to support student success.

The following sources were selected to enable students to identify actionable improvements and understand the process of proposing changes.
- **Source A:** Teacher-developed school improvement brainstorming graphic organizer
- The school improvement brainstorm organizer includes two sections, "What I Like About My School" and "What Could Be Better." This organization stimulates students to think about not only what they want for their school but also what they already like and the ways those elements could be enhanced.

Exit Ticket Suggestion:
After completing Dimension 1 activities, revisit student responses to the compelling question. Ask students to reflect on their initial thoughts and whether their views have changed based on what they have learned and discussed. Teachers

can utilize a T-chart for students to record initial thinking and wonderings in a "What I Thought" column, and at the conclusion of the lessons, they record ideas in the "What I Think Now" column. Students then compare their initial ideas and how the ideas changed after learning more about advocacy and common good.

Dimension 2

Supporting Question 1

The first supporting question is "What are laws and why do we have them?"

The formative task is as follows:
- Students participate in a class discussion initiated by the supporting question. Students will participate in a Think-Pair-Share discussion to share and build on their understanding.
- Students will listen to a reading of *The School With No Rules* by Dr. Poppy Moon, followed by a guided discussion emphasizing the role of laws in maintaining order, protecting rights, and ensuring fairness.

Teachers may implement this task with the following procedures:
- Present an open-ended question to the class: "What are laws, and why do we have them?"
- Utilize a Think-Pair-Share discussion strategy to stimulate student ideas. (The teacher may wish to relate laws to classroom and school rules to enhance relevancy to learners.)
- Read aloud *The School With No Rules* by Dr. Poppy Moon.
- Lead a guided discussion about the role of laws in maintaining order, protecting rights, and ensuring fairness. Use examples that are relatable to student lives.

The following scaffolds and other materials may be used to support students as they work with sources: The teacher can use differentiated question strategies to accommodate learning levels and encourage student engagement, provide visual aids that compare laws to school rules to make the concept more relatable, utilize differentiated partner groupings, and provide one-on-one support to offer additional help understanding concepts discussed.

The following source was selected to provide a foundation for understanding the purpose and impact of laws.
Source A: Moon, P. (2014). *The school with no rules.* YouthLight.

Supporting Question 2

The second supporting question is "What are the steps in the legislative process?"

The formative task is as follows: Students view the *Schoolhouse Rock* video, "I'm Just a Bill" (Source A) and create a flow chart of the legislative process. It should be emphasized that laws begin as bills and bills begin as *ideas*.

Teachers may implement this task with the following procedures:
- Show "I'm Just a Bill" from *Schoolhouse Rock* (Source A) and encourage note taking during the video.
- Guide students in creating a flow chart of the legislative process as depicted in the video. Emphasize that laws start as bills and bills start as *ideas*. Highlight that students have already generated ideas for improving their community. Use this discussion as an opportunity to clarify student misunderstandings.
- Post the class-developed flow chart of the legislative process on the class idea board for later reference.

The following scaffolds and other materials may be used to support students as they work with sources: The teacher can use premade flow chart templates or partially completed flow charts to guide students in the process.

The following source was selected to illustrate the steps a bill goes through to become a law in an engaging and accessible way.
Source A: Schoolhouse Rock. (2014, August 18). *I'm just a bill* [Video]. YouTube. www.youtube.com/watch?v=SZ8psP4S6BQ (Original work published 1976)

Supporting Question 3

The third supporting question is "How do the different branches of government work together to create laws and govern?"

The formative task is as follows: Students utilize a district-approved textbook or alternative teaching resource to complete a Jigsaw activity exploring the roles and interactions of the three branches of government in the legislative process. Students are divided into small groups to explore different aspects of governance focusing on the roles and responsibilities of the three branches of government—Legislative, Executive, and Judicial—particularly in the law-making process. Initially students are divided into small expert groups assigned to study one of the branches of government from their classroom textbooks. Students then reorganize into new Jigsaw groups, each consisting of one or two members of the initial expert groups. In these new groups, students teach their peers about their expert topic.

Teachers may implement this task with the following procedures:
- Divide students into three "expert" groups, each assigned to one branch of government (Legislative, Executive, and Judicial).
- Each expert group will research their assigned branch and complete their designated section of a teacher-developed graphic organizer for this activity. Graphic organizers should include the roles and responsibilities of each branch of government, their main components, and the ways each branch interacts with the other branches (particularly in the legislative process).
- Divide expert groups into smaller three to four student groupings to share their research and provide peer support.
- Reorganize students into mixed groups where they teach each other about their researched branch.
- Review and discuss the concept of "checks and balances" provided by the structure of our government and the reasons it is important to us as citizens.

The following scaffolds and other materials may be used to support students as they work with sources: The teacher can use visual learning aids (e.g., diagrams or flow charts) that outline the functions of the three branches of government, structured group discussions and discussion prompts, peer teaching opportunities, and formative feedback to support student success.

The following sources were selected to enhance understanding of the roles and interactions within the government.
- **Source A:** District-approved Grade 3 Social Studies textbook
- **Source B:** Teacher-developed Jigsaw organizer
- Additional research materials, if desired

Supporting Question 4

The fourth supporting question is "What role do citizens play in the legislative process, and how can understanding the legislative process help us to advocate for changes in our community?"

The formative task is as follows:
- Students review "I'm Just a Bill," highlighting that laws can be generated by citizens (and students).
- Students are introduced to the legislative simulation and are assigned working committee groups for bill proposal writing. Students begin to brainstorm within their assigned improvement category.

Teachers may implement this task with the following procedures:
- Review "I'm Just a Bill" and reinforce the idea that laws and improvements can originate from citizen suggestions, including those from students.
- Introduce legislation simulation activity. *It is important that students have a thorough understanding of the legislative process to participate in this simulation.*
    - In this simulation activity, inspired by an excerpt from "Three Branches of Government," students will be acting as members of the legislative branch to write and hopefully pass bills into effect in their school community (Ashcroft & Petit, as cited in Roberts et al., 2022). In this simulation activity, students will work in small committee groups to identify an area of improvement, gather support and evidence to support their cause, and manifest a persuasive campaign for their cause.
    - Each of the two third-grade classes will simulate the U.S. Congress, embodying the House of Representatives or the Senate. If you have only one class, divide the class into two groups: one half representing the House and the other half representing the Senate. Each group will contain committees that represent the voice of the people, tasked with constructing arguments for their school improvement

ideas in the form of bills. Committees will present their bill and any additional campaign materials to their respective institution of "Congress" (their classmates).
- Within each institution, students will evaluate the bills presented and conduct a vote to pass one bill to the other institution (the other classroom) to be passed by both senators and representatives.
- "Bills" that have been passed in both the "House of Representatives" and the "Senate" will be presented to an executive board consisting of the school principal and the Parent-Teacher Organization for approval and implementation into the school policy.
- Introduce the concept of working in committees, which will mimic the legislative committees in government. Divide students into effective working groups, or "committees" for investigating school improvement needs and bill proposal writing. Teachers may consider utilizing differentiated grouping methods and/or considering collaborative abilities to ensure balanced group dynamics.
- Revisit the class's school improvement idea board. As a class, review the ideas, and work to categorize and combine student ideas into broader themes such as technology upgrades, playground enhancements, diverse learning environments, cafeteria improvements, etc.
- Assign each group an area of school improvement to advocate for. Encourage groups to discuss feasible solutions that could be realistically implemented into the school.
- Encourage students to think about the problems within their assigned area at school that could be improved (e.g., long lunch lines, broken playground equipment, technologies present in some classrooms but not others, etc.).

The following scaffolds and other materials may be used to support students as they work with sources: To support student success in this activity, teachers can utilize various discussion strategies to engage all learners, provide graphic organizers to help students structure their brainstorming and initial proposal ideas.

The following sources were selected to enhance understanding of the role citizens (and students) can play in the legislative process.
- **Source A:** *Schoolhouse Rock*, "I'm Just a Bill"
- **Source B:** Teacher-made presentation of legislative simulation
- **Source C:** School improvement ideas generated to answer Dimension 1 SQ 3.
- **Supplemental:** *What do you do with an Idea?* by Kobi Yamada

Exit Ticket Suggestion:
Answer the prompt, "Identify one improvement you would like to see in our school. Provide two ideas for making that improvement happen."

Dimension 3

Supporting Question 1

Bell Ringer:
- Ask: "What are the important characteristics of a good bill?" Write down at least three qualities you think every bill should have to be successful. Students will revisit their intuition reflections to this question at the conclusion of Dimension 3.
- Alternatively, utilize a modified Four Corners learning strategy, assigning a characteristic of a good bill (relevance, persuasiveness, feasibility, etc.) and asking students to choose the corner that they feel is the most important. Students should consider which resonates the most with them and be able to justify their choice.

The first supporting question is "How can students make a real difference in their community through the legislative process?"

The formative task is as follows:
- Students will read and review Michigan Senate Bill 397 (Source A) and the "Mastodon Named State Fossil" article (Source B) to discuss and analyze how students can participate in the legislative process through a real-life example.
- Students will "Talk with the Text" by taking notes, posing questions, and highlighting important details to analyze the steps taken by the students in this example. They will also discuss strategies used and challenges faced.
- Students will revisit the posted school improvement suggestions from Dimension 1 and discuss possible steps they could take to advocate for the changes they want to see.

Teachers may implement this task with the following procedures:

- Utilize Michigan Senate Bill 397 (Source A; or a more accessible version of the text) and "Mastodon Named State Fossil" (Source B) to highlight how young people have historically impacted legislation, using the example of students who successfully advocated for the mastodon to become the state fossil of Michigan. State history teachers in other states can locate similar bills for their students to study.
- Have students analyze the steps taken by these students and discuss the strategies used and the challenges faced.
- Revisit the class idea board and posted school improvement suggestions. In small groups, students should discuss possible steps they could take to advocate for the change they want to see. Students should also consider possible oppositions to their school improvement ideas. The teacher may wish to implement committee groupings for class sessions prior to the student legislation simulation, though it is not necessary.

The scaffolds and other materials that may be used to support students as they work with sources can include a modified version of Senate Bill 397 for accessibility, cooperate grouping, or whole class work.

The following sources were selected to illustrate the impact students can have on the legislative process.
- **Source A:** State Fossil: Mastodon, S.B. 397 (Mich. 2002). **www.legislature.mi.gov/documents/2001-2002/billanalysis/House/htm/2001-HLA-0397-a.htm**
- **Source B:** The University Record Archives. (2002, April 22). Mastodon named state fossil. **https://record.umich.edu/articles/mastodon-named-state-fossil/**

Supporting Question 2

The second supporting question is "How can we identify areas for improvement within our school community and gather evidence to support these ideas?"

The formative task is as follows:
- Students form legislative committees and focus on gathering evidence and building support for proposed bills aimed at improving their school community. They will work to identify specific areas for improvement such as playground facilities, off-campus learning experiences, or quality of student lunches. Using various data collection methods such as surveys, student interviews, and visual documentation, students will compile evidence to substantiate their proposals.
- The collected data will serve as the foundation of evidence when students begin drafting bills to be later debated and voted on in a simulated legislative environment.

Teachers may implement this task with the following procedures:
- Reiterate to students the importance of their role in becoming the voice of the students at their school. Legislators do not only pass laws in their own interest, but in the interest of the common good. It is their task to formulate an investigation of the community's feelings on school improvement, gather data to support their arguments, and formulate a persuasive campaign for their cause.
- Introduce students to a variety of methods for surveying the community. This could consist of student interviews with other students, staff, or other members of the school community; student interest surveys; or letters from other students in the school community, voicing their school improvement ideas. (This will look different depending on the level of school involvement.)
- Guide students in manifesting appropriate methods to gather data and evidence to support their cause. For example, if students find that their community wants new playground equipment, students need to gather evidence that the current playground equipment is unsatisfactory. They should also utilize information gathered from their survey of student interest to signify that their concern is shared amongst the community.
- Guide students in evaluating their sources of evidence to ensure that their claims are supported effectively. Evidence could include pictures of broken playground equipment, information from student interest surveys, comparison to other playground equipment in the district, etc.

The scaffolds and other materials that may be used to support students as they work with sources are cooperative grouping, peer review sessions, checklists for effective evidence, examples of effective bills, and teacher conferences.

The following source was selected to provide a bias for understanding school needs and prioritizing improvements.
Source A: Student surveys, interviews with community members, and/or student letters

Supporting Question 3

The third supporting question is "How can we use this evidence to create strong arguments (bills) for improving our school?"

The formative task is as follows:
- Students will develop well-supported legislative proposals for school improvements by drafting bills based on evidence collected from student surveys, interviews, and/or letters. They will utilize a bill proposal writing graphic organizer and template to structure their bills.
- Students will integrate persuasive writing techniques and anticipate potential objections, refining their proposals accordingly.
- Students may also create multimedia materials such as posters to enhance the persuasiveness of their presentations.

Teachers may implement this task with the following procedures:
- Provide an explanation of the structure of a bill including essential components such as the title, preamble (problem), and explanation of the bill.
- Provide students with a bill proposal writing graphic organizer and template that guides them through writing an effective and persuasive bill proposal.
- Guide students in integrating the evidence they gathered from surveys, interviews, and student letters into their bills, modeling how to use data to justify the need for proposed changes. Revisit persuasive writing techniques to strengthen their arguments. Provide examples of effective persuasive language and phrases.
- Conduct small discussions focusing on anticipating potential objections and effectively addressing them within the bill. Encourage students to refine their proposals to address possible objections.
- Encourage students to create supporting multi-media materials such as posters that highlight the benefits of their proposed bills. These projects can further persuade their peers and decision makers.
- Offer tips and practice sessions on effective public speaking and presentation skills to prepare students for presenting their bills in the legislative simulation.

The scaffolds and other materials that may be used to support students as they work with sources are cooperative grouping, writing organizers, bill proposal templates, persuasive argument checklists and teacher conferences.
- This is a model for grades 6–8 which could be simplified for younger learners: Anti-Defamation League. (2020, May 11). *Writing a bill*. www.adl.org/resources/lesson-plan/writing-bill
- This is a guide for teaching persuasive writing techniques in a way that is accessible for younger students: Clark, C. (2024, February 28). *Persuasive writing for kids*. Speech and language kids. www.speechandlanguagekids.com/teach-persuasive-writing-children/

The following sources were selected to support students in creating actionable and evidence-based proposals.
- **Source A:** Teacher-developed bill proposal writing organizer and template
- **Source B:** Student surveys, interviews with community members, and/or student letters

Exit Ticket Suggestion:
After the students' complete activities for Dimension 3, ask them to revisit their initial response to the question "What are the important characteristics of a good bill?" Prompt students to reflect on their initial thoughts and whether their views have changed based on what they have learned and discussed. Have students document their revised thoughts and ideas they have developed. This could be compiled on a digital document as a record of their learning journey.

Dimension 4

Overview

Dimension 4 of the C3 Framework emphasizes the importance of students communicating conclusions and taking informed action based on their civic knowledge. In the civics lesson outlined, Dimension 4 activities are tailored to embody this focus, ensuring that students not only learn about the legislative process but also actively participate in it through a simulation that mirrors real-world legislative activities. This hands-on approach allows students to present their developed bills to a mock legislative body, simulating the real-life experience of lawmakers. The activities culminate in students presenting their successfully passed bills to an executive board, which includes the school principal and the Parent-Teacher Organization. This final presentation requires students to use persuasive communication and advocacy skills to champion their proposals, illustrating the practical application of their civic knowledge and the impact of their voice in a democratic process.

The structure of these activities supports the C3 Framework's goals by providing students with authentic experiences that enhance their understanding of how government functions and their role within it. Throughout this process, students are engaged in critical thinking, problem-solving, and collaborative decision-making, reflecting the core of active civic participation. The lessons also involve evaluating and reflecting on the effectiveness of their advocacy efforts, thereby fostering a deeper understanding of the civic processes and encouraging ongoing engagement. This aligns with the C3 Framework's aim to prepare students for active participation in civic life, making the activities in Dimension 4 not only educational but also transformative in equipping students with the skills necessary for informed civic action.

Supporting Question 1

The first supporting question is "How can we effectively communicate and advocate for our proposals to ensure they make a positive impact on our school community?"

The formative task is as follows: Students will present their proposed bills to classmates to practice and refine their advocacy and communication skills. They will receive and provide feedback on the practicality, persuasiveness, and evidence utilization of each bill. Following peer review sessions, students will have the opportunity to amend their bills based on the feedback provided.

Teachers may implement this task with the following procedures:
- Guide students in preparing and practicing their proposal presentation, focusing on clear articulation of goals, justification using evidence, and persuasive techniques.
- Implement peer review sessions where groups evaluate the content of other bills for effectiveness, providing feedback for improvement.
- Allow groups to revise bills based on feedback and prepare a final version for the legislative simulation activity.

The following scaffolds and other materials may be used to support students as they work with sources: The teacher can use guidelines for effective presentations, feedback forums, checklist for presentations components, and rubrics for peer feedback on effectiveness to support student success.

The following source was selected to help ensure that the students' advocacy efforts are structured, focused, and based on evidence, which is essential for effective communication:
Source A: Teacher-developed effective advocacy and communication guide

Supporting Question 2

The second supporting question is "What factors should we consider when deciding whether to support or oppose a bill?"

The formative task is as follows:
- Students will work together to generate criteria for evaluating legislative bills and participate in legislative voting sessions. This was a student-developed rubric we worked to create together.
- Student committees will present their bills and apply the agreed-upon criteria to vote on each bill. The most highly endorsed bills will advance to a second round of voting in another classroom, simulating the legislative process of

passing bills through both houses of Congress before they reach the executive branch for approval.

Teachers may implement this task with the following procedures:
- Facilitate a session where students brainstorm and agree on a set of criteria for evaluating bills (e.g., relevance, feasibility, impact). Provide guidance and examples of effective criteria to ensure the rubric is comprehensive and applicable.
- Organize mock legislative sessions where students present their bills to the House and Senate (i.e., their classmates), emphasizing effective communication and persuasion.
- Conduct a voting session where students apply these criteria to the proposed bills, deciding whether to support or oppose each bill in their respective institution. Students will cast votes for the two bills that most effectively fulfill the agreed-upon criteria, with the bill receiving the highest endorsements moving on to the other institution.
- Following the initial voting session in both the House of Representatives and the Senate, the bills that received the highest endorsements will undergo a second round of voting in a different classroom (representing the other legislative institution), simulating the legislative process where bills must be passed by both the House and the Senate before advancing to the executive branch for final approval.

The following scaffolds and other materials may be used to support students as they work with sources: The teacher can offer blank templates that outline the basic structure of a rubric to aid in organization of student thoughts, sample rubrics, and differentiated peer grouping to support student success.

The following source was selected to foster critical thinking, decision-making, and analytical assessment.
Source A: Student-generated criteria rubric for evaluating proposed bills

Supporting Question 3

The third supporting question is "How does understanding the legislative process and actively using our voices empower us to make a difference in our community?"

The formative task is as follows:
- Students will prepare and present their approved bills to the executive board which consists of the principal and PTO, to seek final approval. This task emphasizes the culmination of their civic engagement efforts.
- Students will reflect on their experience in the legislative simulation, discussing the effectiveness of their advocacy, what they learned about civic engagement, and how they can use their voices in future advocacy efforts.

Teachers may implement this task with the following procedures:
- Stimulate a formal presentation environment where students present their bills to the executive board (e.g., the principal and the PTO). Encourage board members to engage with the students by asking questions and providing feedback.
- Allow students to receive feedback on their presentation skills and the content of their proposals, emphasizing the importance of engaging with feedback to refine their communication skills.
- In the case of a veto by the executive board, invite students to amend their proposals based on feedback.
- Invite students to reflect on their experience in the legislative simulation.
- Answer: How does understanding the legislative process help us to better advocate for community improvement?

The following scaffolds and other materials may be used to support students as they work with sources: The teacher can use cooperative grouping, graphic organizers to structure idea generation, examples of common language used in bill writing, and teacher conferences to support students in reflection.

The following sources were selected to invite students to effectively reflect on the legislative process and civic responsibility:
Any sources from Dimension 1-4

Summative Performance Task

In this civics inquiry, the summative performance task asks students to demonstrate their understanding of the legislative process, advocacy, and civic engagement by constructing and presenting a comprehensive proposal for school improvement. They will then reflect on their learning process, participation, and the potential real-world impact of their proposals. Each student group will present their final bill to an executive panel consisting of the school principal and PTO members. Presentations should include a detailed explanation of the bill, evidence, and arguments to support it and employ persuasive communication techniques. After the presentations, students will write a reflective essay discussing their experience and learning throughout the unit by revisiting the compelling question "How can we make a difference in our community?" additional questions to prompt student reflection include "How does understanding the legislative process support you in advocating for the needs of your community?" and "Do you think it is important for individuals to participate in their local/community governments?"

Students construct evidence-based arguments for their proposed school improvements by analyzing data and insights gathered through their assessments of school needs and community interest. These arguments include relevant evidence to advocate for meaningful changes that align with the common good. Students' arguments will likely vary but could include proposals such as
- Improving school facilities to enhance safety and engagement
- Introducing new extracurricular programs to support student interests
- Implementing environmental initiatives

To support students in their writing, teachers can provide scaffolds like graphic organizers, sentence starters and checklists for constructing evidence-based arguments. Peer review and teacher conferences can also help refine their ideas and ensure clarity.

To extend their arguments, students actively participate in a dynamic legislative simulation. The assume roles as committee members and legislators, crafting and debating bills in a setting that highlights the importance of civic participation. The immersive activity empowers them to explore their potential to influence policy.

Students have the opportunity to take informed action by presenting their proposed bills to an executive board, including relevant school/district professionals (e.g., the principal, PTO members), emphasizing their ability to advocate effectively for real change in their school community. To understand, students connect their learning about the legislative process to current issues in their school community, analyzing community needs they can address and exploring how meaningful changes are made. To assess, students evaluate the potential impacts and benefits of the proposed improvement bills. They consider the feasibility and effectiveness of their ideas, incorporating feedback from peers. To act, students present their finalized bills to school officials. This presentation serves as an opportunity to embody advocacy as they effectively communicate the value and necessity of their proposals.

References

Anti-Defamation League. (2020, May 11). *Writing a bill*. www.adl.org/resources/lesson-plan/writing-bill

Bradford, M., Freeland, S., Kastl, E., Kooyer, J., McCauley, M., Raven, A., & Welch, S. (2016). *Michigan studies*. Michigan Open Book Project.

Boxer, E. (2020). *The voice that won the vote: How one woman's words made history* (V. Mildenberger, Illus.). Sleeping Bear Press.

Clark, C. (2024, February 28). *Persuasive writing for kids*. Speech and language kids. **www.speechandlanguagekids.com/teach-persuasive-writing-children/**

Gonzalez, J. [Cult of Pedagogy]. (2015, April 15). *The jigsaw method* [Video]. YouTube. **www.youtube.com/watch?v=euhtXUgBEts**

McConnell, D. B. (2009). *Meet Michigan*. Hillsdale Educational Publishers.

Michigan Department of Education. (n.d.). *Michigan K–12 standards for social studies*. **www.misocialstudies.org/**

Moon, P. (2014). *The school with no rules*. YouthLight.

National Council for the Social Studies. (2013). *The college, career, and civic life (C3) framework for social studies state standards: Guidance for enhancing the rigor of K–12 civics, economics, geography, and history*.

Roberts, S. L., Wellenreiter, B. R., Ferreras-Stone, J., Strachan, S. L., & Palmer, K. L. (2022). *Teaching middle level social studies: A practical guide for 4th–8th grade* (3rd ed.). Information Age.

Schoolhouse Rock. (2014, August 18). *I'm just a bill* [Video]. YouTube. **www.youtube.com/watch?v=SZ8psP4S6BQ** (Original work published 1976)

State Fossil: Mastodon, S.B. 397 (Mich. 2002). **www.legislature.mi.gov/documents/2001-2002/billanalysis/House/htm/2001-HLA-0397-a.htm**

The University Record Archives. (2002, April 22). *Mastodon named state fossil*. **https://record.umich.edu/articles/mastodon-named-state-fossil/**

Van Dusen, C. (2023). *If I built a school*. Rocky Pond Books.

Yamada, K. (2023). *What do you do with an idea?* (M. Besom, Illus.). Compendium.

Kate Van Haren

Elementary U.S. History

How do Indigenous athletes, like those who play lacrosse, teach others about the resilience of Indigenous cultures and sovereignty?

Supporting Questions Dimension 2

1. What is the game of lacrosse?
2. Who are the Haudenosaunee?
3. What features make the game of lacrosse unique?

Supporting Questions Dimension 3

1. Why is making and playing lacrosse with traditionally made sticks important to the Haudenosaunee people?
2. How and why do the Haudenosaunee play lacrosse today?
3. What are the similarities and differences between how the Haudenosaunee played in the past and how they play today?

Supporting Questions Dimension 4

1. How do the Haudenosaunee people inform other people about the importance of lacrosse?
2. What sports/activities are important to the Indigenous peoples who live on the land around your community today?
3. What lessons can all people learn from Indigenous peoples who share their sports and activities with all people?

Elementary U.S. History

How do Indigenous athletes, like those who play lacrosse, teach others about the resilience of Indigenous cultures and sovereignty?	
Standards and Content	**C3 Standards:** D2.Civ.10.3-5. Identify the beliefs, experiences, perspectives, and values that underlie their own and others' points of view about civic issues. D2.Civ.14.3-5. Illustrate historical and contemporary means of changing society. D2.Geo.4.3-5. Explain how culture influences the way people modify and adapt to their environments. D2.Geo.7.3-5. Explain how cultural and environmental characteristics affect the distribution and movement of people, goods, and ideas. D2.His.2.3-5. Compare life in specific historical time periods to life today. D2.His.3.3-5. Generate questions about individuals and groups who have shaped significant historical changes and continuities. D2.His.5.3-5. Explain connections among historical contexts and people's perspectives at the time. D2.His.16.3-5. Use evidence to develop a claim about the past. **NCSS Themes:** ❶ Culture ❷ Time, Continuity, and Change ❿ Civic Ideals and Practices
Staging the Compelling Question	**Dimension 1:** Brainstorm activities enjoyed with family and community throughout the year. Create illustrations or written descriptions of these activities. Share and discuss traditions in class or small groups. Analyze reasons for participating in these traditions and investigate how they have changed over time. Examine historical photographs (such as school sports) to evaluate why traditions evolve and determine their significance.

Dimension 2

Supporting Question 1	Supporting Question 2	Supporting Question 3
What is the game of lacrosse?	Who are the Haudenosaunee?	What features make the game of lacrosse unique?
Formative Performance Task	**Formative Performance Task**	**Formative Performance Task**
Record notes on the *who, what, where, when, why,* and *how* graphic organizer.	Identify the original homeland of the Haudenosaunee using historical and contemporary maps. Create a diagram of the six nations that form the Haudenosaunee Confederacy and explain their relationships. Define tribal sovereignty using specific examples from Haudenosaunee governance. Analyze the significance of Haudenosaunee passports as an expression of sovereignty by examining primary sources documenting their international use.	Study an image of a statue in La Crosse, Wisconsin. The city is named after the game. Design your own statue or monument using information from the graphic organizers.

Featured Sources	Featured Sources	Featured Sources
Source A: *Roots: Exploring the History of Lacrosse*, 0:00–3:45 **Source B:** *Spirit Game: Pride of a Nation*, 2:45–4:00	**Source A:** *Roots of Lacrosse*, 6:00–9:30 **Source B:** *Spirit Game*, 7:20–9:45 **Source C:** *Spirit Game*, 17:00–18:40	**Source A:** Photograph of lacrosse statue

Exit Ticket Suggestion:
Students will use their notes to write one- or two-sentence summaries that answer the who, what, when, where, why, and how sections of their graphic organizers.

Dimension 3

Bell Ringer:
Students will share the sentences they created the exit activity during the previous day. This will serve as review for the upcoming activities.

Supporting Question 1	Supporting Question 2	Supporting Question 3
Why is making and playing lacrosse with traditionally made sticks important to the Haudenosaunee people?	How and why do the Haudenosaunee play lacrosse today?	What are the similarities and differences between how the Haudenosaunee played in the past and how they play today?
Formative Performance Task	**Formative Performance Task**	**Formative Performance Task**
Record notes from the video.	On the outline of a lacrosse stick, write down your current understandings and answers to the questions.	Create Venn diagrams displaying the similarities and the differences between how the game was played in the past and how it is played today.
Featured Sources	**Featured Sources**	**Featured Sources**
Source A: *Roots of Lacrosse*, 0:00–5:45 **Source B:** *Spirit Game*, 22:00–24:50	**Source A:** *Spirit Game*, 4:15–6:20 **Source B:** *Spirit Game*, 13:25–20:00 **Source C:** *Spirit Game*, 47:49–49:45 **Source D:** *Spirit Game*, 54:00–55:20 **Source E:** *Spirit Game*, 1:05:00–1:07:00 **Source F:** *Spirit Game*, 2:03:00–2:05:00 (*Note.* The teacher is welcome to choose which clips to use if time is limited.)	**Source A:** *Spirit Game*, 13:25–17:00 **Source B:** *Spirit Game*, 54:00–55:20 **Source C:** *Spirit Game*, 59:00–1:02 **Source D:** *Spirit Game*, 1:03:40–1:05:20 **Source E:** *Spirit Game*, 1:13:00–1:19:00 (*Note.* If only able to show one video, the clip in Source E is recommended.)

Dimension 4

Supporting Question 1	Supporting Question 2	Supporting Question 3
How do the Haudenosaunee people inform other people about the importance of lacrosse?	What sports/activities are important to the Indigenous peoples who live on the land around your community today? How and why do the Haudenosaunee play lacrosse today?	What lessons can all people learn from Indigenous peoples who share their sports and activities with all people?
Formative Performance Task	**Formative Performance Task**	**Formative Performance Task**
Take notes about how the Haudenosaunee people spread their knowledge to other people.	Compare the game of lacrosse played by the Ho-Chunk to a sport that is commonly played in your area.	Create an acrostic poem about lessons you learned from completing this activity. Share the poem with the wider school community.
Featured Sources	**Featured Sources**	**Featured Sources**
Source A: *Haudenosaunee Keep Olympic Dreams alive* [Video] **Source B:** *Roots of Lacrosse*, 14:35–18:45 **Source C:** "President Joe Biden and the White House Support Indigenous Lacrosse Team for the 2028 Olympics" [Article]	**Source A:** *Ho-Chunk Lacrosse: Discovering the Ancient Native American Sport* [Video]	**Source A:** Venn diagrams from supporting question 2

Summative Performance Task	**ARGUMENT** How do Indigenous athletes, like those who play lacrosse, teach others about the resilience of Indigenous cultures and sovereignty? Compose poems exploring the cultural and historical significance of lacrosse to the Haudenosaunee. Present these poetic interpretations to demonstrate how lacrosse connects past and present Haudenosaunee contributions to American life. Analyze how traditional games reflect and preserve cultural values through discussion of poetic themes and historical evidence.
	EXTENSION Practice lacrosse techniques and gameplay, then analyze personal experiences in relation to Haudenosaunee players' cultural perspectives and spiritual connections shared throughout the lesson.
Taking Informed Action	**UNDERSTAND** Investigate Indigenous games and athletic traditions within local Indigenous nations, focusing on their cultural significance and evolution across generations.
	ASSESS Analyze contributions of Indigenous athletes to American sports by examining biographies from the North American Indigenous Athletic Hall of Fame.
	ACT Create and present athletic trading cards highlighting Indigenous athletes' achievements and their role in preserving and celebrating cultural traditions through sport.

Overview

Inquiry Description
This inquiry begins with an exploration of the game of lacrosse and its deep connection to the Haudenosaunee people. Students will learn how lacrosse reflects the enduring history and cultural resilience of this Indigenous nation. These activities will serve as a model for students to explore how local Indigenous nations use sports and other traditional activi-

ties to preserve their cultures and teach others about the important role they play in their communities.

In Dimension 1, students will explore key terminology in the compelling question. They will consider how and why generations of family and community members continue to engage in and adapt different activities and games that have been performed for generations. This will allow students to begin to understand the importance of lacrosse for the Haudenosaunee people.

Students will learn important content in Dimension 2. At the end of this section, students will be able to answer the following questions: What is lacrosse? Who are the Haudenosaunee? How is lacrosse unique? This builds background knowledge for a deeper dive into the cultural significance of the game. This background knowledge is essential for Dimension 3.

In Dimension 3, students explore the meaning of lacrosse to the modern Haudenosaunee people. Students will gain this knowledge by listening to the stories and experiences of players and other people involved in the game. In the first supporting question, students will consider why traditional stick making is important and how the Haudenosaunee people play lacrosse today compared to the past. Students will listen to players explain what meaning the game has for them today and watch footage of games. This will help students be able to explain which aspects of the game have changed and which ones have stayed the same.

Dimension 4 focuses on cultural exchange. Students will explore how the Haudenosaunee share their knowledge of lacrosse on the international stage and learn about sports and activities important to Indigenous communities in their own area. Through this, they will identify lessons we can all learn from Indigenous traditions. The culminating performance task asks students to connect the dots. They will use their learning to explain how studying lacrosse helps us understand the significance of the Haudenosaunee people in American history. The unit includes extension activities (e.g., playing lacrosse, creating trading cards of Indigenous athletes) and encourages further exploration of Indigenous cultures in local communities.

This lesson is intended to take around five days in a fifth-grade classroom. The students had around 45 minutes per day to complete all the activities. Most of the clips in this inquiry come from two films. The first film, *Spirit Game: Pride of a Nation* (2017), is available through various streaming services. The other film, *Roots of Lacrosse* (2020), is available on YouTube. This lesson also uses other clips and resources. Links to these sources are provided throughout the lesson.

Structure of the Inquiry

Dimension 1: The "hook" activity and introduction to the compelling question
Dimension 2: Content (using C3 Framework, NCSS Themes, state/district curriculum)
Dimension 3: Primary, secondary, documentary sources to evaluate
Dimension 4: Action plan and implementation with authentic assessment

Dimension 1

Staging the Compelling Question

Students will be given the prompt, "What activities do you enjoy doing with your family and your community each year?" On a blank piece of paper, students can draw or write about some of these activities. As an entire class or in small groups, students should discuss what they have either drawn or written on their paper.

After this initial discussion, the class should discuss reasons why people engage in these activities. The teacher should record these responses on a space where all students can see responses.

Students will then be asked if people celebrate or engage in the activity the exact same way when the celebration first started. If possible, the teacher should collect photographs of school or community activities from past and present to share with students. The best examples would be of school sports activities. Students can also think about the examples in their drawings or descriptions. The teacher should engage students in a discussion about why certain aspects of traditions change and why some aspects stay the same.

Dimension 2

Supporting Question 1

The first supporting question is "What is the game of lacrosse?"

The formative task is as follows: On a teacher-provided graphic organizer, students will record notes that answer the following questions: who, what, when, where, why, and how? The teacher should remind students that they will be watching two clips so they should leave room for more notes.

Teachers may implement this task with the following procedures: Students should take notes in each box as they are watching the video clips.

The following scaffolds and other materials may be used to support students as they work with sources:
- The teacher can provide guidance about how much information should be provided in each box. For example, the teacher may ask students to record two notes in each box.
- After the film clip, the teacher can lead a group discussion about what students have written. Students who struggled to find information on their own can write answers from other students.

The following sources were selected to complete the tasks:
- **Source A:** Premier Lacrosse League. (2020, November 24). *Roots: Exploring the history of lacrosse.* [Video]. YouTube. www.youtube.com/watch?v=JxM5mcuCR8M (0:00–3:45)
- **Source B:** Spirer, P., & Baxter, P. (Directors). (2017). *Spirit game: Pride of a nation* [Film]. One Bowl Productions. (2:45–4:00)

Supporting Question 2

The second supporting question is "Who are the Haudenosaunee?"

The formative task is as follows: The teacher will lead a group discussion to make sure students understand the important facts about the Haudenosaunee Nation. For example:
- "Where is the original homeland of the Haudenosaunee?" New York
- "What groups are part of the Haudenosaunee Confederacy?" Seneca, Cayuga, Oneida. Onondaga, Mohawk, and Tuscarora
- "What is tribal sovereignty?" Indigenous people have their own governments, so they have the right to make decisions and choices that affect their communities. These choices often help different Indigenous groups like the Haudenosaunee preserve their culture and protect their land.
- "Why is being able to travel on a Haudenosaunee passport so important to the players?" A passport shows that the Haudenosaunee are an independent nation, even though their land is within the United States. When they use their passports in another country, it shows the world they want the Haudenosaunee culture to be recognized.
- By engaging in a group discussion, the teacher can make sure that students understand the information. They can take time necessary to clarify information that might be confusing to students.

The following sources were selected to complete the tasks:
- **Source A:** World Wood Day. (2017, October 26). *Roots of Lacrosse by IWCS* [Video]. YouTube. https://youtu.be/GCyv_4TYf2Q?si=xZQV7CimOI3KpXAF (6:00–9:30)
- **Source B:** *Spirit Game*, 7:20–9:45 (*Note*. This clip focuses on how the Haudenosaunee team use their own passport to travel to other countries in 2010, they were not allowed to use their passports to travel internationally, so they decided not to travel. This clip is an excellent example of how Indigenous sovereignty plays out in modern times. This clip may require some discussion for students not familiar with the term.)
- **Source C:** *Spirit Game*, 17:00–18:40

Supporting Question 3

The third supporting question is "What features make the game of lacrosse unique?"

The formative task is as follows:
- Students will discuss why the city of a La Crosse, Wisconsin, which is named after the game, chose to design the statue with the features they identify in the image.
- Students will have a chance to design their own statue using facts they learned from completing the other formative tasks.

Teachers may implement this task with the following procedures:
- Although students may discuss ideas with other students, they should complete this activity individually. This will also enable teachers to assess student understanding of lacrosse's rules and cultural significance.
- Students should be given the opportunity to teach other students about their statues either in small groups or as a whole class. If possible, teachers can display the images.

The following scaffolds and other materials may be used to support students as they work with sources: The teacher can decide the amount of detail that needs to be in the statue. For example, the teacher can determine how many features must be in the image. Students can also explain their drawings either through writing or group discussion.

The following source was selected to complete the tasks:
Source A: Highsmith, C. M. (2016) *Statue in downtown La Crosse, Wisconsin of two Winnebago Tribe members playing lacrosse, the game that the tribe invented and after which the city on the Mississippi River is named* [Photograph]. Library of Congress. www.loc.gov/item/2016631276/

Exit Ticket Suggestion: Students can use their notes to write one or two sentences describing *who, what, when, where, why,* and *how* of the game of lacrosse. Students' graphic organizers and their drawings can help provide details to be able to answer these questions.

Note. Either collect student work or make sure that they keep their work so they can access it during the next class period. This work will be necessary for completing future activities.

Dimension 3

Supporting Question 1

Bell Ringer:
- Students share the sentences that they wrote yesterday with a partner or small group.
- Students can discuss how their answers were similar and how they were different from their peers

The first supporting question is "Why is making and playing lacrosse with traditionally made sticks important to the Haudenosaunee people?"

The formative task is as follows: Students will record notes from the video clips. These notes will be used to help them complete the formative performance task for supporting question 2.

Teachers may implement this task with the following procedures: Notes can be taken on a scrap piece of paper, or the teacher can create a graphic organizer. They should focus on how the lacrosse stick is made and what significance a traditional lacrosse stick has to players.

The following scaffolds and other materials may be used to support students as they work with sources:
- If students need additional prompts, the teacher can ask the following questions:
  - What materials are the sticks made of, and what do they symbolize?
  - How does making sticks using traditional methods remind craftspeople of their ancestors?
- Students can share answers, and the teacher can record them where all students can see them. This way, students who are struggling to come up with answers on their own will have some answers to help them on the next assignment.

The following sources were selected to complete the tasks:
- **Source A:** *Roots of Lacrosse*, 0:00–5:45
- **Source B:** *Spirit Game*, 22:00–24:50

Supporting Question 2

The second supporting question is "How and why do the Haudenosaunee play lacrosse today?"

The formative task is as follows: On the outline of a lacrosse stick, students will write down their current understandings and answers to the question.

Teachers may implement this task with the following procedures:
- Students should record notes that help answer the supporting questions next to their answers from supporting question 1.
- On a piece of paper with an outline of a lacrosse stick, students will write down their current understandings and answers to the question. Students should record what they think are the most important ideas and make a small poster with what they think are the most important ideas from their notes sheet.

The following scaffolds and other materials may be used to support students as they work with sources:
- Students can share answers, and the teacher can record them where all students can see them. This way students who are struggling to come up with answers on their own will have some answers to help them on the next assignment.
- The teacher can determine how many ideas or notes need to be included on the small poster.

The following sources were selected to complete the tasks:
- **Source A:** *Spirit Game*, 4:15–6:20
- **Source B:** *Spirit Game*, 13:25–20:00
- **Source C:** *Spirit Game*, 47:49–49:45
- **Source D:** *Spirit Game*, 54:00–55:20
- **Source E:** *Spirit Game*, 1:05:00–1:07:00
- **Source F:** *Spirit Game*, 2:03:00–2:05:00
- *Note.* The teacher is welcome to choose selected clips from this list if time is limited.

Supporting Question 3

The third supporting question is "What are the similarities and differences between how the Haudenosaunee played in the past and how they play today"

The formative task is as follows: Students will complete a Venn diagram comparing how and why people played lacrosse in the past compared with how and why they play the game today.

Teachers may implement this task with the following procedures: The teacher should either distribute or have students take out their graphic organizers and drawings from the previous day's activities. State that these sheets and the students' posters will be helpful to fill in the Venn diagram.

The scaffolds and other materials may be used to support students as they work with sources:
- Students can work in pairs to complete the Venn diagram.
- The teacher can determine how many ideas or notes need to be included on Venn diagram.

The following sources were selected to complete the tasks:
- **Source A:** *Spirit Game*, 13:25–17:00
- **Source B:** *Spirit Game*, 54:00–55:20
- **Source C:** *Spirit Game*, 59:00–1:02:00
- **Source D:** *Spirit Game*, 1:03:40–1:05:20
- **Source E:** *Spirit Game*, 1:13:00–1:19:00
- *Note.* All of these clips show footage of various different games the Nationals play throughout the season. If only able to show one video, the clip in Source E is recommended. It is the semifinal match between the Haudenosaunee and the United States. It helps students visualize that the Haudenosaunee and the United States are two sovereign nations.

Exit Ticket Suggestion: Students' Venn diagrams will serve as the exit ticket for this lesson. The teacher should use these diagrams to check for student understanding. (Students will need to use their Venn diagrams for the next day's activities.)

Dimension 4

Overview

For this inquiry, Dimension 4 has been designed to give opportunities to learn more about local Indigenous communities and their efforts to preserve and teach others about their traditions and cultures. Just like the Haudenosaunee, other Indigenous nations have adapted traditional activities for their present-day communities. In this lesson, students learned about the Ho-Chunk Nation, the original inhabitants of the land where the school is located. As a nation of the Eastern Woodlands, lacrosse was and remains important to the Ho-Chunk Nation. Indigenous nations from other regions of the United States use different games and activities. The final activity asks students to write acrostic poems explaining the importance of lacrosse to both the Haudenosaunee and the Ho-Chunk Nation.

Teachers are highly encouraged to adapt supporting questions 2 and 3 and incorporate sources that explore the histories and modern contributions of their local Indigenous communities. Teachers are highly encouraged to reach out to local Indigenous communities to learn more information that will enhance this inquiry unit.

Bell Ringer: Students can share their Venn diagrams with each other. Students can share facts that were similar and what new things they learned from their partners.

Supporting Question 1

The first supporting question is "How do the Haudenosaunee people inform other people about the importance of lacrosse?"

The formative task is as follows:
- Students will discuss how playing in the Olympics will allow the Haudenosaunee to share their history and culture with the rest of the world.
- Students will discuss how other Indigenous people feel playing lacrosse, even if lacrosse is not a traditional sport of their nation.

Teachers may implement this task with the following procedures:
- After watching the video *Haudenosaunee Nationals Keep Olympic Dreams in Focus,* students will engage in a group discussion. Examine the Haudenosaunee role in bringing lacrosse to the Olympics and analyze how international competition enables them to share their history and culture with the world community. The ability of the Haudenosaunee to play on an international stage will allow them to share their history and culture with the world community.
- After students watch the second clip (Source B), analyze how players describe their emotional and cultural connections to lacrosse, including their sense of ancestral connection, physical well-being, stress relief, and desire to preserve the tradition for future generations.
- Read the article in Source C. This focuses students on examining how the Haudenosaunee use opportunities like Olympic participation and media coverage to educate others about both lacrosse's cultural significance and their sovereign status.

The following scaffolds and other materials may be used to support students as they work with sources: During the discussion, the teacher can make sure that students understand the important ideas in the videos and take time to clear up misunderstandings as they come up.

The following sources were selected to complete the tasks:
- **Source A:** WGRZ-TV. (2022, January 20). *Haudenosaunee Nationals keep Olympic dreams in focus.* [Video]. YouTube. www.youtube.com/watch?v=sMFxV4NIaVQ&ab_channel=WGRZ-TV
- (*Note.* As time progresses towards the 2028 Olympics, the teacher may be able to find updated videos.)
- **Source B:** *Roots of Lacrosse* , 14:30–18:45
- **Source C:** Pells, E. (2023, December 6). President Joe Biden and the White House support Indigenous lacrosse team for the 2028 Olympics. *AP News.* https://apnews.com/article/lacrosse-olympics-biden-haudenosaunee-8ebf449d752db21b807ceee9c174b937

Supporting Question 2

The second supporting question is "What sports/activities are important to the Indigenous peoples who live on the land around your community today?"

The formative task is as follows: Compare the game of lacrosse played by the Ho-Chunk to a sport that is commonly played in your area.

Teachers may implement this task with the following procedures:
- Students can record notes as they are watching the video (Source A). After, the teacher should discuss key ideas from the video.
- Students can use their Venn diagrams and previous work to help them fill in their second Venn diagram.

The following scaffolds and other materials may be used to support students as they work with sources:
- Students can work in pairs to complete the Venn diagram.
- The teacher can determine how many ideas or notes need to be included on Venn diagram.

The following source was selected to complete the tasks:
Source A: Discover Wisconsin. (2023, February 5). *Ho-Chunk lacrosse: Discovering the ancient Native American sport* [Video]. YouTube. www.youtube.com/watch?v=tY6sTejFBZg&ab_channel=DiscoverWisconsin

Supporting Question 3

The third supporting question is "What lessons can all people learn from Indigenous peoples who share their sports and activities with all people?"

The formative task is as follows: Students will create acrostic poems about lessons they learned from completing this activity. These poems can be shared with the wider school community.

Teachers may implement this task with the following procedures:
- Students should come up with a vocabulary word that they think is a good description of the game of lacrosse. It will be helpful to provide students with the instructions so they can pick a word that facilitates creative thinking. Words between five and eight letters tend to work best.
- If students have learned about the activities of another nation, the teacher can have the students use words from that specific activity. Students could also choose words that describe both activities.
- Students can use all work completed in other parts of the inquiry to help them complete this work.

The following scaffolds and other materials may be used to support students as they work with sources:
- Students who are struggling to come up with a word can use a teacher-provided word. For example, students could just use the word "lacrosse."
- Students can come up with individual words instead of writing entire sentences.
- Students should be given the opportunity to share their poems.

Summative Performance Task

The game of lacrosse plays an important role in Haudenosaunee culture. Lacrosse is played by many other Indigenous nations across the Eastern Woodlands of the United States. Indigenous peoples in other regions of the United States also have games and traditions that have evolved over generations. In addition to learning about the Haudenosaunee, it is important that students learn about the Indigenous peoples within their own communities. Dimension 4 supporting question 2 has been designed as a place to investigate local communities.

It is also important to acknowledge that there is a rich history of Indigenous athletes who have competed in all kinds of sports. These athletes have used their chosen sports to showcase their diverse talents and cultures. The North American Indigenous Athletics Hall of Fame provides biographies of athletes and other individuals who have contributed to the growth of sports in United States history.

For example, the following members of the Haudenosaunee had successful careers in other sports:
- Asa Shenandoah (Lumbee/Tuscarora/Onondaga): rowing
- Ayana O'Kimosh (Oneida/Menominee/Arikara): wrestling
- David Powless (Oneida): football
- Dennis J. Danforth (Oneida): boxing

One possible activity is for students to create trading cards about the individuals to share with the rest of the class.

Featured Source:
North American Indigenous Athletics Hall of Fame, http://www.naiahf.org

At this point in the inquiry, students have examined the cultural significance of Indigenous sports, particularly lacrosse, through the lens of the Haudenosaunee people. They have analyzed historical and contemporary sources about lacrosse's role in preserving cultural traditions and expressing Indigenous sovereignty.

Students should be expected to demonstrate the breadth of their understandings and their abilities to use evidence from multiple sources to support their claims. In this task, students construct an evidence-based argument addressing the compelling question "How do Indigenous sports, such as lacrosse, reflect the rich history and resilience of Indigenous peoples of the United States?"

Students' arguments will likely vary, but could include any of the following:
- Indigenous sports like lacrosse serve as living traditions that connect past to present, demonstrating how Indigenous peoples maintain cultural practices while adapting to contemporary contexts.
- Through international competition and sovereignty expressions like Haudenosaunee passports, Indigenous nations use sports to assert their political and cultural identity.
- Traditional games provide Indigenous communities with ways to pass down cultural values, maintain spiritual connections, and strengthen community bonds across generations.

To support students in their writing, teachers can provide source organizers that help students connect evidence to claims. Students may also benefit from sentence stems that help them make explicit connections between sporting traditions and cultural resilience.

To extend their arguments, students can engage in firsthand experience with traditional games. Where lacrosse equipment is available, students practice the game and reflect on players' perspectives. Alternatively, students participate in other group games to analyze themes of teamwork and community building.

Students have the opportunity to Take Informed Action by serving as cultural ambassadors within their school community. To understand, students can examine how Indigenous peoples use sports to maintain and share cultural traditions. To assess, students can evaluate how contemporary Indigenous athletes and communities use sports to educate others about their heritage and values. To act, students can create presentations or events that share their learning about Indigenous sporting traditions with the broader school community.

References

Discover Wisconsin. (2023, February 5). *Ho-Chunk lacrosse: Discovering the ancient native American sport* [Video]. YouTube. **www.youtube.com/watch?v=tY6sTejFBZg&ab_channel=DiscoverWisconsin**

Highsmith, C. M. (2016) *Statue in downtown La Crosse, Wisconsin of two Winnebago Tribe members playing lacrosse, the game that the tribe invented and after which the city on the Mississippi River is named* [Photograph]. Library of Congress. **www.loc.gov/item/2016631276/**

Pells, E. (2023, December 6) President Joe Biden and the White House support Indigenous lacrosse team for the 2028 Olympics. AP News. **https://apnews.com/article/lacrosse-olympics-biden-haudenosaunee-8ebf449d752db21b807ceee9c174b937**

Premier Lacrosse League. (2020, November 24). *Roots: Exploring the history of lacrosse.* [Video]. YouTube. **www.youtube.com/watch?v=JxM5mcuCR8M**

Spirer, P., & Baxter, P. (Directors). (2017). *Spirit game: Pride of a nation* [Film]. One Bowl Productions.

WGRZ-TV. (2022, January 20). *Haudenosaunee Nationals keep Olympic dreams in focus.* [Video]. YouTube. **www.youtube.com/watch?v=sMFxV4NIaVQ&ab_channel=WGRZ-TV**

World Wood Day. (2017, October 26). *Roots of Lacrosse by IWCS* [Video]. YouTube. **https://youtu.be/GCyv_4TYf2Q?si=xZQV7CimOI3KpXAF**

STARLYNN NANCE AND TAYLOR HAWES-GULDENPFENNIG

Middle School World History

Does China make the world flat?

Supporting Questions Dimension 2
1. Did the physical geography of Ancient China present ancient people with challenges?
2. How did the accomplishments of the different dynasties prohibit or encourage the Silk Road?
3. What was the purpose of the Silk Road, and did it cause cultural diffusion to take place?

Supporting Questions Dimension 3
1. Can you identify the causes of sweatshops and distinguish between two main types of labor markets (regarding sweatshops)?
2. Describe three ethical approaches that are used to analyze moral problems and apply the three ethical approaches to sweatshops
3. Evaluate three policy options for dealing with sweatshops.

Supporting Questions Dimension 4
1. Using our new information, do you see an issue in our community that is similar to the content from our unit?
2. Now that the class has chosen [issue], what is this class going to do about it?
3. Now that the class has the solution, what does implementation look like?

Middle School World History

	Does China make the world flat?
Standards and Content	**C3 Standards:** D2.His.1.6-8. Analyze connections among events and developments in broader historical contexts **NCSS Themes:** ❷ Time, Continuity, and Change ❼ Production, Distribution, and Consumption ❾ Global Connections
Staging the Compelling Question	**Dimension 1:** Look at the three examples of art, and list terms that represent each piece of art on a teacher-made graphic organizer (see narrative after the IDM for an example). In a Think-Pair-Share (TPS) activity, discuss your answers. Then, create a Mind Map using the terms you used and heard about the three pictures of art. From the Mind Maps, list words that are being repeated. As a class, determine one word that represents all three pictures of art. Use your knowledge from the lesson to answer the compelling question: Does China make the world flat? **Featured Sources:** *Camel and rider* (sculpture from Middlebury College Museum of Art) *Illustrated map* (from History.com) *Mural* (from *Chinese Social Sciences Today*)

Dimension 2

Supporting Question 1	Supporting Question 2	Supporting Question 3
Did the physical geography of Ancient China present ancient people with challenges?	How did the accomplishments of the different dynasties prohibit or encourage the Silk Road?	What was the purpose of the Silk Road, and did it cause cultural diffusion to take place?
Formative Performance Task	**Formative Performance Task**	**Formative Performance Task**
Analyze the physical features that characterize Ancient China. Locate neighboring countries, cities, deserts, mountain ranges, and bodies of water. Draw the Silk Road on the map. What continent is this Ancient China on?	Create a Gallery Walk that lists the major accomplishments of the Shang, Zhou, Qin, and Han dynasties. Visit each gallery to fill out the teacher-made graphic organizer. Answer the question: Did these accomplishments prohibit or encourage the Silk Road?	Define "cultural diffusion." Annotate the chapter and sections associated with the Silk Road Answer the supporting question using a Mind Map.
Featured Sources	**Featured Sources**	**Featured Sources**
Source A: Map of Ancient China *Note.* The teacher can use maps from teacher sources, the textbook, or an online source if needed.	**Source A:** Teacher-developed slides that cover the major accomplishments of the Shang, Zhou, Qin, and Han dynasties. Follow your district or state standards or objectives for this content.	**Source A:** District-approved World History textbook *Note.* The teacher can use any secondary source to complete the formative performance task for supporting question 3.

Exit Ticket Suggestion:
After the students complete Dimension 1 (Staging Question) and Dimension 2 (Content), design an exit ticket for students to evaluate their new knowledge of Ancient China. Design a Four Corners activity answering the compelling question, "Does China make the world flat?" Corner one represents "yes it does 100%," corner two represents "no, it does not at all," corner three represents "it sort of does," and corner four represents "undecided." The students will examine the content from the class and walk to the corner that best explains claim. Students discuss with peers why they chose the corner. The teacher will facilitate the Teacher Talk allowing one spokesperson from each group to discuss their corner's thoughts and evidence (from Dimension 1 and Dimension 2).

Dimension 3

Suggested Bell Ringer:
Ask the students as a whole class to explain what would make the world flat? Have the students write the answers to the following questions: "Does China still have a Silk Road or have business in trade? How do you know?" (Students may give examples of electronics, clothes, etc.) Students will share answers with the class. Have the students write the answers to the next set of questions on their paper: "Are any of your clothes or shoes made in China?" Have the students describe their prior knowledge about trade with China throughout the world. (Answers will vary but hopefully they discuss sweatshops.)

Supporting Question 1	Supporting Question 2	Supporting Question 3
Can you identify the causes of sweatshops and distinguish between two main types of labor markets (regarding sweatshops)?	Describe three ethical approaches that are used to analyze moral problems and apply the three ethical approaches to sweatshops.	Evaluate three policy options for dealing with sweatshops.
Formative Performance Task	**Formative Performance Task**	**Formative Performance Task**
Annotate the reading in Source A with teacher-created Metacognitive Markers. (e.g., ! = something interesting; ____ = main idea; ? = I have a question about this; Circle a word = need a definition/explanation) Discuss each Metacognitive Marker used in the directions. Answer the supporting question using a teacher-made graphic organizer. Compare and contrast the visuals in Source B on the teacher-made graphic organizer.	Answer the supporting question in Jigsaw Groups using a teacher-made graphic organizer then in a Share Out group. Group 1: Ethical Approach 1 Group 2: Ethical Approach 2 Group 3: Ethical Approach 3 Discuss three statements from #7 on page 83 of Source C with your group then with the class. Read Source B and answer the questions.	In TPS groups, source and annotate/close read Source A. In TPS groups, read and annotate Source B and answer questions on a piece of paper. Watch *China Blue* (Source C) and write quotations from the documentary in a teacher-made graphic organizer. Review Source B. How would you change your answers?
Featured Sources	**Featured Sources**	**Featured Sources**
Source A: Activity 6.1 Sweatshops and Labor Markets (Wight & Morton, 2007, pp. 93–98) **Source B:** Visual 6.1 Features of Sweatshop and 6.2 Market Structures (Wight & Morton, 2007, pp. 89–90)	**Source A:** Visual 6.3 Approaches to Ethical Issues (Wight & Morton, 2007, p. 91) **Source B:** Activity 6.2 Two Perspectives on Sweatshops (Wight & Morton, 2007, pp. 101–102) **Source C:** Lesson 6 (Wight & Morton, 2007, pp. 81–106)	**Source A:** Visual 6.4 The Market Approach (Wight & Morton, 2007, p. 92) **Source B:** Activity 6.3 What Should We Do About Sweatshops? (Wight & Morton, 2007, pp. 103–106) **Source C:** *China Blue* [Film]

Artificial Intelligence (AI) Enhancement

Suggested Bell Ringer for AI Enhancement:
When were the material we used in the lesson and the documentary made? Do you think this information is still the same today? How can we find out? Has anyone had a historical conversation with AI? Can you describe that? What types of questions do you ask? To learn more than a definition or basic facts, how do you frame the questions? Having a conversation with AI is different than searching Google. How?

Enhancement from Taylor for Dimension Three:
- Identify where your tennis shoes were made by checking the tag in your shoes. Share out with a partner and then as a whole group the locations on your shoes using a word cloud generator, writing on the whiteboard, or even pinning on a digital map via resources such as Padlet (**https://padlet.com/**).
- In pairs or small groups, read the article, "The Cost of Fast Fashion" (Anastasia, 2017), annotating with the Metacognitive Markers.
- Complete a Graffiti Wall activity and then a Gallery Walk around the room to review others' responses. Graffiti Wall topics might include but are not limited to the causes for the rise of fast fashion, factors that led to fast fashion becoming a three-billion-dollar industry, effects of fast fashion on workers and on the environment, and connections between fast fashion and the Silk Road.
- Create a Frayer Model definition of "fast fashion."
- Participate in a whole class discussion: What are the main ideas discussed in the article regarding the impacts of fast fashion? How does globalization contribute to the rise of fast fashion? What are some of the environmental and social costs mentioned in the article? How does the concept of the Silk Road relate to globalization and trade, and how might it be contrasted with modern global supply chains in the context of fast fashion?
- Summarize the costs of fast fashion and its connections to globalization and historical trade routes.
- Discuss potential solutions or actions individuals can take to address the negative impacts of fast fashion.
- *Exit Ticket:* Write a short reflection on what you found the most surprising or concerning about the article and how it has influenced your views on consumer choices. Write your response on a sticky note and post it to the door of the classroom on your way out of the room.

Dimension 4

Supporting Question 1	Supporting Question 2	Supporting Question 3
Using our new information, do you see an issue in our community that is similar to the content from our unit?	Now that the class has chosen [issue], what is this class going to do about it?	Now that the class has the solution, what does implementation look like?
Formative Performance Task	**Formative Performance Task**	**Formative Performance Task**
Create a list of issues that relate to the compelling question. Discuss each issue and how it relates to the content from Dimensions 2 and 3 using evidence from the lessons to compare the issues with the content. (Can be written in a student-made graphic organizer).	List solutions related to issue selected from SQ1. Choose a solution and develop an action plan.	Write the issue and solution on the board for all students to refer to during this lesson. Choose an implementation plan and complete the plan as written.
Featured Sources	**Featured Sources**	**Featured Sources**
Sources from Dimensions 1–3	Sources from Dimensions 1–3 and answers from SQ1	Sources from Dimensions 1–3 and answers from SQ1 and SQ2

Summative Performance Task	**ARGUMENT** *Does China make the world flat?* Using content from Dimensions 1–3 in a P.E.E.L. paragraph, answer the compelling question. **EXTENSION** Use AI to develop more knowledge about sweatshops by using appropriate questions in a conversation-style activity rather than a question-and-answer situation. Question the AI answers and correct the answers, if necessary.
Taking Informed Action	**UNDERSTAND** Connect the past to the present by using the content to choose a similar problem from the present in their community. **ASSESS** Develop a plan of action to solve the problem in their community. **ACT** Implement the plan of action to solve the problem in their community.

Overview

Inquiry Description

This inquiry leads students through an investigation of ancient dynasties and trade in Ancient China. Focusing on the Silk Road, students will use the historical knowledge from the Silk Road to compare trade on the Silk Road with trade in China in the early 2000s. Students will engage with primary sources, secondary sources, documentary film, and case studies to evaluate sweatshops using their new knowledge. The extension lesson will use artificial intelligence (AI) to have an academic conversation with AI about sweatshops today. The students will move to the present day to create a plan of action and implement a solution to a problem they see in the community. Students will go through all four dimensions of the C3 Framework.

This inquiry highlights the following standard:
- D2.His.1.6-8 Analyze connections among events and developments in broader historical contexts

This inquiry is expected to take 12–15 days with 50-minute class periods. The inquiry time frame could expand if teachers think their students need additional instructional experiences (e.g., supporting questions, formative performance tasks, featured sources, writing, watching documentary clips). Teachers are encouraged to adapt the inquiry to meet the needs and interests of their students. This inquiry lends itself to AI, differentiation, and modeling of historical thinking skills while assisting students in reading and viewing a variety of sources.

Structure of the Inquiry

Dimension 1: The "hook" activity and introduction to the compelling question
Dimension 2: Content (using the C3 Framework, NCSS Themes, state/district curriculum)
Dimension 3: Primary, secondary, and documentary sources to evaluate (Using a lesson plan from Wight, J. B., & Morton, J. S. (2007). What should we do about sweatshops? In *Teaching the ethical foundations of economics.* National Council on Economic Education.)
Dimension 4: Action plan and implementation with authentic assessment

Dimension 1

Staging the Compelling Question

In staging the compelling question,
- Take the pictures from the three featured sources and put the pictures on PowerPoint or Google Slides for the students to look at without any information about the art or its source.
- Have the students look at the three pictures of art from China.
- On a teacher-made graphic organizer (example below), individually have the students list terms the three pictures of art represent.
- In a Think-Pair-Share (TPS) activity, have the students discuss their answers.
- Have a whole class Teacher Talk (TT) over the conversations in the TPS.
- From the whole class TT, have the students in the TPS create a Mind Map using the terms they used and heard about the three pictures of art.
- From the Mind Maps, list words that are being repeated within the groups. As a class determine one word that represents all three pictures of art.
- For an exit ticket, have the students use their knowledge from the lesson to answer the compelling question: "Does China make the world flat?"

Note. From this staging activity, the goal is to facilitate a TT that will result in the terms "globalization," "trade," "economics," etc.

Artwork Analysis Graphic Organizer
Directions: Analyze the artwork for a minute and then complete the graphic organizer. Complete the graphic organizer for each piece of art. We will share out as a class after your individual work time.

What do you see?	What does it mean?

The following sources were selected to complete the tasks:
- **Source A:** Camel and Rider. [Terracotta sculpture]. (618–906). Middlebury College Museum of Art Visual Descriptions Highlights Tour. https://sites.middlebury.edu/museumvisualdescriptions/camel-and-rider/
- **Source B:** Map from History.com Editors. (2023, June 6). *Silk road.* www.history.com/topics/ancient-middle-east/silk-road
- **Source C:** Mural from Pei, S. (2017, June 1). *History of art on silk road revealed by cultural exchange.* Chinese Social Sciences Today. www.csstoday.com/Item/4490.aspx

Dimension 2

Supporting Question 1

The first supporting question is "Did the physical geography of Ancient China present ancient people with challenges?"

The formative task is as follows:
- Analyze the physical features that characterize Ancient China
- Locate neighboring countries, cities, deserts, mountain ranges, and bodies of water.
- Answering: What continent is this Ancient China on?

Teachers may implement this task with the following procedures:
- Using a map from your curriculum, have the students complete the formative tasks.
- This can be done in groups, centers, a Gallery Walk or as a whole class activity.

The following scaffolds and other materials may be used to support students as they work with sources: The teacher can use cooperative grouping, data driven differentiation, or teacher conferences to support students. Using 1-1 instruction is an option for students during this lesson. The teacher can implement formative assessments to check objectives during the tasks.

The following sources were selected to complete the tasks:
- **Source A:** Map of Ancient China from the teacher sources from the text.
- *Note.* The teacher can use maps from an online source if needed

Supporting Question 2

The second supporting question is "How did the accomplishments of the different dynasties prohibit or encourage the Silk Road?"

The formative task is as follows:
- On a teacher-made graphic organizer, list the major accomplishments of the Shang, Zhou, Qin, and Han dynasties.
- Answer: Did these accomplishments prohibit or encourage the Silk Road?

Teachers may implement this task with the following procedures:
- The teacher will make a Graphic Organizer for the teacher-made Gallery Walk
- Choral Response can be found at: **https://kyocare.com/choral-responding-a-versatile-aba-technique-to-engage-students/**
- The second supporting question begins a study into the dynasties of Ancient China with a focus on the relationship with the Silk Road. With a teacher-made Graphic Organizer and Gallery Walk, the students will experience each of the major dynasties. After completing the Gallery Walk and finishing their Graphic Organizer, the students will answer the supporting question as a teacher facilitated Teacher Talk.
- I ask the students, "What accomplishments do you think prohibited the Silk Road?" pausing as they highlighted the answers on the Graphic Organizer. I asked the students, "what accomplishments do you think encouraged the Silk Road?" and paused as they circled the answers on the Graphic Organizer. I then directed the students how to participate in the Teacher Talk using the two sentence stems so they would identify the dynasty and back up their claim with evidence (from the Gallery Walk and textbook).
- I model for the students how to use the two sentence stems, I stated, "(Blank) dynasty prohibited the Silk Road by (adding your evidence to complete the sentence) or (blank) dynasty encouraged the Silk Road by (adding your evidence to complete the sentence)." Students answered each sentence stem, and I would Cold Call students to agree or disagree with student A's claim. Student B would agree or disagree and have to back up their answer with more evidence. It took the students a bit to get in a rhythm of answering their classmates back but after a few minutes, more students grew confident in sharing their claims and debating answers. At the end of the Teacher Talk, I reviewed the content of the dynasties with the students in a Choral Responding exit ticket.

The following scaffolds and other materials may be used to support students as they work with sources: The teacher can use cooperative grouping, data driven differentiation, or teacher conferences to support students. Using 1-1 instruction is an option for students during this lesson. The teacher can implement formative assessments to check objectives during the tasks.

The following source was selected to complete the tasks:
Source A: Teacher-made slides from district and/or state curriculum standards

Supporting Question 3

The third supporting question is "What was the purpose of the Silk Road, and did it cause cultural diffusion to take place?"

The formative task is as follows:
- Using the district-approved textbook, in groups, have the students define "cultural diffusion."
- Then instruct the students to annotate the chapter and sections associated with the Silk Road.
- Answer the supporting question using a Mind Map.

Teachers may implement this task with the following procedures: Using the teacher-made graphic organizer, the students can complete the formative tasks in groups, centers, a Gallery Walk or as a whole class activity, or a choose your own adventure (tiered differentiation).

The following scaffolds and other materials may be used to support students as they work with sources: The teacher can use cooperative grouping, data driven differentiation, or teacher conferences to support students. Using 1-1 instruction is an option for students during this lesson. The teacher can implement formative assessments to check objectives during the tasks.

The following sources were selected to complete the tasks:
- **Source A**: District-approved World History textbook
- *Note*. The teacher can use any secondary source to complete the formative assessment for supporting questions 3.

Exit Ticket Suggestion: After the students complete Dimension 1 (Staging Question) and Dimension 2 (content), have them complete an exit ticket using their new knowledge of Ancient China. Have the students participate in a Four Corners activity answering the compelling question, "Does China make the world flat?" Corner one will be the claim, "Yes, it does 100%." Corner two will be the claim, "No, it does not at all." Corner three will be the claim, "It sort of does." Corner four will be the claim "undecided." The teacher will have the students walk to one of the four corner claims. Each corner will discuss why they chose the corner claim using evidence from the unit. The teacher will facilitate the Teacher Talk allowing one spokesperson from each group to discuss their corner's thoughts and evidence (from Dimension 1 and Dimension 2) that backs up their group's corner answer.

The Four Corners activity explanation is #29: Lambert, K. (2012, April). *Tools for formative assessment techniques to check understanding and processing activities.* https://www.utwente.nl/en/examination/faq-testing-assessment/60formativeassessment.pdf

---

Dimension 3

Supporting Question 1

Bell Ringer:
- Ask: What would make the world flat? There is no right answer, but after some suggested (literal or figurative) answers ask the students if China still has a Silk Road or has business in trade? Ask how they know? (Students may give examples of electronics, clothes, etc.) Then say, "are any of your clothes or shoes made in China?" Ask what the students know about trade with China throughout the world? (Answers will vary but hopefully they discuss sweatshops).
- Begin the lesson with saying, expanding on what we learned about Ancient China and how the Silk Road evolved through different challenges and successes, let's think about current history and trade.

The first supporting question is "Can you identify the causes of sweatshops and distinguish between two main types of labor markets (regarding sweatshops)?"

The formative task is as follows:
- Using Source A, have the students annotate the reading with teacher created Metacognitive Markers. (For Example: ! is the symbol for something interesting; @ is the symbol for main idea; ? is the symbol for I have a question about this; and circling a word will symbolize that the student needs a definition/explanation.)
- Whole class Teacher Talk over the reading (focus on Metacognitive Markers) and questions from the reading. Have students discuss each Metacognitive Marker.
- Have a mini-Teacher Talk where students fill in a teacher-made Graphic Organizer to answer the supporting question (objectives) above. Use Visual 6.1 and 6.2 (Source B) to summarize the information.

Teachers may implement this task with the following procedures:
- Using the lesson plan (What should we do about sweatshops?) published by the Council for Economic Education (CEE), follow the plan as written in this section of the inquiry.
- The lesson was inspired by the CEE, but some directions were changed to fit the inquiry. The teacher should follow the formative performance tasks and use the CEE document "What should we do about sweatshops?" (Wight & Morton, 2007) as a resource.
- Questions and answers are in the CEE document to help teachers with instruction.

The scaffolds and other materials that may be used to support students as they work with sources can be cooperative groups or whole class work.

The following sources were selected to complete the task:
- **Source A:** Activity 6.1 Sweatshops and Labor Markets (pp. 93-98)
- **Source B:** Visual 6.1 and 6.2 (pp. 89-90)
- Both sources are from Wight, J. B., & Morton, J. S. (2007). What should we do about sweatshops? In *Teaching the ethical foundations of economics*. National Council on Economic Education.

Supporting Question 2

The second supporting question is "Describe three ethical approaches that are used to analyze moral problems and apply the three ethical approaches to sweatshops."

The formative task is as follows:
- Use the instructional strategy Jigsaw for the students to accomplish the answers to the supporting questions (objectives) above. Create a graphic organizer for the students to transfer information from the share out groups to use in a whole class discussion.
  - Group 1: Ethical Approach 1
  - Group 2: Ethical Approach 2
  - Group 3: Ethical Approach 3
- Students will Jigsaw to the Share Out Group and teach each other the approaches.
- After each Share Out group has completed the teaching section, the teacher will give the Share Out group the 3 statements from #7 on page 83 of Source C to read and discuss as a group, then as a whole class. The students will review answers 5, 6, and 7 from the day before by placing these questions on a PowerPoint/slides presentation. (These were multiple choice questions.) Review the correct answers.
- After the review, give the students the Activity 6.2. Have the groups read each perspective and answer the questions. Whole class Teacher Talk over the answers

Teachers may implement this task with the following procedures:
- Using the lesson plan published by the Council for Economic Education (CEE), follow the plan as written in this section of the inquiry.
- The lesson was inspired by the CEE, but some directions were changed to fit the inquiry. The teacher should follow the formative performance tasks and use the CEE document as a resource.
- Questions and answers are in the CEE document to help teachers with instruction.

The scaffolds and other materials that may be used to support students as they work with sources are cooperative grouping.

The following sources were selected to complete the tasks:
- **Source A:** Visual 6.3 (p. 91)
- **Source B:** Activity 6.2 (pgs. 101-102)
- **Source C:** Lesson 6 (pp. 81–106)

All sources are from Wight, J. B., & Morton, J. S. (2007). What should we do about sweatshops? In *Teaching the ethical foundations of economics*. National Council on Economic Education.

Supporting Question 3

The third supporting question is "Evaluate three policy options for dealing with sweatshops."

The formative task is as follows:
- Display or give the students Visual 6.4. Have the students in a TPS group source and annotate/close read the document.
- Give the TPS groups the Activity 6.3 to read and annotate. Then have the TPS group answer the questions.
- Watch the documentary film titled *China Blue* from PBS Independent Lens. Have the students use a teacher-made Graphic Organizer to write down quotes to back up the clip questions and so they can use it in the summative activity. https://www.youtube.com/watch?v=o9gO9MgSO7A
    - 00:00:00–00:02:18
        - Teacher Talk Questions:
            - When was it filmed? (Sourcing)
            - Why was it filmed? (Contextualization)
            - What do you find important about this clip?
            - How does this clip relate to the content from the lessons?
    - 00:02:19–00:17:15
        - Teacher Talk Questions:
            - What does your group find most important about this clip?
            - How does it relate to the content we have been studying?
            - Do you think these types of issues or similar types of issues could be found during the Silk Road? (Even though it was ancient times.)
            - Do you think this type of sweatshops exist in the US today?
- Go back to the questions from Activity 6.3. After watching the film clips, ask students how would you change your answers? Have the TPS groups add to their answers, then complete a whole class Teacher Talk.

Note. If the teacher wants to show the entire documentary, this is encouraged to show a teenager perspective and firsthand account of working in a sweatshop. However, this lesson does not include any instruction past the time stamps above.

Teachers may implement this task with the following procedures:
- Using the lesson plan published by the Council for Economic Education (CEE), follow the plan as written in this section of the inquiry.
- The lesson was inspired by the CEE, but some directions were changed to fit the inquiry. The teacher should follow the formative performance tasks and use the CEE document as a resource.
- Questions and answers are in the CEE document to help teachers with instruction.

The scaffolds and other materials that may be used to support students as they work with sources are cooperative grouping.

The following sources were selected to complete the tasks:
- **Source A:** Visual 6.4 (p. 92)
- **Source B:** Activity 6.3 (pgs. 103-106)
- **Source C:** Documentary *China Blue*
- **Sources A** and **B** are from Wight, J. B., & Morton, J. S. (2007). What should we do about sweatshops? In *Teaching the ethical foundations of economics*. National Council on Economic Education.

Artificial Intelligence (AI) Enhancement

Suggested Bell Ringer for AI Enhancement:
When was the material we used in the lesson and the documentary made? Do you think this information is still the same today? How can we find out? Has anyone had a historical conversation with AI? Can you describe that? What types of questions do you ask? To learn more than a definition or basic facts, how do you frame the questions? Having a conversation with AI is different than searching Google. How?

Note. The sources used in the lessons for Dimension 3 are from the early 2000s. To bring this to the current time, the students are going to use AI to get more information about sweatshops that is more current. Before starting this section, the teachers should instruct the students on how to use the AI tool, how to generate engineering prompts (using Bloom's Taxonomy stems is helpful for students), and how to follow all district policies for AI use. This section of the inquiry is optional but encouraged. Using the activities, visuals, and the documentary film clips, have the students engage in an academic conversation with AI. The teachers can do this as a whole class, where the teacher is using the AI on the screen but having the students create the engineering prompts using the sources prior to the conversation. Other options are for students to complete as a homework assignment or a project.

Enhancement from Taylor for Dimension Three (from Chapter 6)
This enhancement lesson seeks to provide students another tangible connection between the Silk Road and modern globalization. To begin, I had students identify where their tennis shoes were made. This can be done by checking the tag contained within their shoes relatively easily during class. Additionally, students could check the tag on their t-shirts to provide more variety in their responses, since many students wear the same brand of shoes. I had students share out with a partner and then as a whole group the locations on their shoes. This can be done visually as a class using a word cloud generator, writing on the whiteboard, or even pinning on a digital map via resources such as Padlet. I then facilitated a whole group discussion, asking questions such as "Describe what you see" and "What does this tell us about globalization?" Students should be able to make connections between the variety of locations (predominantly in countries located in Asia or South America) and that of previously learned content about sweatshops, globalization, and the Silk Road.

After completing the introductory activity, I divided students either into pairs or small groups and gave every student a copy of the article, "The Real Cost of Fast Fashion" (Anastasia, 2017). Students can read the article in pairs, or as a small group, annotating with their Metacognitive Markers. After completing their annotations, I directed students' attention to the posters hanging up around the room. I informed students that we now are going to complete a Graffiti Wall activity (see Figure 6.3). This means that students go around the room to each poster and answer whatever question or prompt is present at that station. (Example responses or sentence stems can be provided on each poster to guide students.) After each group had the opportunity to share out on all posters, I provided students time to conduct a Gallery Walk around the room to review others' responses. Graffiti Wall topics could include but are not limited to the causes for the rise of fast fashion, factors that led to fast fashion becoming a three-billion-dollar industry, effects of fast fashion on workers and on the environment, as well as connections between fast fashion and the Silk Road. After reviewing the Graffiti Wall, students created a Frayer Model definition of "fast fashion" using what they learned from the article. During group work time, I rotated around the room, assessing student work and conferencing with groups to ensure they were on task and generating quality ideas.

Once all groups completed their Graffiti Wall and Frayer Model definition, I facilitated a whole class discussion, allowing students to ask questions or provide additional insights. I asked students questions such as, "What are the main ideas discussed in the article regarding the impacts of fast fashion?" "How does globalization contribute to the rise of fast fashion?" "What are some of the environmental and social costs mentioned in the article?" and "How does the concept of the Silk Road relate to globalization and trade, and how might it be contrasted with modern global supply chains in the context of fast fashion?" I asked students to summarize what they had learned about the costs of fast fashion and its connections to globalization and historical trade routes. We then discussed potential solutions or actions individuals could take to address the negative impacts of fast fashion. These discussions brought up ideas such as shopping at thrift stores rather than buying new or boycotting major brands that neglect their workers or the environment and buying from small businesses instead. Students even made connections to the documentary viewed previously in class regarding sweatshops.

As an Exit Ticket, I had students write a short reflection on what they found most surprising or concerning about the article and how it has influenced their views on consumer choices. These responses were collected on a sticky note and then posted to the door of the classroom on their way out of the room. While not necessary, this engaging enhancement provides students with valuable opportunities to discover meaningful connections between historical trade routes, contemporary global supply chains, and their own consumer choices.

Dimension 4

Overview

Dimension 4 is where the students take over and develop real life skills. They create their own inquiry connecting the past to the present. As teachers, we want them to take over and own their learning. This dimension is for teachers to be silent and to teach through questioning. This lesson has been tested in secondary classrooms at different grades and was a very successful way to have students take over their own learning. Ask yourself, if I give them an answer of how to implement, is that *really* inquiry? Try this method out so that students can develop skills and learn in an environment where mistakes are okay and where working together can make a difference.

Supporting Question 1

The first supporting question is "Using our new information, do you see an issue in our community that is similar to the content from our unit?"
Note. The teacher does not suggest any answers or give hints. The teacher is only supposed to ask questions so the students can experience inquiry and civic engagement.

The formative task is to create a list of issues that relate to the compelling question and discuss each issue and how it relates to the content from Dimensions 2 and 3 using evidence from the lessons to compare the issues with the content. (This can be written in a student-made graphic organizer.)

Teachers may implement this task with the following procedures:
- Students will make a list of issues that come to mind on the board or in a shared document that everyone can see and type on. (I suggest using the board.)
- Students discuss each issue and how it relates to the content that was taught in the unit in groups. The groups will use evidence from the lessons to compare the issues with the content. This can be in a student-made graphic organizer.
- The teacher will facilitate a Teacher Talk with the students about their findings. Then ask the class which issue is more like the content? After the class has picked one, that is the issue they will be using for their plan of action.

The following sources were selected to complete the tasks:
All sources from Dimensions 1–3 can be used during this lesson.

Supporting Question 2

The second supporting question is "Now that the class has chosen [issue], what is this class going to do about it?"
Note. Classes will have different issues and different solutions. The teacher does not suggest any answers or give hints. The teacher is only supposed to ask questions so the students can experience inquiry and civic engagement.

The formative task is to list solutions related to issue selected from SQ1 then choose a solution and develop an action plan.

Teachers may implement this task with the following procedures:
- Students will make a list of solutions that comes to mind on the board or in a shared document that everyone can see and type on. (I suggest using the board.)
- The teacher facilitates this discussion without input. Every solution the students suggest is equal and will be placed on the board. After an exhaustive list, the teacher then gives the boundaries from school/district policy, the principal, the department, etc.
- Using the boundaries, the students decide which of the solutions will not be able to be completed and the teacher crosses them off.
- After the students' conversation is complete, they will have one solution that is policy friendly.
- Ask the students, how are you going to accomplish this? What is the plan? How are you going to implement it using the boundaries we have set?

The following sources were selected to complete the tasks:
- Students will create a portfolio that develops a plan of action and how they will implement it.
- This is student led. No rubrics or input from the teachers.

Supporting Question 3

The third supporting question is "Now that the class has the solution, what does implementation look like?"
Note. Classes will have different issues and different solutions. The teacher does not suggest any answers or give hints. The teacher is only supposed to ask questions so the students can experience inquiry and civic engagement.

The formative task is to write the issue and solution on the board for all students to refer to during this lesson. Then, choose an implementation plan and complete the plan as written.

Teachers may implement this task with the following procedures:
- Students will make a list of solutions that come to mind on the board or in a shared document that everyone can see and type on. (I suggest using the board.)
- The teacher facilitates this discussion without input. Every implementation plan that the students suggest is equal and will be placed on the board. After an exhaustive list, the teacher then reminds the students of the boundaries from school/district policy, the principal, the department, etc.
- Using the boundaries, the students decide which of the implementation plans will not be able to be completed and the teacher crosses them off.
- After the students' conversation is complete, they will have one implementation plan that is policy friendly.
- Ask the students, "How are you going to accomplish this? What is the implementation plan? How are you going to implement it using the boundaries we have set?"

The following sources were selected to complete the tasks:
- Students will create a portfolio that develops a plan of action and how they will implement it.
- This is student led. No rubrics or input from the teachers.

Summative Performance Task

In this inquiry, there are two summative performance tasks. One is to write the P.E.E.L. paragraph (or use a format of writing that is in your curriculum) (ISC Learn, n.d.) to answer the compelling question. This ideally can be assigned after completing Dimension 3. The second summative performance task is the authentic assessment. This is the action plan and implementation in Dimension 4. Because AI is going to be an important tool to use, any inquiry can be extended to have academic conversations with an AI tool. I prefer Perplexity (www.perplexity.ai/) to use in social studies courses, but please follow district guidelines and work with the AI prior to implementing it.

ARGUMENT *Does China make the world flat?* Using content from Dimensions 1–3 in a P.E.E.L. paragraph, answer the compelling question.

EXTENSION Students will use AI to develop more knowledge about sweatshops by using appropriate questions in a conversation-style activity rather than a question-and-answer situation. Students will be able to question the AI answers and correct the answers, if necessary.

UNDERSTAND Students will connect the past to the present by using the content to choose a similar problem from the present, in their community.

ASSESS Students will develop a plan of action to solve the problem from the community.

ACT Students will implement the plan of action to solve the problem from the community.

References

A Middlebury Blog (n.d.). *Camel and rider.* Middlebury College Museum of Art Visual Descriptions Highlights Tour. https://sites.middlebury.edu/museumvisualdescriptions/camel-and-rider/

Adams, N. E. (2015, July). *Bloom's taxonomy of cognitive learning objectives. Journal of the Medical Library Association* 103(3). 152-153. doi: **10.3163/1536-5050.103.3.010**

Allyn, P. (2019, March 7). *Let's commit to celebrating the read-aloud year-round.* National Council of Teachers of English. **https://ncte.org/blog/2019/03/celebrating-the-read-aloud/**

Anastasia, L. (2017, September 4). *The real cost of fashion.* Upfront Scholastic. **https://upfront.scholastic.com/pages/archives/articles/the-real-cost-of-cheap-fashion.html?language=english#1070L**

Council for Economic Education (n.d.). *What should we do about sweatshops?* **https://www.socialstudies.com/pdf/JCE122EX.pdf**

Council Of Chief State School Officers & National Governors' Association. (2009) *Common Core State Standards Initiative.* United States. https://www.loc.gov/item/lcwaN0010852/

Digital Inquiry Group (n.d.) *Reading like a historian.* **https://inquirygroup.org/history-lessons**

Dorr, H. (2023). *How to set up learning centers: A comprehensive guide for teachers.* TeachStarter. **https://www.teachstarter.com/us/blog/how-to-set-up-learning-centers-classroom/**

Francis, E. M. (2017, May 9). *What is depth of knowledge?* ASCD Blog. **https://www.ascd.org/blogs/what-exactly-is-depth-of-knowledge-hint-its-not-a-wheel**

Gregory, G. H. & Chapman, C.M. (2012). *Differentiated instructional strategies: One size does not fit all.* Sage Publications.

Gonzalez, J. (2015, April 15). *4 things you don't know about the jigsaw method.* Cult of Pedagogy. **https://www.cultofpedagogy.com/jigsaw-teaching-strategy/**

Henry, L. (2024). *Building reading comprehension through think-alouds.* Read, Write, Think. National Council of Teachers of English. **https://www.readwritethink.org/classroom-resources/lesson-plans/building-reading-comprehension-through**

History Editors. (2023, June). *Silk road.* https://www.history.com/topics/ancient-middle-east/silk-road

ISC Learn (n.d.). *How to use PEEL writing in your assignments.* www.icslearn.co.uk/blog/study-advice/how-to-use-peel-writing-in-your-assignments/

Johnson, R. T. & Johnson, D. W. (1994). An overview of cooperative learning. In J. Thousand, A. Villa & A. Nevid (Eds.), *Creativity and collaborative learning* (pp. 1-21). Brookes Press.

Jwyks. (n.d.). *Strategy #1—the graffiti wall (engagement strategies series).* Musings from the Middle School. **https://musingsfromthemiddleschool.org/2016/01/strategy-1-the-graffiti-wall-engagement-strategies-series.html**

Lambert, K. (2012, April). *Tools for formative assessment techniques to check understanding and processing activities.* https://www.utwente.nl/en/examination/faq-testing-assessment/60formativeassessment.pdf

Marks, M. (2021). China blue documentary English version [Video file]. *YouTube*. https://www.youtube.com/watch?v=IsRIjiPz5Tk

National Council for the Social Studies. (2013). *College, career, and civic life (C3) framework for social studies state standards.* www.socialstudies.org/c3

National Council for the Social Studies (n.d.). *National curriculum standards for social studies.* https://www.socialstudies.org/standards/national-curriculum-standards-social-studies-introduction

Padlet (n.d.). *Make beautiful boards to collect, organize, and present anything.* https://padlet.com/

Pei, S. (2017, June 1). *History of art on silk road revealed by cultural exchange.* Chinese Social Sciences Today. http://www.csstoday.com/Item/4490.aspx

Silver, R. G. (2012). *First graphic organizers: Reading. Scholastic teaching resources.* https://bpsassets.weebly.com/uploads/9/9/3/2/9932784/graphic_organizers_1-3.pdf

Swan, K., Lee, J., Grant, S. G. (Eds.). (2018). *Teaching the College, Career, and Civic Life (C3) Framework: Part two.* National Council for the Social Studies, 2018.

Teaching Tolerance (n.d.). *Strategy: Thinking notes.* https://www.learningforjustice.org/sites/default/files/general/Thinking%20Notes.pdf

The University of Adelaide (n.d.). *Mind mapping.* Writing Centre Learning Guide. https://www.adelaide.edu.au/writingcentre/sites/default/files/docs/learningguide-mindmapping.pdf

Wisconsin Department of Public Instruction (n.d.). *Frayer Model.* https://dpi.wi.gov/sites/default/files/imce/ela/bank/6-12_L.VAU_Frayer_Model.pdf

CAMERON PACK

High School World History

Can the home front determine a war?

Supporting Question Dimension 2
1. How did capital and resources work with a country at war?

Supporting Questions Dimension 3
1. After entering the war, what happened to the goods and services of a country?
2. How did economic decisions affect the well-being of individuals, businesses, and society during World War II in Germany and the United Kingdom?

Supporting Questions Dimension 4
1. Using our new information, do you see an issue in high school that can have awareness brought to it through the use of propaganda?
2. Now that you have chosen [issue], how will you bring awareness?
3. Now that the class has the solution, what does implementation look like?

High School World History

	Can the home front determine a war?
Standards and Content	**C3 Standards:** D2.Eco.6.9-12. Generate possible explanations for a government role in markets when market inefficiencies exist. D2.Eco.7.9-12. Use benefits and costs to evaluate the effectiveness of government policies to improve market outcomes. **NCSS Themes:** ❷ Time, Continuity, and Change ❼ Production, Distribution, and Consumption ❾ Global Connections
Staging the Compelling Question	**Dimension 1:** Who is the Michelin Man? Describe him. What does he have to do with food? How can he help with WWII? Watch the video from Tasting History with Max Miller. Get into Think-Pair-Share (TPS) groups and answer the following questions: From the video, what three pieces of information stood out to you? Of the three, which one was most important to the war effort? Why? **Source:** *Why a Tire Company Gives Out Food's Most Famous Award* (video)

Dimension 2

Supporting Question 1
How did capital and resources work with a country at war?
Formative Performance Task
Determine the definition of "human capital," "physical capital," "natural resources," and "home front." Analyze how these terms relate to a country at war.

Exit Ticket Suggestion: Use a P.E.E.L. paragraph (or another writing format used by the teacher) to answer "Why are human capital, physical capital, and natural resources important to a country?"

Dimension 3

Supporting Question 1	Supporting Question 2
After entering the war, what happened to the goods and services of a country?	How did economic decisions affect the well-being of individuals, businesses, and society during WWII in Germany and the United Kingdom?
Formative Performance Task	**Formative Performance Task**
Complete the United Kingdom National Archives Lesson Plan and conduct a Gallery Walk with the propaganda posters displayed around the classroom, using a teacher-made source guide to direct questions and answers. Discuss the answers as a class through Teacher Talk. Complete the Germany Home Front Lesson Plan. Post pictures of German Propaganda on the smart board and identify the behavior the propaganda seeks to influence on a white board. Award points to the winning group. Discuss answers at the end through Teacher Talk.	Watch segments of *Mien Leben für Irland* and complete a Think-Pair-Share based on the viewing. Engage in class discussion about the various uses of propaganda and its impact on individuals, businesses, and society. Participate in an E-Gallery Walk to answer the supporting question, using information from the Teacher Talk, texts, and other resources to complete a teacher-made source guide. Discuss the answers as a class through a brief Teacher Talk.
Featured Sources	**Featured Sources**
Source A: *The Home Front*, The National Archives **Source B:** *Nazi Posters 1939-1945*, German Propaganda Archive	**Source A:** *Mein Leben für Irland* (video) **Source B:** World War 2 – The Home Front, Home Front History **Source C:** *Simon Partner: The WWII Home Front in Japan*, Duke Today **Source D:** *The stomach for the fight: the food policies used by the Nazis to maintain control in the Third Reich*, HistoryExtra.

Dimension 4

Supporting Question 1	Supporting Question 2	Supporting Question 3
Using our new information, do you see an issue at our school that is similar to the content from our unit?	Now that you have chosen [issue], what are you going to do about it?	Now that you have the solution, what does implementation look like? How will one bring awareness to the school?
Formative Performance Task	**Formative Performance Task**	**Formative Performance Task**
List issues that come to mind on the board or in a shared document visible to all participants. Discuss each issue in groups, analyzing its connection to the content taught in the unit (e.g., scarcity of resources in war, use of propaganda to solve resource issues, applying propaganda to raise awareness of school issues). Engage in a Teacher Talk. Choose an issue from the school that impacts you and aim to raise awareness while attempting to influence peers' opinions, adhering to school/district policies and guidelines provided by the teacher.	Develop a plan to raise awareness of the chosen issue. Outline how to accomplish the goal within the established boundaries, focusing on the methods and steps to implement the plan.	Create a project using propaganda to raise awareness of an issue that affects you, selecting a format such as posters, podcasts, commercials, or digital pamphlets, while working within the parameters set by the teacher.
Featured Sources	**Featured Sources Student Created**	**Featured Sources Student Created**
All previous sources.	Students will brainstorm what they can do to bring awareness once they have an issue in mind.	Students will create something to bring awareness to an issue in the school.

Summative Performance Task	**ARGUMENT** *Can the home front determine a war?* Using content from Dimensions 1–3 in a P.E.E.L. paragraph, answer the compelling question. Use evidence from each dimension to develop your claim.
	EXTENSION Students can look at resources such as the National Archives from the UK to try to find more primary sources about how the soldiers used the guides to help with the war effort.
Taking Informed Action	**UNDERSTAND** Students will connect historical content to contemporary issues by selecting a similar problem within their high school or community.
	ASSESS Students will devise a comprehensive plan of action to address the identified problem found in the school.
	ACT Students will actively implement their action plan to resolve the school issue, applying their learning in a practical context.

Overview

Inquiry Description

This IDM inquiry guides students in examining the home front economies during World War II, specifically in the UK and Germany, focusing on the resources required to secure victory. Students will analyze historical sources from the home front to determine how scarcity can affect their lives and how propaganda was used to motivate the people to solve these issues. Then, they take these skills with propaganda and apply it to a problem found in their high school. Through analyzing primary and secondary sources, students will assess how home front propaganda can sway public opinion. Furthermore, students will transition to the present day to devise and implement ways to bring awareness to issues observed within their high school, just like how the UK and Germany used propaganda to motivate their populations during WWII. This inquiry encompasses all four dimensions of C3 Framework.

Duration: 9 days (50-minute class periods)

Educators have the flexibility to extend the inquiry as needed by incorporating additional instructional elements such as supporting questions, formative performance tasks, featured sources, writing assignments, or documentary clips. It is recommended that teachers customize the inquiry to align with the unique needs and preferences of their students. This inquiry framework promotes differentiation and fosters the growth of historical thinking skills by assisting students in critically evaluating a range of sources.

Structure of the Inquiry

Dimension 1: The "hook" activity and introduction to the compelling question, along with a video about history and cooking.
Dimension 2: Frayer Model activity in which students teach students.
Dimension 3: Primary sources of propaganda used to motivate populations in war, and film showing effective propaganda across battle lines.
Dimension 4: Action plan and implementation with authentic assessment.

Dimension 1

Staging the Compelling Question

Teachers may implement this task with the following procedures:
- On a white board, write the compelling question, "Can the home front determine a war?"
- On the smart board, show a bell ringer slide with a picture of the Michelin Man and three questions:
  - Who is the Michelin Man?
  - Does he have anything to do with food?
  - How could he help World War II?
- Have the students answer these questions to the best of their ability but only give them the answer to Question 1 if they do not figure it out. Leave Questions 2 and 3 unanswered.
- The students will watch *Why a tire company gives out food's most famous award.*
- The students will conduct a Think-Pair-Share activity answering "What stood out to you in the video?" and "What was Michelin's most important contribution to the war effort?"
- Teacher will show the definition of "capital."
- Students will create a list of all the capital a country has.

The following source was selected to complete the tasks:
Miller, M. [Tasting History with Max Miller] (2024, February 20). *Why a tire company gives out food's most famous award* [Video]. YouTube. www.youtube.com/watch?v=-Y_TWPbmiRE&t=934s

Dimension 2

Supporting Question 1

Bell Ringer:
Pick a common word or slang in the students' vernacular. Ask them to define it. What are examples of it? What are non-examples of it? What characteristics does this word have? The reason to do this as the bell ringer is because the main activity for this lesson is the Frayer Model, where students will have to figure out what non-examples are for vocabulary terms. Students struggle finding non-examples because it is out of their comfort zone. So, finding a slang term that they think is funny and using that term to pick out non-examples works well to get their minds thinking about what exactly "non-examples" are.

The first supporting question is "How did capital and resources work with a country at war?"

The formative task is as follows:
Cooperative Groups of students create Frayer Models for human capital, physical capital, natural resources, and home front. Putting their assigned term in the center of the paper, with the definition, examples, characteristics, and non-characteristics in each corner for the students to work together to complete. Discuss these answers as a class and correct any information needed with a Teacher Talk. Ask the groups to list examples of resources (after discussing the types of capital and natural resources in the Frayer Models) that are used to produce goods and services. Discuss as a class and correct any information needed with another short Teacher Talk.

Teachers may implement this task with the following procedures:
- In cooperative groups, give each group one of the four terms (four groups in total), and have them complete a Frayer Model. A Frayer Model has a vocabulary term in the center of the page, and the words "definition," "characteristics," "examples," and "non-examples" in each corner. For more about the Frayer Model, see **https://dpi.wi.gov/sites/default/files/imce/ela/bank/6-12_L.VAU_Frayer_Model.pdf**
- Once the groups have completed this task, break them into Jigsaw groups, with an expert group.
- Each member of the expert group presents their findings on the white board, teaching the rest of the class their definition.

The following scaffolds and other materials may be used to support students as they work with sources:
- To assist students effectively, teachers can employ cooperative grouping or differentiation based on student need.
- Providing one-on-one instruction is also a viable approach within this lesson.
- Utilizing formative assessments to monitor progress towards objectives throughout the tasks can aid in maintaining student engagement and understanding.

Exit Ticket Suggestion:
Have the students use a P.E.E.L. paragraph (or another writing format used by the teacher) answering "Why are human capital, physical capital, and natural resources important to a country?"

Dimension 3

Supporting Question 1

Bell Ringer:
- Describe to the students that World War III has broken out and that all the men from ages 18-41 have been drafted. Note that big cities in the region are under constant threat of air raids.
- Ask the students: "What role will women take on in this new reality?"
- Ask the students: "What should be done with the children with this constant threat looming overhead?"

The reason for this line of questioning for the bell ringer is to get the students thinking about why the children of London had to be sent to the countryside during World War II and why it was essential for women to take over traditionally male roles in England when the men were sent to fight.

The first supporting question is "After entering the war, what happened to the goods and services of a country?"

The formative task is as follows:
- Cooperative groups will complete a Gallery Walk featuring propaganda posters from the United Kingdom during World War II and complete a source guide. Print out the posters on pages 6, 7, 10-12, 15, 17 of Source A. The students will move in groups from one poster to the other, answering questions for the corresponding posters as they go.
- Cooperative groups will examine German propaganda posters from Source B shown on the smartboard. The groups will be given whiteboards to make their informed guesses about what the posters may be trying to convey. If the group guesses correctly, give them a point. Team with the most points at the end wins.

Teachers may implement this task with the following procedures:
- Historical propaganda posters (printouts or digital images)
- Projector or whiteboard (if displaying digitally)
- Printed handouts or digital source guides for analysis
- Markers, pens, or digital tools for note-taking
- Whiteboard or chart paper for group discussions
- Classroom space for group work or a Gallery Walk

The following sources were selected to complete the tasks:
- **Source A:** The National Archives. (2021, September 2). *The home front*. www.nationalarchives.gov.uk/education/resources/home-front/
- **Source B:** Bytwerk, R. (2023, August 2). *Nazi posters: 1939-1945*. German Propaganda Archive. https://research.calvin.edu/german-propaganda-archive/posters3.htm

Supporting Question 2

Bell Ringer:
- Play the film *Mien Leben für Irland* from 00:00:04 to 00:04:30. Then have the students complete a Think-Pair-Share activity to answer what they believe is happening in the film and why.
- Then play the film from 01:15:39 to 01:17:15. Then have the students complete a Think-Pair-Share activity to answer what they believe is happening in the film and why.

This film is German propaganda aimed at the Irish population to convince them to rebel against the British for crimes the British were actually committing in not such an over-dramatized way. This bell ringer will get the students thinking about the rights and wrongs of history, along with how to use propaganda to try to solve problems for oneself or cause problems for one's enemies.

The second supporting question is "How did economic decisions affect the well-being of individuals, businesses, and society during WWII in Germany and the United Kingdom?"

The formative task is as follows: The teacher will create an e-Gallery Walk for students to answer the supporting question. Using the information from the Teacher Talk and other texts, students will complete a teacher-made source guide. Discuss the answers as a class with a Teacher Talk.

The following sources were selected to complete the tasks:
- **Source A:** Kimmich, M. W. (Director). (1941). *Mein leben für Irland* [Film]. Tobis Film. Internet Archive. https://archive.org/details/1941-Mein-Leben-fuer-Irland
- **Source B:** *World War 2 – The home front*. (2015). Home Front History. www.homefronthistory.com/the-home-front
- **Source C:** Hicks, S. (2003, March 20). *Simon Partner: The WWII Home Front in Japan*. Duke.edu. https://today.duke.edu/2003/03/japan_lecture0321.html
- **Source D:** Pine, L. (2022, October 27). *The stomach for the fight: the food policies used by the Nazis to maintain control in the Third Reich*. History Extra. www.historyextra.com/period/second-world-war/nazi-germany-food-policies-second-world-war-shortages-propaganda-black-market-ersatz-hunger-plan/ (Reprinted from "The stomach for the fight: The food policies used by the Nazis to maintain control in the Third Reich," 2022, *BBC History Magazine*, 23[10], 58-64)

Dimension 4

Overview

Dimension 4 empowers students to cultivate practical skills and bridge historical knowledge with present-day contexts. Here, students are encouraged to craft their inquiries, fostering a sense of ownership over their learning journey. In this phase, teachers transition to a facilitative role, guiding through questioning rather than direct instruction. It emphasizes the importance of allowing students to navigate their learning path independently. By refraining from providing direct answers and promoting collaborative problem-solving, students can enhance their skills in a supportive environment that values learning from mistakes and teamwork.

However, it is not the only way to have the students create an action plan and implement that plan. I recommend looking at inquiries from the C3 Teachers website (**https://c3teachers.org/inquiries/**) or *Teaching the College, Career, and Civic Life (C3) Framework: Part Two* (Swan et al., 2018).

Supporting Question 1

The first supporting question is "Using our new information, do you see an issue at our school that is similar to the content from our unit?" *Note.* The teacher does not suggest any answers or give hints. The teacher is only supposed to ask questions so the students can experience inquiry and civic engagement.

The formative task is as follows:
- Students will make a list of issues that come to mind on the board or in a shared document that everyone can see and type on. (I suggest using the board.)
- Students discuss each issue and how it relates to the content that was taught in the unit in groups. Examples include the following: scarcity of resources in war, use of propaganda to solve resource issues. Now use propaganda to bring awareness to issues in school.
- The teacher will facilitate a Teacher Talk with the students about their findings. Allow students to individually pick an issue from the school that affects them to bring awareness to and try to influence their peers' opinion.

Supporting Question 2

The second supporting question is "Now that you have chosen [issue], what are you going to do about it?" *Note.* Classes will have different issues and different solutions. The teacher does not suggest any answers or give hints. The teacher is only supposed to ask questions so the students can experience inquiry and civic engagement.

The formative task is as follows:
- The teacher gives the boundaries from school/district policy, the principal, the department, etc.
- Ask the students how they plan to bring awareness. Ask the students, "how are you going to accomplish this? What is the plan? How are you going to implement it using the boundaries we have set?"

Supporting Question 3

The third supporting question is "Now that you have the solution, what does implementation look like? How will one bring awareness to the school?" *Note.* Classes will have different issues and different solutions. The teacher does not suggest any answers or give hints. The teacher is only supposed to ask questions so the students can experience inquiry and civic engagement.

The formative task is as follows:
Students will begin creating something that will bring awareness to an issue that affects them by using propaganda. This could be in the form of posters, podcasts, commercials, digital pamphlets. Whatever the students want to do within the parameters that have been set. The teacher is not to influence their choice or creativity.

Summative Performance Task

In this inquiry unit, students will engage in two distinct summative performance tasks. The first task involves crafting a response to the compelling question utilizing the P.E.E.L. paragraph structure or an equivalent format specified in the curriculum document. This task is designed to be completed after the exploration in Dimension 3. The second task, an authentic assessment, requires the creation and execution of an action plan detailed in Dimension 4.

Task Breakdown:
- **ARGUMENT** Students will formulate a response to the inquiry "Can a home front determine a war?" by constructing a P.E.E.L. paragraph. This response must integrate evidence from Dimensions 1-3 to support their claim effectively.
- **EXTENSION** Utilizing the Frayer Model, students will define and dissect the concepts of "human capital," "physical capital," "natural resources," and "home front." Working in expert groups, students will teach their peers about these concepts and explore their interconnectedness.

Learning Objectives:
- **UNDERSTAND** Students will connect historical content to contemporary issues by selecting a similar problem within their high school.
- **ASSESS** Students will devise a comprehensive plan of action to address the identified problem found in the school.
- **ACT** Students will actively implement their action plan to resolve the school issue, applying their learning in a practical context.

References

Bytwerk, R. (2023, August 2). *Nazi posters: 1939-1945*. German Propaganda Archive. https://research.calvin.edu/german-propaganda-archive/posters3.htm

Hicks, S. (2003, March 20). *Simon Partner: The WW II home front in Japan*. Duke Today. https://today.duke.edu/2003/03/japan_lecture0321.html

IMDb.com. (1941, February 17). *Mein Leben für Irland*. IMDb.com. (1941, February 17). *Mein Leben für Irland*. IMDb. https://www.imdb.com/title/tt0033895/

Kimmich, M. W. (Director). (1941). *Mein leben für Irland* [Film]. Tobis Film. Internet Archive. https://archive.org/details/1941-Mein-Leben-fuer-Irland

Miller, M. [Tasting History with Max Miller] (2024, February 20). *Why a tire company gives out food's most famous award* [Video]. YouTube. www.youtube.com/watch?v=-Y_TWPbmiRE&t=934s

The National Archives. (2021, September 2). *The home front*. www.nationalarchives.gov.uk/education/resources/home-front/

Pine, L. (2022, October 27). *The stomach for the fight: the food policies used by the Nazis to maintain control in the Third Reich*. History Extra. www.historyextra.com/period/second-world-war/nazi-germany-food-policies-second-world-war-shortages-propaganda-black-market-ersatz-hunger-plan/ (Reprinted from "The stomach for the fight: The food policies used by the Nazis to maintain control in the Third Reich," 2022, *BBC History Magazine, 23* [10], 58–64)

Swan, K., Lee, J., & Grant, S. G. (2018). *Inquiry design model: Building inquiries in social studies*. National Council for the Social Studies; C3 Teachers.

World War 2—The home front. (2015). Home Front History. www.homefronthistory.com/the-home-front

TAYLOR HAWES-GULDENPFENNIG

Grade 12 Sociology

Can you see the world through others' eyes?

Supporting Questions Dimension 2
1. How does economics relate to sociology?
2. How does inequality lead to conflict?
3. What happened during the Age of Imperialism?
4. What does it mean to remove a people?

Supporting Questions Dimension 3
1. What happens when people move and cultures collide?
2. Did imperialism affect everyone in the same way?

Grade 12 Sociology

	Can you see the world through others' eyes?
Standards and Content	**C3 Standards:** D2.Soc.15.9-12. Identify common patterns of social inequality. D2.Soc.16.9-12. Interpret the effects of inequality on groups and individuals. D2.Soc.17.9-12. Analyze why the distribution of power and inequalities can result in conflict. D2.Soc.18.9-12. Propose and evaluate alternative responses to inequality. **NCSS Themes:** ❶ Culture ❹ Individual Development and Identity ❺ Individuals, Groups, Institutions ❻ Power Authority and Governance
Staging the Compelling Question	**Dimension 1:** Students will be completing a digital discussion board utilizing the district's chosen learning management system (LMS). Students will view a video on YouTube that shows Disney's "Let it Go" (2013), after it has been run through Google Translate, translating the lyrics into different languages. Then it was translated back into English. Students will create their original post answering the discussion questions. Then students will respond to at least one other classmate within the discussion board. Once students have posted, the teacher will interact with all posts, posing questions for further discussion. Students are required to respond to the teacher with new information. **Discussion Board Questions:** • If no written alphabet existed in the English language, how would you text? • How do you communicate as a community with no letters? • Explain how proper translation and understanding is vital in avoiding confusion and cultural misunderstandings. **Featured Source:** *"Let It Go" from Frozen according to Google Translate* (Video)

Dimension 2

Supporting Question 1	Supporting Question 2	Supporting Question 3	Supporting Question 4
How does economics relate to sociology?	How does inequality lead to conflict?	What happened during the Age of Imperialism?	What does it mean to remove a people?
Formative Performance Task	**Formative Performance Task**	**Formative Performance Task**	**Formative Performance Task**
Define key terms related to the unit of study on a Frayer Model graphic organizer. View instructional videos for key terms and make connections between economics and sociology via Cornell Notes.	Define the term "culture." Analyze data regarding social inequalities in society. Discuss what the data tells us about how inequality leads to conflict.	Analyze the impact of Imperialism on Africa after the Berlin Conference.	Analyze the impact of the Indian Removal Act (1830) on Indigenous people of the United States by viewing sources on the topic.
Featured Sources	**Featured Sources**	**Featured Sources**	**Featured Sources**
Source A: Frayer Model graphic organizer **Source B:** Cornell Note template **Source C:** Teacher-developed instructional videos	**Source A:** Iceberg image **Source B:** United Nations data *Note.* Teachers can select data that they feel is relevant, from any source.	**Source A:** Political cartoons on the Berlin Conference **Source B:** Map of the Scramble for Africa **Source C:** Berlin Conference artwork	**Source A:** Video defining "settler colonialism" **Source B:** Map of the Trail of Tears **Source C:** Andrew Jackson's Message to Congress (1830) **Source D:** Supreme Court Cases: *Cherokee Nation v. Georgia* (1831) and *Worcester v. Georgia* (1832) **Source E:** Arguments for Resettlement—Emerson **Source F:** Trail of Tears artwork; Robert Lindeneux (1942) **Source G:** Cave Johnson letter to Andrew Jackson **Source H:** Address from the Cherokee to Congress (July 1830)

Dimension 3

Supporting Question 1	Supporting Question 2
What happens when people move and cultures collide?	Did imperialism affect everyone in the same way?
Formative Performance Task	**Formative Performance Task**
Analyze sources regarding residential schools in Canada.	Research the experiences of other Indigenous cultures around the world. Compare and contrast these experiences with those in Canada.
Featured Sources	**Featured Sources**
Source A: Quotations by Nicholas Davin & Duncan Campbell Scott **Source B:** Map of Residential Schools **Source C:** Description of Daily Life **Source D:** Survivor Account of Paul Dixon **Source E:** Excerpt from "The Lonely Death of Chanie Wenjack" **Source F:** Attempts at Reconciliation **Source G**: Clips from the documentary film, *We Were Children* • 0:00–5:00 • 5:00–14:00 • 15:00–17:35	**Source A:** Teacher-developed list of acceptable Indigenous nations for students to research

Dimension 4

Summative Performance Task	**ARGUMENT** *Can you see the world through others' eyes?* Construct an argument (P.E.E.L. paragraph) that evaluates the need to study, remember, and/or celebrate this expedition using specific claims and relevant evidence from sources while acknowledging competing views.
	EXTENSION Have students research and study another time period in history where inequality led to conflict. Identify what the inequality was, how it ultimately led to conflict, and describe the way conflict was resolved.
Taking Informed Action	**UNDERSTAND** Investigate an issue plaguing your local community and possible solutions.
	ASSESS Evaluate the potential solutions to the issue, weighing the possible drawbacks and benefits.
	ACT Write an essay proposing your solution to resolving inequality in our society.

Overview

Inquiry Description

This inquiry leads students through an investigation of conflict, power, and identity as it relates to the experiences Indigenous peoples had in Canada throughout history.

This inquiry highlights the following additional standards:

NCSS Themes:
- Culture
- Individual Development and Identity
- Individuals, Groups, Institutions
- Power Authority and Governance

C3 Standards:
D2.Soc.15.9-12. Identify common patterns of social inequality.
D2.Soc.16.9-12. Interpret the effects of inequality on groups and individuals.
D2.Soc.17.9-12. Analyze why the distribution of power and inequalities can result in conflict.
D2.Soc.18.9-12. Propose and evaluate alternative responses to inequality.

It is important to note that this inquiry requires prerequisite knowledge of imperialism, colonialism, and the policies made surrounding Indigenous peoples in North America (i.e., Indian Removal Act, Trail of Tears, etc.).

Note. This inquiry is expected to take 10 50-minute class periods. The inquiry time frame could expand if teachers think their students need additional instructional experiences (e.g., supporting questions, formative performance tasks, featured sources, writing). Teachers are encouraged to adapt the inquiry to meet the needs and interests of their students. This inquiry lends itself to differentiation and modeling of historical thinking skills while assisting students in reading the variety of sources.

Structure of the Inquiry
In addressing the compelling question—"Can you see the world through others' eyes?"—students work through a series of supporting questions, formative performance tasks, and featured sources in order to construct an argument supported by evidence while acknowledging competing perspectives.

Dimension 1

Staging the Compelling Question

In staging the compelling question—"Can you see the world through others' eyes?"—students will complete a digital discussion board utilizing the district's chosen learning management system (LMS). Students will view a video on YouTube that shows Disney's "Let it Go" (2013), after it has been run through Google Translate, and translated into different languages. Then it was translated back into English. Students will create their original post answering the discussion questions. Then, students will respond to at least one other classmate within the discussion board. Once students have posted, the teacher will interact with all posts, posing questions for further discussion. Students are required to respond to the teacher with new information.

Discussion Board Questions:
- Summarize what happened in the video.
- Why is proper translation important?
- How does this help avoid confusion, and cultural misunderstandings?

Featured Source: Reese, M. K. [Twisted Translations]. (2014). *"Let it go" from Frozen according to Google Translate (Parody)* [Video]. YouTube. https://www.youtube.com/watch?v=2bVAoVlFYf0

Dimension 2

Supporting Question 1

The first supporting question—"How does economics relate to sociology?"—helps students define key terms related to the unit that are typically found in economics classes. By identifying and defining these key terms, students are able to make connections between economics and the study of sociology.

The formative task is defining key terms related to the unit prior to learning new information.

Teachers may implement this task with the following procedures:
- Students will define key terms necessary for understanding unit content and complete Frayer models for the following terms: "scarce resources," "conflict," "identity," "stratification," "inequality."
- After each term, they will view an instructional video in which the teacher will review important information for each term, ensuring that students have correct responses.
- During these videos, students will complete a notes section of their assignment so that they can remain engaged during the instructional videos.
- For the "exit ticket," students will complete a discussion board with their initial answer to the compelling question, "Can you see the world through others' eyes?" Students should use the vocabulary terms as well as their notes from the instructional videos to formulate their responses.

The following sources were selected to help students organize the information they are learning in an easy-to-understand fashion. These graphic organizers and note templates will allow students to track information and contain in one place for use throughout the unit as a whole. Teachers should add or subtract, excerpt, modify, or annotate sources in order to respond to student needs or teacher preferences.
- **Source A:** Frayer Model graphic organizer
- **Source B:** Cornell Note taking template
- **Source C:** Teacher-developed instructional videos for each of the key terms

Supporting Question 2

The second supporting question—"How does inequality lead to conflict?"—helps students define "identity" as it relates to culture. Students will analyze how being a cultural outsider can lead to inequalities that will ultimately cause conflict between people.

The formative task is to analyze images, data, and statistics from the United Nations and to determine what inequalities exist in society today. Teachers can have students post their findings and analysis in a discussion board on their district provided LMS, or this can be completed as a whole class discussion.

Teachers may implement this task with the following procedures:
- Students will analyze an image of an iceberg to write their own definition for the term "culture."
- Students participate in either a whole group discussion or via a digital discussion board post.
- Students will analyze data regarding social inequalities in our society.
- Discussion Board Questions:
    - Write a definition for the term "culture" using the image provided.
    - How does this relate to identity?
    - Describe things that are important in shaping your cultural identity. What would it feel like if these things were taken away from you?

To scaffold work and support student needs, teachers may implement grouping, stations, or jigsawing of data analysis.

The following sources were selected to show students common inequalities at a global level and how these inequalities or competition for resources or cultural identities can lead to conflict.
- **Source A:** an image of an iceberg covered in identifying traits; SOPTV ED. (2017). *Iceberg concept of culture*. PBS Learning Media. https://kcpt.pbslearningmedia.org/resource/a353a4ba-cd56-4999-97dd-0e40e11a7211/iceberg-concept-of-culture-images-and-pdfs/

- **Source B:** United Nations. (n.d.). *Inequality—Bridging the divide.* https://www.un.org/en/un75/inequality-bridging-divide

Supporting Question 3

The third supporting question—"What happened during the Age of Imperialism?"— helps students begin to contextualize how inequality and differences in culture can lead to conflict. Students will consider a recent modern issue and trace its roots historically. To begin, students will look at the developments during the Age of Imperialism, as global powers sought dominance around the world, particularly in Africa.

The formative task is analyzing political cartoons, maps, and artwork to learn what happened after the "Scramble for Africa" during the Berlin Conference (1830).

Teachers may implement this task with the following procedures:
- View a video that defines the term "imperialism."
- Analyze a set of sources (e.g., political cartoon, map, artwork) related to imperialism in Africa.
- Write a definition and assess the impact of imperialism on the world.

The following sources were selected to provide students a quick refresher over the Age of Imperialism. Students should have previously learned about this era in history during their World History classes. However, it is important to remind students about imperialism, as it is this mindset that sets up future policies and decision-making regarding Indigenous nations in North America.
- **Source A:** video over the term "imperialism"; Shibusawa, N. (2021a, February 19). *What is imperialism?* [Video]. Choices Program, Brown University. www.choices.edu/video/what-is-imperialism/
- **Source B:** political cartoon regarding the Berlin Conference; [Cartoon of Otto von Bismark cutting a cake labeled "Afrique"]. (1885). BBC Bitesize. www.bbc.co.uk/bitesize/articles/zrfjqfr#zqssf82
- **Source C:** map of Africa; Chmielewski, K. (n.d.). *Colonization of Africa by Europeans (as of the early 1900s)* [Map]. Britannica Kids. https://kids.britannica.com/kids/article/Scramble-for-Africa/632997

Supporting Question 4

The fourth supporting question—"What does it mean to remove a people?"—helps students begin to corroborate how inequality and differences in culture can lead to conflict. Students will consider a recent modern issue and trace its roots historically. Having already analyzed a global example in Africa, students now will zoom in further to a national example regarding the policy of the Indian Removal Act (1830) in the United States.

The formative task is analyzing primary and secondary sources to determine arguments for and against the Indian Removal Act by Andrew Jackson (1830).

Teachers may implement this task with the following procedures:
- View a video that defines the term "settler colonialism."
- Analyze a set of primary and secondary sources related to the Indian Removal Act (1830).
- Assess the impact of removing a people on one's culture and identity.

To scaffold work and support student needs, teachers may implement grouping, Gallery Walk stations, or jigsawing of source analysis.

The following sources were selected to provide students a quick refresher over the Indian Removal Act (1830). Students should have previously learned about this era in history during their American History classes. However, it is important to remind students about this topic, as they soon will look at an example in Canada that far outlasted that of the United States.
- **Source A:** video about the term "settler colonialism"; Shibusawa, N. (2021b, February 19). *Why is it important to say "settler colonialism" instead of "westward expansion"?* [Video]. Choices Program, Brown University. www.choices.edu/video/why-is-it-important-to-say-settler-colonialism-instead-of-westward-expansion/
- **Sources B–F:** primary and secondary sources regarding the Indian Removal Act; New Visions for Public Schools. (n.d.). *Indian removal act stations.* https://curriculum.newvisions.org/social-studies/course/us-history/1103a-building-a-nation/indian-removal-act-stations/

Dimension 3

Supporting Question 1

The first supporting question—"What happens when people move and cultures collide?"—helps students continue to corroborate how inequality and differences in culture can lead to conflict. Students will consider a recent modern issue and trace its roots historically. Having already analyzed a global example in Africa and an American example with the Indian Removal Act (1830), students will now look at another example in Canada. However, the residential school system in Canada far outlasted that of the United States, continuing until 1997 when the last residential school closed.

The formative task is analyzing primary and secondary sources to understand the impact of residential schools in Indigenous culture in Canada.

Teachers may implement this task with the following procedures:
- Analyze a set of primary and secondary sources related to the residential schools.
- Students assess the impact of residential schools on Indigenous culture and identity.
- Discuss attempts at apology and reconciliation from the Canadian government.

To scaffold work, and support student needs, teachers may implement grouping, Gallery Walk stations, or jigsawing of source analysis.

The following sources were selected to provide students an understanding of policies put forth by the Canadian government to strip Indigenous tribes of their cultural identity. These sources were also chosen to illustrate the more recent attempts by the Canadian government at reconciliation and apology for past policies.
- **Source A:** Quotations by Nicholas Davin & Duncan Campbell Scott; Facing History & Ourselves. (2020, July 28). *"Until there is not a single Indian in Canada."* www.facinghistory.org/en-ca/resource-library/until-there-not-single-indian-canada
- **Source B:** Map of residential schools; The Canadian Encyclopedia. (2021, August 6). *Residential schools in Canada interactive map.* www.thecanadianencyclopedia.ca/en/article/residential-schools-in-canada-interactive-map
- **Source C:** Description of daily life; Merasty, J., & Carpenter, D. (2022, September 15). Life inside a Catholic-run residential school for Canadian Indigenous Children. *Time.* https://time.com/6213238/canada-residential-school-indigenous-children-excerpt/
- **Source D:** Survivor account of Paul Dixon; Dixon, P. (2023, September 29). *I spent 10 years in residential schools. This is what I want my grandchildren to know.* CBC First Person. www.cbc.ca/news/canada/montreal/first-person-facing-genocide-mohawk-institute-la-tuque-residential-school-1.6527631
- **Source E:** Excerpt from "The Lonely Death of Chanie Wenjack" (1967); Adams, I. (1967). The lonely death of Chanie Wenjack. *Maclean's.* https://macleans.ca/society/the-lonely-death-of-chanie-wenjack/
- **Source F:** Attempts at reconciliation
  - National Centre for Truth and Reconciliation, University of Manitoba, https://nctr.ca/
  - School District 27 Residential Schools and Reconciliation. (2014, December 6). *Canadian federal government apology to First Nations* [Video]. YouTube. www.youtube.com/watch?v=xCpn1erz1y8
- **Source G:** Clips from the documentary film, *We Were Children*; Wolochatiuk, T. (Director). (2012). *We were children* [Film]. Eagle Vision; eOne Television; National Film Board of Canada.
  - 0:00–5:00
  - 5:00–14:00
  - 15:00–17:35

Supporting Question 2

The second supporting question—"Did imperialism affect everyone in the same way?"—helps students compare and contrast the experiences of Indigenous peoples of North America to other Indigenous peoples from around the globe.

The formative task is to research another Indigenous nation from a teacher-provided list. Students must focus their research on specific questions related to the key terms from the very beginning of the unit. Teachers can have students post their findings and analysis in a discussion board on their district-provided LMS, or this can be completed as a whole class discussion or presentation

Teachers may implement this task with the following procedures:
- Students will sign up for a research topic.
- Students research their chosen topic utilizing the research and discussion prompts.
- Students compare and contrast the experiences of their chosen Indigenous nation with that of Indigenous nations in Canada.
- Students discuss or present research findings to the class.
- Student Research Questions:
    - According to your research, what inequality did you find?
    - What stratification issue was there?
    - What conflict was there?
    - How did this conflict impact your chosen group's identity?
    - Compare and contrast your group's experiences with that of Indigenous people in Canada. What is the same? What is different? Why do you think this is?

To scaffold work and support student needs, teachers may assign certain Indigenous nations to specific students or may allow students to submit their own nation for research.

The following source was created to provide students a jumping off point on global Indigenous nations. This can be administered in person or via a digital sign-up sheet or website.
Source A: A teacher-developed list of Indigenous nations for students to research

Dimension 4

Summative Performance Task

At this point in the inquiry, students have examined identity and culture as well as inequalities throughout our society. As a result of these inequalities, there is inherent conflict that can lead to one group seeking control over another. Students have utilized their sociological skills by tracing the roots of inequality through a specific historical event starting with the Age of Imperialism, then to the Indian Removal Act, and ending with residential schools in Canada. Their case study allowed them to apply their knowledge of history to a modern issue.

Students should be expected to demonstrate the breadth of their understandings and their abilities to use evidence from multiple sources to support their claims. In this task, students will answer the compelling question—"Can you see the world through others' eyes?"—via an extended written response.

Students' arguments will likely vary but could include any of the following:
- You cannot see the world through someone else's eyes in a way that is beneficial to those around you. There are experiences and opinions that one cannot feel or have due to where or how they were raised.
- It is not possible to fully understand someone, as each person is unique and has their own thoughts, feelings, experiences, and perspectives.
- No one person can fully comprehend the entirety of another person's being or experience.
- It is possible to see the world through others' eyes to an extent, and only if you are truly open to seeing more than just what you would like to see.
- Seeing the world in others' eyes exactly the way they do is impossible, but understanding their history and the challenges they face is a close second. You have to be willing to understand, and willing to know that, while you may not understand, you can still try.

To support students in their writing, teachers can provide a written response template, such as P.E.E.L. (Point, Evidence, Explain, Link) or C.E.R. (Claim Evidence Reason), and a writing rubric so that students understand what is expected. Additionally, teachers can allow students to review their peers' writing prior to submitting their work for assessment.

To extend their arguments, students can research another instance where inequality led to conflict throughout history. Teachers could encourage students to find a more recent example in history or perhaps a current event that illustrates this concept.

Action Question: Propose and evaluate alternate responses to inequality.

Taking Informed Action

Action Task: Write an essay to propose and evaluate an alternate response to inequality.

Structure of Taking Informed Action:
Taking informed action tasks have three steps to prepare students for informed, reasoned, and authentic action. The steps ask students to (1) understand the issues evident from the inquiry in a larger and/or current context, (2) assess the relevance and impact of the issues, and (3) act in ways that allow students to demonstrate agency in a real-world context.

For this inquiry, students have the opportunity to take informed action by drawing on their understanding of inequality and conflict in order to address an issue in their community.

UNDERSTAND Students identify and research an alternate response to inequality.

ASSESS Students evaluate the potential solutions, weighing the possible drawbacks and benefits.

ACT Students propose an alternate response to inequality. This could be done through raising awareness, social media posting, letters to local government, etc.

CIVIC THEME This task reflects the civic theme of community. When students engage in community-building civic action, they expand understanding of others in their community (whether local or global in scope) and cooperate with others towards shared concerns.

Note About Ways to Take Informed Action
This inquiry has a suggested taking informed action task. Teachers and students are encouraged to revise or adjust the task to reflect student interests, the topic or issue chosen for the task, time considerations, etc. Taking informed action can manifest in a variety of forms and in a range of venues. They can range from small actions (e.g., informed conversations) to big (e.g., organizing a protest). These actions may take place in the classroom, the school, the local community, across the state, and around the world. What is important is that students are authentically applying the inquiry to an out-of-classroom context. Actions should reach people outside of the classroom.

References

Adams, I. (1967). The lonely death of Chanie Wenjack. *Maclean's*. https://macleans.ca/society/the-lonely-death-of-chanie-wenjack/

The Canadian Encyclopedia. (2021, August 6). *Residential schools in Canada interactive map*. www.thecanadianencyclopedia.ca/en/article/residential-schools-in-canada-interactive-map

[Cartoon of Otto von Bismark cutting a cake labeled "Afrique"]. (1885). BBC Bitesize. www.bbc.co.uk/bitesize/articles/zrfjqfr#zqssf82

Chmielewski, K. (n.d.). *Colonization of Africa by Europeans (as of the early 1900s)* [Map]. Britannica Kids. https://kids.britannica.com/kids/article/Scramble-for-Africa/632997

Dixon, P. (2023, September 29). *I spent 10 years in residential schools. This is what I want my grandchildren to know*. CBC First Person. www.cbc.ca/news/canada/montreal/first-person-facing-genocide-mohawk-institute-la-tuque-residential-school-1.6527631

Facing History & Ourselves. (2020, July 28). *"Until there is not a single Indian in Canada."* www.facinghistory.org/en-ca/resource-library/until-there-not-single-indian-canada

Merasty, J., & Carpenter, D. (2022, September 15). Life inside a Catholic-run residential school for Canadian Indigenous Children. *Time*. https://time.com/6213238/canada-residential-school-indigenous-children-excerpt/

New Visions for Public Schools. (n.d.). *Indian removal act stations*. https://curriculum.newvisions.org/social-studies/course/us-history/1103a-building-a-nation/indian-removal-act-stations/

Reese, M. K. [Twisted Translations]. (2014). *"Let it go" from Frozen according to Google Translate (Parody)* [Video]. YouTube. https://www.youtube.com/watch?v=2bVAoVlFYf0

School District 27 Residential Schools and Reconciliation. (2014, December 6). *Canadian federal government apology to First Nations* [Video]. YouTube. www.youtube.com/watch?v=xCpn1erz1y8

Shibusawa, N. (2021a, February 19). *What is imperialism?* [Video]. Choices Program, Brown University. www.choices.edu/video/what-is-imperialism/

Shibusawa, N. (2021b, February 19). *Why is it important to say "settler colonialism" instead of "westward expansion"?* [Video]. Choices Program, Brown University. www.choices.edu/video/why-is-it-important-to-say-settler-colonialism-instead-of-westward-expansion/

SOPTV ED. (2017). *Iceberg concept of culture*. PBS Learning Media. https://kcpt.pbslearningmedia.org/resource/a353a4ba-cd56-4999-97dd-0e40e11a7211/iceberg-concept-of-culture-images-and-pdfs/

United Nations. (n.d.). Inequality—Bridging the divide. www.un.org/en/un75/inequality-bridging-divide

Wolochatiuk, T. (Director). (2012). *We were children* [Film]. Eagle Vision; eOne Television; National Film Board of Canada.

Chapter 10

Additional Lessons for Elementary and Secondary Teachers

Introduction

Chapter 10 is divided into elementary and secondary sections for convenience. Each IDM inquiry is created by teachers and teacher educators who use these inquires in their own classes. The first section is for elementary teachers (and possibly for middle school teachers). The elementary section includes the topics of the Jamestown Colony and migration.

Our first contributor, Nancy B. Sardone is a former teacher and teacher educator. Nancy has written several lesson plans for Scott Roberts's *Hollywood or History?* book series and has adapted a lesson from the book series to help students learn more about the real Pocahontas. Using a variety of primary and secondary sources, including the 1995 Disney film, *Pocahontas*, students are asked to determine if they think the filmmakers "rewrote history" or were simply using artistic license in their depiction of this famous individual in American history. Scott Roberts uses this lesson plan in his Social Studies methods classes, and the lesson has been adapted and used by many of his students in their third- to fifth-grade pre-student teaching placements throughout the state of Michigan.

The second IDM inquiry was developed by two of Scott's former students, Chloe Thompson and Meghan Beauchamp, and was used in their pre-student teaching program. The lesson is multidisciplinary, focusing on economics, geography, and civics. The lesson is also based on the *Hollywood or History?* strategy, where students analyze the film *Ice Age* (2002) to help understand migration patterns of both humans and animals. After watching the film, students use this knowledge to help them understand how immigration has led to the growth of their home state. Their fourth graders also took informed action by writing state officials and asking to help with conservation efforts for wildlife that may be impacted by the population growth of humans based on what they learned from the lesson.

The second section includes secondary IDM inquiries about World War I and the Holocaust. The first and second inquiries are focused on World War I and written by Cameron Pack and Jackson Margargee. Cameron is a tenth-grade teacher, head wrestling coach, and Staff Sergeant in the Army Reserves. Cameron begins his inquiry by asking the students, "What did the Lost Generation lose?" His inquiry uses art to discuss identities and disillusionment of societal norms by the WWI generation. By using a world history lens, the students watch clips from *All Quiet on the Western Front* (1979) and read from the text *All Quiet on the Western Front* (1928). Students use art to answer the supporting and compelling questions and to think critically about identity during war.

Jackson Margargee is a senior in the Social Studies Program at the University of Central Missouri. In his IDM inquiry, he uses artificial intelligence (AI) to help students address the causes of WWI and also learn historical thinking skills and critical literacy to question an author's thesis, bias, or lack of voices. Mastering how to develop quality questions, students converse with AI to answer not only supporting questions but also student-created questions like, "Whose voices are missing from the textbook?" Additionally, this IDM uses documentaries to allow students to gain content knowledge and hear from historians about this historical era. Students watch clips of the History Hit documentaries *Six Key Steps to World War One* (2023) and *How the Assassination of Archduke Franz Ferdinand Unfolded, with Dan Snow* (2014) to gain insight concerning the assassination through WWI's aftermath and answer the supporting and compelling question.

Our last contributor, Katie Engemann, is a high school teacher who teaches different social studies courses including world history and the Holocaust. Starlynn Nance was Katie's faculty advisor and social studies professor. Katie completed the Holocaust Genocide and Human Rights program through Penn State funded by the National Endowment for the Humanities in 2023. Using her new content knowledge and assistance from her former professor, Katie and Starlynn developed an inquiry that asks the students, "Under what circumstances would breaking the law be justified?" The film used in the inquiry is *The Courageous Heart of Irena Sendler* (2009), which makes visible the actions of an upstander and bystander. The clips focus on students identifying these behaviors toward Jewish people as documented in different areas. Dimension 3 includes a lesson from the United States Holocaust Memorial Museum where students analyze primary sources in more detail about the main behaviors toward Jewish people during World War II. Dimension 4 starts with a twist where Starlynn included AI to help students begin to develop good questioning to dialogue about bystanders, upstanders, and others in the past and present with AI.

NANCY B. SARDONE

Grade 5 History

Did the filmmakers of *Pocahontas* rewrite history?

Supporting Questions Dimension 2
1. Who was Chief Powhatan?
2. Who was Captain John Smith?
3. Who was Pocahontas?
4. Why did the English sail to the New World and settle in Jamestown, Virginia?

Supporting Questions Dimension 3
1. Is the filmmaker's visual portrayal of Pocahontas similar to or different than that of historians?
2. Is Captain John Smith's description of his capture similar to or different than that of historians?
3. Is the filmmaker's active portrayal of the relationship between Pocahontas and John Smith similar to or different than that of historians?

Supporting Questions Dimension 4
1. What is one reason that the filmmakers made a romanticized version of the film *Pocahontas*?
2. Why do filmmakers alter narratives?

Grade 5 History

	Did the filmmakers of *Pocahontas* rewrite history?
Standards and Content	**C3 Standards:** D2.His.6.3-5. Describe how people's perspectives shaped the historical sources they created. D2.His.10.3-5. Compare information provided by different historical sources about the past. D3.4.3-5. Use evidence to develop claims in response to compelling questions. D4.1.3-5. Construct arguments using claims and evidence from multiple sources. D4.2.3-5. Construct explanations using reasoning, correct sequence, examples, and details with relevant information and data. **NCSS Theme:** ❷ Culture
Staging the Compelling Question	**Dimension 1:** Explain what "dramatic license" or "artistic license" means. Think of examples in stories or films where you may have experienced "dramatic license" or "artistic license" on the part of the filmmaker or storyteller.

Dimension 2

Supporting Question 1	Supporting Question 2	Supporting Question 3	Supporting Question 4
Who was Chief Powhatan?	Who was Captain John Smith?	Who was Pocahontas?	Why did the English sail to the New World and settle in Jamestown, Virginia?
Formative Performance Task	**Formative Performance Task**	**Formative Performance Task**	**Formative Performance Task**
Investigate Chief Powhatan using the provided sources and take notes. In a class discussion, describe the similarities and differences between the sources.	Investigate Captain John Smith using the provided sources and take notes. In a class discussion, describe the similarities and differences between the sources.	Investigate Pocahontas using the provided sources and take notes. In a class discussion, describe the similarities and differences between the sources.	Review the lyrics from the opening song of the film. Compare the lyrics to the Historic Jamestown account. Take notes. In a class discussion, describe the similarities and differences between the sources.
Featured Sources	**Featured Sources**	**Featured Sources**	**Featured Sources**
Source A: Powhatan, National Park Service **Source B:** Chief Powhatan, *Pocahontas* (10:00–12:30)	**Source A:** Captain John Smith, National Park Service **Source B:** Captain John Smith, Historic Jamestowne **Source C:** Captain John Smith, *Pocahontas* (0:58–4:33)	**Source A:** Pocahontas: Her Life and Legend, National Park Service **Source B:** Pocahontas, *Pocahontas* (7:52–10:00)	**Source A:** New World reasoning, *Pocahontas* (0:00–1:46) *Note.* Use closed captioning or printed lyrics **Source B:** History of Jamestown, Historic Jamestowne

Dimension 2 Exit Ticket:
Share your findings about Chief Powhatan, John Smith, Pocahontas, and the reasons why the English sailed to the New World. Describe the attributes of the people investigated. What is one unifying theme among all sources?

Dimension 3

Bell Ringer:
Describe the one unifying theme among all sources investigated in Dimension 2 (e.g., powerful, adventurous, leaders, unafraid, proud). Now, describe the reason for the journey of the English people to the New World (e.g., greed, power, enterprising, unafraid, powerful). What do you suppose happens when powerful reasons and powerful, unafraid people collide?

Supporting Question 1	Supporting Question 2	Supporting Question 3
Is the filmmaker's visual portrayal of Pocahontas similar to or different than that of historians?	Is Captain John Smith's description of his capture similar to or different than that of historians?	Is the filmmaker's active portrayal of the relationship between Pocahontas and John Smith similar to or different than that of historians?
Formative Performance Task	**Formative Performance Task**	**Formative Performance Task**
Explore the provided sources. Describe how the sources visually portray Pocahontas. In a class discussion, describe the similarities and/or differences between the sources. Take notes.	Investigate the provided sources. In a class discussion, describe the similarities and/or differences between the sources. Take notes.	Investigate the provided sources. In a class discussion, describe the similarities and/or differences between the sources. Take notes.
Featured Sources	**Featured Sources**	**Featured Sources**
Source A: Pocahontas photo gallery, Disney **Source B:** "Life Portrait of Pocahontas," Virginia Museum of History & Culture **Source C:** "Disney Loose With Facts About Pocahontas," *The Spokesman Review* **Source D:** Obituary for Shirley "Little Dove" Custalow McGowan	**Source A:** "Chronology of Powhatan Indian Activity," National Park Service (Read Pre-1607–1609) **Source B:** *A True Relation* by Captain John Smith (1608), pp. 43–49 **Source C:** *The Double Life of Pocahontas* by Jean Fritz (1983), p. 16	**Source A:** "Chronology of Powhatan Indian Activity," National Park Service (Read Pre-1607–1618) **Source B:** Pocahontas and John Smith kiss, *Pocahontas* (1:01:00–1:03:00) **Source C:** "Savages" and Pocahontas' Sacrifice, *Pocahontas* (1:05:35–1:09:27) **Source D:** *Pocahontas and the Powhatan Dilemma* by Camilla Townsend (2005), pp. 85–87

Dimension 3 Close Activity:
Share your findings in an open class discussion. Describe the differences in the ways the film portrays Pocahontas compared to the Virginia Historical Society and the image and words of Shirley "Little Dove" Custalow McGowan. Discuss the similarities or differences between the Historic Jamestown chronology of events and John Smith's book regarding his capture. Discuss the similarities or differences between the Historic Jamestowne chronology of events and a film clip regarding the relationship between John Smith and Pocahontas.

Exit Ticket:
Why do you suppose people have different views of events?

Dimension 4

Bell Ringer: Share your responses to the exit ticket prompt: Why do you suppose people have different views of events?

Supporting Question 1	Supporting Question 2
What is one reason that the filmmakers made a romanticized version of the film *Pocahontas*?	Why do filmmakers alter narratives?
Formative Performance Task	**Formative Performance Tasks**
Watch the two provided sources. Take notes. Discuss as a class.	Read the two provided sources. Take notes. Discuss as a class.
Featured Sources	**Featured Sources**
Source A: Pocahontas and John Smith Kiss, *Pocahontas* (1:01:00–1:03:00) **Source B:** "Disney Loose With Facts About Pocahontas," *The Spokesman Review*	**Source A:** "10 Historical Movies Criticized for Their Accuracy & Realism," ScreenRant **Source B:** "Filmmakers Manipulate History? So Did Shakespeare," *The New York Times*

Summative Performance Task	**ARGUMENT** *Did the filmmakers of the film* Pocahontas *rewrite history?* Construct an argument (three-paragraph essay) that evaluates the need to study, remember, and/or celebrate this investigation using specific claims and relevant evidence from sources while acknowledging competing views.
	EXTENSION Work in groups to rewrite one of the historical inaccuracies depicted in the film *Pocahontas*. This can be completed in the format of choice (e.g., oral presentation, slide deck, or puppet show).
Taking Informed Action	**UNDERSTAND** Research historical inaccuracies that are portrayed in popular films as truth.
	ASSESS Examine the money made by film studios despite their inaccurate portrayal of historical events.
	ACT Write a letter to the president of the Motion Picture Association (www.motionpictures.org/) explaining your view about altering historical events through artistic/dramatic license in films.

Overview

Inquiry Description

This inquiry leads students through an investigation of how and why filmmakers alter films, using the film *Pocahontas* as the lens. Students will consider historians' views of how the filmmakers portrayed an inaccurate version of the relationship between Pocahontas and Captain John Smith when the English settled in Native American territory in Jamestown, Virginia, 1607.

This inquiry highlights the following standards:

C3 Standards:
- D2.His.6.3-5: Describe how people's perspectives shaped the historical sources they created.
- D2.His.10.3-5: Compare information provided by different historical sources about the past.
- D3.4.3-5: Use evidence to develop claims in response to compelling questions.
- D4.1.3-5: Construct arguments using claims and evidence from multiple sources.
- D4.2.3-5: Construct explanations using reasoning, correct sequence, examples, and details with relevant information and data.

NCSS Theme ❷ Culture

This inquiry is expected to take five (5) 50-minute class periods. The inquiry time frame could expand if teachers think their students need additional instructional experiences (e.g., supporting questions, formative performance tasks, featured sources, writing). Teachers are encouraged to adapt the inquiry to meet the needs and interests of their students. This inquiry lends itself to differentiation and modeling of historical thinking skills while assisting students in engaging in a variety of sources.

Structure of the Inquiry

Dimension 1: The hook activity and introduction of the compelling question.

Dimension 2: Content (using C3 Framework standards). Students learn about important people such as Chief Powhatan, his daughter Pocahontas, and Captain John Smith, and the reasons why the English sailed from London and settled in Jamestown, Virginia. This builds background knowledge for a deeper understanding of the historical events.

Dimension 3: Primary and secondary sources to formulate arguments about the use of the filmmakers' technique of artistic or dramatic license. Students explore the filmmakers' examples of artistic or dramatic license by comparing historians' views with the filmmakers' visual portrayals, comparing historians' accounts of John Smith to his own written version, and comparing historians' views with the filmmakers' portrayal of the relationship between Pocahontas and John Smith. This helps students see the freedom filmmakers take in departing from the facts to create an effect. This also helps students to understand that people have different views of events.

Dimension 4: Taking informed action through formal presentation and letter writing. Students explore reasons why filmmakers depart from the historical accuracy of an event. They look at what was gained by making a more romanticized version of the Pocahontas story. They are also given clips from the film that corroborate historians' accounts of what happened, such as John Smith's capture and release. This is done so students can see if the filmmakers rewrote history or if they simply embellished one storyline (e.g., the relationship between Pocahontas and Smith).

Dimension 1

Staging the Compelling Question

In staging the compelling question, students explore the filmmaking technique of artistic or dramatic license as key concepts. Students are asked to recall examples of films or stories that use this technique.

Dimension 2

Supporting Question 1

The first supporting question is "Who was Chief Powhatan?"

The formative task is to investigate Chief Powhatan using the provided sources and take notes. In a class discussion, students are asked to describe the similarities and differences between the sources.

Teachers may implement this task with the following procedures: Students need to take notes as they investigate each source.

The following scaffolds and other materials may be used to support students as they work with sources: The teacher can provide a graphic organizer if needed for students, or students can simply use their own notebooks for notetaking.

The following sources were selected to complete the task:
- **Source A:** National Park Service (2024b, March 19). *Powhatan.* https://www.nps.gov/people/powhatan.htm
- **Source B:** Goldberg, E., & Gabriel, M. (Directors). (1995). *Pocahontas.* [Motion Picture]. Walt Disney Studios Motion Pictures. (10:00-12:30)

Supporting Question 2

The second supporting question is "Who was Captain John Smith?"

The formative task is to investigate Captain John Smith using the provided sources and take notes. In a class discussion, students are asked to describe the similarities and differences between the sources.

Teachers may implement this task with the following procedures: Students need to take notes as they investigate each source.

The following scaffolds and other materials may be used to support students as they work with sources: The teacher can provide a graphic organizer if needed for students or students can simply use their own notebooks for notetaking.

The following sources were selected to complete the task:
- **Source A:** National Park Service. (2024a, February 23). *John Smith.* https://www.nps.gov/people/john-smith.htm
- **Source B:** Historic Jamestowne. (n.d.). *John Smith.* https://historicjamestowne.org/history/pocahontas/john-smith/
- **Source C:** *Pocahontas* (0:58–4:33)

Supporting Question 3

The third supporting question is "Who was Pocahontas?"

The formative task is to investigate Pocahontas using the provided sources and take notes. In a class discussion, students are asked to describe the similarities and differences between the sources.

Teachers may implement this task with the following procedures: Students need to take notes as they investigate each source.

The following scaffolds and other materials may be used to support students as they work with sources: The teacher can provide a graphic organizer if needed for students or students can simply use their own notebooks for notetaking.

The following sources were selected to complete the task:
- **Source A:** Stebbins, S. J. (2022, September 4). *Pocahontas: Her life and legend.* National Park Service. https://www.nps.gov/jame/learn/historyculture/pocahontas-her-life-and-legend.htm
- **Source B:** *Pocahontas* (7:52–10:00)

Supporting Question 4

The fourth supporting question is "Why did the English sail to the New World and settle in Jamestown, Virginia?"

The formative task is to review the lyrics from the opening song of the film (Source A). Compare the lyrics to the Historic Jamestowne account (Source B). In a class discussion, describe the similarities and differences between the sources.

Teachers may implement this task with the following procedures: Students need to take notes as they investigate each source.

The following scaffolds and other materials may be used to support students as they work with sources: The teacher can provide a graphic organizer if needed for students or students can simply use their own notebooks for notetaking.
The following sources were selected to complete the task:
- **Source A:** *Pocahontas* (0:00–1:46); *Note.* Turn on closed captioning or print out the lyrics so students can read the song lyrics.
- **Source B:** Historic Jamestowne. (n.d.). *History of Jamestown.* https://historicjamestowne.org/history/history-of-jamestown/

Dimension 2 Exit Ticket:
After completing Dimension 2 activities, ask students to share their findings about Chief Powhatan, John Smith, Pocahontas, and the reasons why the English sailed to the New World. Describe the attributes of the people investigated.

What is one unifying theme among all sources?

Dimension 3

Supporting Question 1

Bell Ringer:
- Students are asked to describe the one unifying theme among all sources investigated in Dimension 2 (e.g., powerful, adventurous, leaders, unafraid, proud).
- Now, describe the reason for the journey of the English people to the New World (e.g., greed, power, enterprising, unafraid, powerful).
- What do you suppose happens when powerful reasons and powerful, unafraid people collide?

The first supporting question is "Is the filmmaker's visual portrayal of Pocahontas similar to or different than that of historians?"

The formative task is as follows: Have students explore Disney's photo gallery (Source A), the Virginia Historical Society (Source B), a newspaper article from *The Spokesman-Review* (Source C) about the film's inaccuracies pertaining to Pocahontas and John Smith, and the obituary image of Shirley "Little Dove" Custalow McGowan (Source D). Describe how the sources visually portrayed Pocahontas. In a class discussion, describe the similarities and/or differences between the sources.

Teachers may implement this task with the following procedures: Students need to take notes as they investigate each source.

The following scaffolds and other materials may be used to support students as they work with sources: The teacher can provide a graphic organizer if needed for students or students can simply use their own notebooks for note taking.

The following sources were selected to complete the task:
- **Source A:** Disney. (n.d.). *Pocahontas photo gallery.* http://princess.disney.com/pocahontas-photo-gallery
- **Source B:** Virginia Museum of History & Culture. (n.d.). *Life portrait of Pocahontas.* https://virginiahistory.org/learn/life-portrait-pocahontas
- **Source C:** Rochman, B. I. (1995, April 24). Disney loose with facts about Pocahontas. *The Spokesman-Review.* https://www.spokesman.com/stories/1995/apr/24/disney-loose-with-facts-about-pocahontas/
- **Source D:** [Obituary for Shirley "Little Dove" Custalow McGowan]. (2021). Vincent Funeral Home. https://www.vincentfh.com/obituaries/Shirley-Little-Dove-Mcgowan/#!/Obituary

Supporting Question 2

The second supporting question is "Is John Smith's description of his capture similar to or different than that of historians?"

The formative task is as follows: Have students investigate the Historic Jamestowne chronology of events (Source A), John Smith's book (Source B), and a historian's account regarding Smith's capture (Source C). In a class discussion, describe the similarities and/or differences between the sources.

Teachers may implement this task with the following procedures: Students need to take notes as they investigate each source.

The following scaffolds and other materials may be used to support students as they work with sources: The teacher can provide a graphic organizer if needed for students or students can simply use their own notebooks for notetaking.

The following sources were selected to complete the task:
- **Source A:** Read to Pre-1607 to 1609 in Stebbins, S. J. (2020, August 24). *Chronology of Powhatan Indian Activity.* National Park Service. https://www.nps.gov/jame/learn/historyculture/chronology-of-powhatan-indian-activity.htm
- **Source B:** Read pp. 43–49 in Smith, J. (1866). *A true relation.* Wiggin and Lunt. www.loc.gov/item/rc01002803/ Original work published 1608)

- Paraphrased: "We went ashore and within a quarter of an hour, I hear a loud cry and a hollowing of Indians. I was struck with an arrow on the right thigh; Indians drew their bows which I prevented in discharging a French pistol. 20 or 30 arrows were shot at me but fell short. I discharged my pistol and killed a few. They killed my group of men. They captured me."
- **Source C:** Read p. 16 in Fritz, J. (1983). *The double life of Pocahontas* (E. Young, Illus.). Putnam Juvenile Press.
  - Paraphrased: 1607—Smith and others were on an expedition when they were surprised by a hunting party of Pamunkey Indians. They attacked; Smith fired back with his pistol and killed two Indians. Smith was captured.

Supporting Question 3

The third supporting question is "Is the filmmaker's active portrayal of the relationship between Pocahontas and John Smith similar to or different than that of historians?"

The formative task is as follows: Have students investigate the Historic Jamestowne chronology of events (Source A), two film clips (Source B, Source C), and a historian's perspective regarding the relationship between John Smith and Pocahontas (Source D). In a class discussion, describe the similarities and/or differences between the sources.

Teachers may implement this task with the following procedures: Students need to take notes as they investigate each source.

The following scaffolds and other materials may be used to support students as they work with sources: The teacher can provide a graphic organizer if needed for students or students can simply use their own notebooks for note taking.

The following sources were selected to complete the task:
- **Source A:** Read to Pre-1607 to 1618 in Stebbins, S. J. (2020, August 24). *Chronology of Powhatan Indian Activity*. National Park Service. https://www.nps.gov/jame/learn/historyculture/chronology-of-powhatan-indian-activity.htm
- **Source B:** Pocahontas and John Smith kiss, *Pocahontas* (1:01:00–1:03:00)
- **Source C:** "Savages" and Pocahontas's Sacrifice, *Pocahontas* (1:05:35–1:09:27)
- **Source D:** Read pages 85–87 in Townsend, C. (2005). *Pocahontas and the Powhatan dilemma*. Hill and Wang Publishers.
  - Paraphrased: 1610—Pocahontas married Kocoom. He was a warrior, from the nearby Patowomeck nation. Pocahontas married Kocoom by choice. Within a few years, Kocoom disappeared.

Dimension 3 Close Activity: After completing Dimension 3 activities, ask student to share their findings in an open class discussion. Describe the differences in the ways the film portrays Pocahontas compared to the Virginia Historical Society and the image and words of Shirley "Little Dove" Custalow McGowan. Discuss the similarities or differences between the Historic Jamestowne chronology of events and John Smith's book regarding his capture. Discuss the similarities or differences between the Historic Jamestowne chronology of events and a film clip regarding the relationship between John Smith and Pocahontas.

Exit Ticket: Ask students to respond to the following prompt: Why do you suppose people have different views of events?

Dimension 4

Overview

Bell Ringer: Students are asked to share their responses to the exit ticket prompt: Why do you suppose people have different views of events?

Supporting Question 1

The first supporting question is "What is one reason that the filmmakers made a romanticized version of the film *Pocahontas*?"

The formative task is as follows: Watch the *Pocahontas* film clip of the relationship between Pocahontas and John Smith (Source A). Then read the newspaper article (Source B). Discuss as a class.

Teachers may implement this task with the following procedures: Students need to take notes as they investigate each source. The following scaffolds and other materials may be used to support students as they work with sources: The teacher can provide a graphic organizer if needed for students or students can simply use their own notebooks for note taking.

The following sources were selected to complete the task:
- **Source A:** Pocahontas and John Smith kiss, *Pocahontas* (1:01:00–1:03:00)
- **Source B:** Rochman, B. I. (1995, April 24). Disney loose with facts about Pocahontas. *The Spokesman-Review.* https://www.spokesman.com/stories/1995/apr/24/disney-loose-with-facts-about-pocahontas/

Supporting Question 2

The second supporting question is "Why do filmmakers alter narratives?"

The formative task is to read the two provided sources and then discuss as a class.

Teachers may implement this task with the following procedures: Students need to take notes as they investigate each source.

The following scaffolds and other materials may be used to support students as they work with sources: The teacher can provide a graphic organizer if needed for students or students can simply use their own notebooks for note taking.

The following sources were selected to complete the task:
- **Source A:** Mutuc, P. (2023, October 14). 10 historical movies criticized for their accuracy & realism. *ScreenRant.* https://screenrant.com/historical-movies-inaccuracies-criticism/
- **Source B:** Toplin, R. B. (2013, September 3). Filmmakers manipulate history? So did Shakespeare. *The New York Times.* https://www.nytimes.com/roomfordebate/2013/09/03/when-movies-trade-on-real-life/filmmakers-manipulate-history-so-did-shakespeare

Summative Performance Task

At this point in the inquiry, students have examined the ways in which filmmakers use the artistic/dramatic technique and why. Students explored reasons why filmmakers depart from the historical accuracy of an event. They looked at what was gained by making a more romanticized version of the Pocahontas story. They were also given clips from the film that corroborate historians' accounts of what happened, such as John Smith's capture and release. This was done so students can see if the filmmakers rewrote history or if they simply embellished one storyline (e.g., the relationship between Pocahontas and Smith).

Students should be expected to demonstrate the breadth of their understandings and their abilities to use evidence from multiple sources to support their claims. In this task, students are asked to construct an argument (three-paragraph essay) that evaluates the need to study, remember, and/or celebrate this investigation using specific claims and relevant evidence from sources while acknowledging competing views.

Students' arguments will likely vary, but could include any of the following:
- Making money is a major reason that filmmakers alter the historical accuracy of an event so the film attracts more viewers.
- Some films alter major storylines, while others alter only minor storylines.

To extend their arguments, work in groups to rewrite one of the historical inaccuracies depicted in the film *Pocahontas*. This can be completed in the format of choice (e.g., oral presentation, slide deck, or puppet show).

Students have the opportunity to Take Informed Action:

UNDERSTAND: Research historical inaccuracies that are portrayed in popular films as truth.

ASSESS: Examine the money made by film studios despite their inaccurate portrayal of historical events.

ACT: Write a letter to the president of the Motion Picture Association (**https://www.motionpictures.org/**) explaining your view about altering historical events through artistic/dramatic license in films.

References

Disney. (n.d.). *Pocahontas photo gallery.* http://princess.disney.com/pocahontas-photo-gallery

Feest, C. (1990). *The Powhatan tribes: Indians of North America.* Chelsea House Publishers.

Fritz, J. (1983). *The double life of Pocahontas* (E. Young, Illus.). Putnam Juvenile Press.

Goldberg, E., & Gabriel, M. (Directors). (1995). *Pocahontas.* [Motion Picture]. Walt Disney Studios Motion Pictures.

Historic Jamestowne. (n.d.). *History of Jamestown.* https://historicjamestowne.org/history/history-of-jamestown/

Historic Jamestowne. (n.d.). *John Smith.* https://historicjamestowne.org/history/pocahontas/john-smith/

Mutuc, P. (2023, October 14). 10 historical movies criticized for their accuracy & realism. *ScreenRant.* https://screenrant.com/historical-movies-inaccuracies-criticism/

National Council for the Social Studies. (2013). *The college, career, and civic life (C3) framework for social studies state standards: Guidance for enhancing the rigor of K-12 civics, economics, geography, and history.*

National Park Service. (2024a, February 23). *John Smith.* https://www.nps.gov/people/john-smith.htm

National Park Service (2024b, March 19). *Powhatan.* https://www.nps.gov/people/powhatan.htm

[Obituary for Shirley "Little Dove" Custalow McGowan]. (2021). Vincent Funeral Home. https://www.vincentfh.com/obituaries/Shirley-Little-Dove-Mcgowan/#!/Obituary

Rochman, B. I. (1995, April 24). Disney loose with facts about Pocahontas. *The Spokesman-Review* https://www.spokesman.com/stories/1995/apr/24/disney-loose-with-facts-about-pocahontas/

Sardone, N. (2018). Debunking myths in U.S. history: Will the real story of Pocahontas please rise? In S. Roberts and C. Elfer (Eds.), *Hollywood or history? An inquiry-based strategy for using film to teach United States history* (pp. 3–14). Information Age.

Smith, J. (1866). *A true relation.* Wiggin and Lunt. www.loc.gov/item/rc01002803/ (Original work published 1608)

Stebbins, S. J. (2020, August 24). *Chronology of Powhatan Indian Activity.* National Park Service. https://www.nps.gov/jame/learn/historyculture/chronology-of-powhatan-indian-activity.htm

Stebbins, S. J. (2022, September 4). *Pocahontas: Her life and legends.* National Park Service. https://www.nps.gov/jame/learn/historyculture/pocahontas-her-life-and-legend.htm

Toplin, R. B. (2013, September 3). Filmmakers manipulate history? So did Shakespeare. *The New York Times.* https://www.nytimes.com/roomfordebate/2013/09/03/when-movies-trade-on-real-life/filmmakers-manipulate-history-so-did-shakespeare

Townsend, C. (2005). *Pocahontas and the Powhatan dilemma.* Hill and Wang Publishers.

Virginia Museum of History & Culture. (n.d.). *Life portrait of Pocahontas.* https://virginiahistory.org/learn/life-portrait-pocahontas

Meghan Beauchamp and Chloe Thompson

Grade 4 Economics, Geography, and Civics

How has migration and immigration affected the world in the past, present, and future?

Supporting Questions Dimension 1
- What factors influence population growth and decline?
- How can immigration and migration be defined?
- Why is immigration and migration valuable to the economy?

Supporting Questions Dimension 2
- From where, to where, and why did people migrate to the United States?
- Are land and resource use affected by immigration and migration? If so, how?
- What are some examples of push/pull factors in our state?

Supporting Questions Dimension 3
- What role does immigration play in our community?
- How do we identify and explain trends of immigration and migration?
- How can we use our voices to educate others on the environmental impacts of immigration and migration?

Supporting Questions Dimension 4
- In what ways does analyzing the community-level effects of immigration and migration contribute to our understanding of economic transformations?
- What factors should be considered when identifying trends of immigration and migration?
- How can we show our support to those who dedicate their work to environmental conservation?

Grade 4 Economics, Geography, and Civics

	How has migration and immigration affected the world, in the past, present, and future?
Standards and Content	**C3 Standards:** D1.5.3-5. Determine the kinds of sources that will be helpful in answering compelling and supporting questions, taking into consideration the different opinions people have about how to answer the questions. D2.Civ.12.3-5. Explain how policies are developed to address public problems. D2.Eco.2.3-5. Identify positive and negative incentives that influence the decisions people make. D2.Geo.9.3-5. Analyze the effects of catastrophic environmental and technological events on human settlements and migration. D3.4.3-5. Use evidence to develop claims in response to compelling questions. D4.2.3-5. Construct explanations using reasoning, correct sequence, examples, and details with relevant information and data. **NCSS Theme:** ❸ People, Places, Environments
Staging the Compelling Question	**Dimension 1:** Using the Think-Pair-Share strategy, students reflect, discuss, and write their initial responses to the compelling question.

Dimension 1

Supporting Question 1	Supporting Question 2	Supporting Question 3
What factors influence population growth and decline?	How can immigration and migration be defined?	Why is immigration and migration valuable to the economy?
Formative Performance Task	**Formative Performance Task**	**Formative Performance Task**
Analyze different factors that contribute to population growth and decline Research a continent to determine population density and push/pull factors that have led to population change. Answer: What are some push/pull factors that have caused population growth and decline in your continent?	Evaluate the impact of push/pull factors on a specific individual. Read and discuss the experience of migration based on the life of an immigrant. Answer: How can we relate Luz's story to the push/pull factors we have discovered as population geographers?	Evaluate the economies of your assigned continent as it pertains to immigration and migration. Discuss how different continents' economies are impacted by immigration and migration patterns.
Featured Sources	**Featured Sources**	**Featured Sources**
Source A: *How Populations Grow and Change: Crash Course Geography #33* [Video] by CrashCourse **Source B:** Teacher-developed checklist	**Source A:** *The Boy from Mexico: An Immigration Story of Bravery and Determination* by Edward Dennis **Source B:** *Residents in South El Paso Worry About Impact of Migrants on Their Neighborhood* [Video] by KTSM 9 NEWS.	**Source A:** Social studies notebook T-chart

Exit Ticket Suggestion:
Upon completion of the Dimension 1 activities, revisit student responses to the compelling question. Ask students to retrieve their social studies notebooks and begin to reflect on their views based on their newfound knowledge.

Dimension 2

Supporting Question 1	Supporting Question 2	Supporting Question 3
From where, to where, and why did people migrate to the United States?	Are land and resource use affected by immigration and migration? If so, how?	What are some examples of push/pull factors in our state?
Formative Performance Task	**Formative Performance Task**	**Formative Performance Task**
Engage in a *Hollywood or History?* analysis about if the film *Ice Age* shows an accurate depiction of the push/pull factors of migration.	Watch the documentary *Mysteries of the Great Lakes* to compare the factors for migration discussed to those ideas that were suggested in the film *Ice Age*.	Explore the push/pull factors that have led to migration to and from the state, province, or local area.
Featured Sources	**Featured Sources**	**Featured Sources**
Source A: *Ice Age* (2002)	**Source A:** *Mysteries of the Great Lakes* (2008) **Source B:** Social studies notebook Venn diagram	**Source A:** A book about state history; e.g., *It Happened in Michigan* (2019)

Exit Ticket Suggestion:
After completing the activities outlined in Dimension 2, have students complete an exit ticket answering the prompt, "Identify two or three scenarios in which immigration and migration can occur and the effects of each."

Dimension 3

Bell Ringer:
Ask: "How would you define a trend?" Write down at least two characteristics a trend needs. This paragraph will be revisited at the conclusion of Dimension 3.

Supporting Question 1	Supporting Question 2	Supporting Question 3
What role does immigration play in our community, and what evidence can we gather from it to support an argument?	How do we identify and explain trends of immigration and migration and gather evidence to support these trends?	How can students use their voice to educate others on the environmental impacts of immigration and migration?

Formative Performance Task	Formative Performance Task	Formative Performance Task
Discuss and analyze how immigration affects our community through a real-life example.	Conduct an investigation and gather data to analyze and predict the past, present, and future of immigration and migration in different world regions.	Investigate how various species (human or animal) migrate from place to place and the impact these migrations have on the environment.
Featured Sources	**Featured Sources**	**Featured Sources**
Source A: Interview	**Source A:** Teacher-created WebQuest **Source B:** *Migration Data Hub*	**Source A:** Social studies notebook Venn diagram **Source B:** Local nature centers

Exit Ticket Suggestion: After the students complete the activities outlined in Dimension 3, ask them to revisit their initial responses to "How would you define a trend?" Prompt students to reflect on their thoughts and whether their views have changed based on what they learned and discussed. Have students document their revised thoughts in their social studies notebooks.

Dimension 4

Supporting Question 1	Supporting Question 2	Supporting Question 3
In what ways does analyzing the community-level effects of immigration and migration contribute to our understanding of economic transformations?	What factors should be considered when identifying trends of immigration and migration?	How can we show our support to those who dedicate their work to restoring populations such as sturgeons?
Formative Performance Task	**Formative Performance Task**	**Formative Performance Task**
Create a YouTube video to teach the public or another class in their school about how immigration and migration impacts their community.	Take action "inside the walls of the classroom" by collaboratively developing trend identification criteria and conduct your own trend analyses.	Write a handwritten letter to a key figure at your state Department of Natural Resources, sharing your experiences at a local nature center to express support for nature conservation efforts.
Featured Sources	**Featured Sources** **Student Created**	**Featured Sources**
Source A: Clips from class interview **Source B:** Notes from class interview from social studies notebook	**Source A:** *Migration Data Hub* **Source B:** Notes on trends from social studies notebook	**Source A:** Key figure in state's Department of Natural Resources **Source B:** Notes from social studies notebook on the field trip to the nature center

Summative Performance Task	**ARGUMENT** How has migration and immigration affected the world, in the past, present, and future? Compose a written argument that answers the compelling question by presenting specific claims and applicable evidence drawn from historical sources, all while recognizing different points of view.
	EXTENSION Create a pamphlet detailing the outcome of migration on places of their choice, closing in on the impact on how land and resources were affected, as well as the dynamics of push/pull factors.

Taking Informed Action	**UNDERSTAND** Connect your learning about migration and immigration to current instances within your own community by identifying ways in which your community is impacted by migrants and by understanding how migration trends can be leveraged to make economic changes.
	ASSESS Examine the costs and benefits of immigration and migration. Evaluate the potential impacts of trends in immigration and migration considering location and outcomes of implementing change.
	ACT Write a letter to Randy Claramunt, the Chief of the Fisheries Division at the Michigan Department of Natural Resources, that outlines support for their efforts (Michigan Department of Natural Resources)
	* Locate your state's Department of Natural Resources to determine a significant role to whom students can write a letter.

Overview

Inquiry Description

This inquiry leads students through an exploration of civic, economic, and geographic engagement focusing on how students can actively participate and make impactful changes within their environment. Utilizing a comprehensive understanding of economic concepts and advocacy, students will investigate the role of citizens in shaping public policy and governance based on this knowledge. This lesson incorporates a variety of activities to help students understand the topic of migration of both humans and animals to eventually effectively advocate for community changes.

The lessons in this inquiry lend themselves to cross-curricular learning experiences utilizing persuasive writing, literature studies, film analysis, data analysis, and civic learning. It is estimated to take 5 days with 50-minute class periods. This inquiry lends itself to collaboration, hands-on learning, civic engagement, and ongoing reflection and can be adapted to meet the needs and interests of learners.

Structure of the Inquiry

Dimension 1: Introduction to the compelling question and activities that stimulate thinking about economics and geography
Dimension 2: Civic, Geographic, and Economic Content (using C3 Framework, NCSS themes, state/district curriculum)
Dimension 3: Using primary, secondary, and student-obtained sources to formulate arguments based in evidence (e.g., text and video analysis, interviews)
Dimension 4: Taking informed action through writing to a person in a leadership position at the state level.

Dimension 1

Staging the Compelling Question

Begin the unit by posing the unit's compelling question to the class, "How has migration and immigration affected the world, in the past, present, and future?" Give time to complete the Think-Pair-Share discussion. Begin by giving students time to reflect and write their initial responses. Pair students in groups of two to three to discuss their ideas about the impact of migration and immigration on a given place. Once students have been given adequate time to share their initial thoughts, collect their written responses. Upon completion of the activities in Dimension 1, revisit the compelling question. Distribute students' initial responses and provide time for them to reflect on their views based on their newfound knowledge. Students will document their revisions and ideas. The updated thoughts should be compiled into their social studies notebooks as a record of their learning journey.

Supporting Question 1

The first supporting question is "What factors influence population growth and decline?"

The formative task is as follows:

- Students will analyze different factors that contribute to population growth and decline by roleplaying as population geographers. In small groups, students will be assigned a continent where the focus of the research is to determine the population density and the push/pull factors affecting such population change.
- Research will be conducted using school-provided technology. The required data will be provided via a teacher-made checklist. Data collected will be written and organized in their social studies notebooks.

Teachers may implement this task with the following procedures:
- Tell students they are going to be taking on the role of a geographer.
- Introduce the concept of a population density and push/pull factors. Students should be told *population density* is a measure of population per unit of land area. In the United States, we would use the population per square mile. Then explain what push/pull factors are. *Push factors* are things that push people out of an area. These include war, famine, and natural disasters. *Pull factors* are things that cause people to want to move to a different area. This could include a good economy, political freedom, religious freedom, or a better job. Then show the video *How Populations Grow and Change: Crash Course Geography #33* (Source A) to reinforce student understanding.
- Students will analyze different continents and the ways that push/pull factors have led to population change. Students will research this information using school-approved technology. Divide students into small groups and provide them with a checklist (Source B) to help in their research. The checklist could include items such as "continent under study," "population density of the continent," "three push factors that cause people to leave the continent" and "three pull factors that cause people to move to the continent."
- Students will write the answers to the checklist in their social studies notebooks.

The following scaffolds and other materials may be used to support students as they work with sources: The teacher can use cooperative grouping, pre-made checklist templates, and specific websites to help students locate population density and push/pull factors. The teacher can utilize this activity to assess student understanding of the important vocabulary discussed above.

The following sources were selected to provide a comprehensive understanding of population density and push/pull factors. This will provide students with foundational knowledge of economic and geographic concepts to build upon in later lessons.
- **Source A:** CrashCourse. (2021, November 8). *How populations grow and change: Crash course geography #33* [Video]. YouTube. www.youtube.com/watch?v=JpAiBg0hrfQ
- **Source B:** Teacher-developed checklist.

Supporting Question 2

The second supporting question is "How can immigration and migration be defined?"

The formative task is as follows:
- Students will read *The Boy from Mexico: An Immigration Story of Bravery and Determination* by Edward Dennis (Source A) and participate in an interactive read aloud to define "immigration" and "migration."
- While reading, ask the following questions so that students understand why people migrate or immigrate:
    - "Using context clues, how could we define 'immigration'?"
    - "How can we relate Luz's story to the factors that we discovered as population geographers?"
    - "What might happen if people didn't have the courage to migrate to a different place?"
- Bridge the historical context of the book with current examples of the impact immigration and migration has on not only places but also people. Such connections can be made by exposing students to interviews with Mexican migrants and people who reside in border countries (Source B).

Teachers may implement this task with the following procedures:
- Introduce *The Boy from Mexico: An Immigration Story of Bravery and Determination* and discuss its context and relevance to modern immigration based on pull and push factors.
- Relate the story to contemporary examples where immigration has led to change in community policies.
- Ask students to write a paragraph about the reasons for immigration and the impact it has on individuals and communities, using examples from the book (Source A) and video clip (Source B).

The following scaffolds and other materials may be used to support students as they work with sources: The teacher can use discussion guides for *The Boy from Mexico: An Immigration Story of Bravery and Determination*, Think-Pair-Share discussion strategies, and writing prompts to help students formulate reflections on the factors of migration.

The following sources were selected to illustrate the significance of push/pull factors on migration.
- **Source A:** Dennis, E. (2022). *The boy from Mexico: An immigration story of bravery and determination.* Dragonfruit.
- **Source B:** KTSM 9 NEWS. (2022, December 20). *Residents in South El Paso worry about impact of migrants on their neighborhood* [Video]. YouTube. www.youtube.com/watch?v=wqz1M8Rp7Lo

Supporting Question 3

The third supporting question is "Why is immigration and migration valuable to the economy?"

The formative task is as follows:
- Students will actively evaluate the economies of their assigned continents as it pertains to immigration and migration compared to countries with different types of different levels of immigration. In their social studies notebooks, students will draw and fill out a T-chart graphic organizer with labels of "[Continent]'s Economy With Immigration and Migration" and "[Continent]'s Economy Without Immigration and Migration" (Source A). An example will be placed on the visualizer for students to reference.
- Once the lists have been generated, students will participate in "Economies Around the World" where the continent groups travel from continent to continent sharing their ideas. Students are encouraged to modify or add to their lists.
- After each continent group has shared with the other groups, a guided discussion will occur where each continent group shares one thing they learned about their economy and one thing they learned about another continent's economy.

Teachers may implement this task with the following procedures:
- Distribute T-chart graphic organizers with the labels "[Continent]'s Economy With Immigration and Migration" and "[Continent]'s Economy Without Immigration and Migration" (Source A).
- Facilitate small group discussions, "Economies Around the World," for knowledge sharing and to encourage peer feedback.
- Guide students in selecting and sharing one thing they learned about their continent's economy and one thing they learned about another continent's economy.

The following scaffolds and other materials may be used to support students as they work with sources: The teacher can use cooperative grouping, T-chart graphic organizers to structure idea generation, and teacher-facilitated whole group discussion to support student success.

The following source was selected to enable students to identify actionable improvements and to understand the process of proposing changes.
Source A: Social studies notebook T-chart

Exit Ticket Suggestion: Upon completion of the Dimension 1 activities, revisit student responses to the compelling question. Ask students to retrieve their social studies notebooks and begin to reflect on their views based on their newfound knowledge.

Dimension 2

Supporting Question 1

The first supporting question is "From where, to where, and why did people migrate to the United States?"

The formative task is as follows:
- Students will take notes of animal migrations based on environmental impacts by watching *Ice Age* (Source A). They should record phrases such as "Whattaya say we head south together" (9:42–9:43) and scenes such as "at 39:10 it starts to snow" (39:10) into their social studies notebooks.
- Compare and contrast the relationship between animal migration and human migration through a guided discussion. Questions should include "What did you notice occurred when it started to snow?" and "How can we relate this to grandparents who leave for somewhere warmer in the winter?"
- Introduce and discuss the concept of *Hollywood or History?* This should lead to a guided discussion about the representation of migration in the movie. Ask questions such as "What elements of the movie do you believe were

realistic?" and "Do you think this movie was an accurate depiction of migration?"

Teachers may implement this task with the following procedures:
- Present an open-ended question to the class "What are the similarities and differences between animal migration and human migration?"
- Utilize a Think-Pair-Share discussion strategy to stimulate student ideas.
- Watch two scenes from the film *Ice Age* (Source A):
  ○ The migration scene in the fall, cool weather where the animals are just beginning to migrate (3:24–7:28)
  ○ The migration scene where they encounter a challenge, in this case, the saber-toothed tigers trying to capture a mammoth (1:00:10–1:08:20)
- Lead a guided discussion about the elements of the movie that students believe to be realistic and not realistic about the reasons for migration.

The following scaffolds and other materials may be used to support students as they work with sources:
- The teacher can use differentiated question strategies to accommodate learning levels and encourage student engagement, provide visual aids that show reasons for both animal and human migrations, utilize differentiated partner groupings, and provide one-on-one support to offer additional help understanding concepts discussed.
- A graphic organizer with sections titled "Realistic Examples for Migration" and "Non-Realistic Examples of Migration" can be used by students while watching the film clips.

The following source was selected to provide a foundation for understanding the reasons for human and animal migrations.
Source A: Wedge, C. (Director). (2002). *Ice age* [Film]. Blue Sky Studies; 20th Century Fox Animation.

Supporting Question 2

The second supporting question is "Are land and resource use affected by immigration and migration? If so, how?"

The formative task is as follows:
- Watch *Mysteries of the Great Lakes* (Source A; available on Amazon Prime and Pluto TV). While viewing, students should construct a bulleted list of environmental impacts such as "A fish that had once dominated the Great Lakes declined by 99%" (9:22–9:27) in their social studies notebooks.
- Revisit the concept of *Hollywood or History?* Another guided discussion should occur. Ask questions such as "Do you believe this documentary to be Hollywood or History?" and "What evidence from the documentary supports your opinion?"
- Compare and contrast notes and ideas discussed with *Ice Age* and with *Mysteries of the Great Lakes*. Ask questions such as "How does the environment change with migration?" and "How did the movie and the documentary compare/contrast in their representation of migration?" The teacher will condense shared student thoughts and ideas via a Venn diagram as they lead the students to do the same in their social studies notebooks (Source B).

Teachers may implement this task with the following procedures:
- Show the documentary *Mysteries of the Great Lakes* (Source A) and encourage notetaking during the video.
- Guide students in comparing the information about migration found in the documentary *Mysteries of the Great Lakes* to that of the film *Ice Age*. Help students in locating evidence from both films. Have students use a Venn diagram (Source B) to help with this comparison.
- Post a class-developed Venn diagram of the similarities and difference found in the ideas of the films and have students copy the final Venn diagram in their social studies notebooks.

The following scaffolds and other materials may be used to support students as they work with sources: The teacher can use pre-made Venn diagram templates or partially completed Venn diagrams to guide students in the process.

The following sources were selected to help students compare and contrast the ideas about migration in the two videos.
- **Source A:** Lickley, D. (Director). (2008). *Mysteries of the Great Lakes* [Film]. Science North.
- **Source B:** Social studies notebook Venn diagram

Supporting Question 3

The third supporting question is "What are some examples of push/pull factors in our state?"

The formative task is as follows:
- The teacher pulls specific sections from a book about state history (Source A), such as "The Griffon Sets Sail" (Burcar, 2019, p. 6) and "Detroit Race Riots" from *It Happened in Michigan* (Burcar, 2019, p. 124).
- After reviewing each section as a whole class, the students will then utilize the alternate teaching resource to make a list of push/pull examples from the teacher's selected sections.
- In addition to their compiled lists, students will also use the selected sections to complete a Jigsaw activity exploring the differences between push/pull factors when it comes to migration and immigration.

Teachers may implement this task with the following procedures:
- Divide students into three "expert" groups, each assigned to one of the teacher-selected push/pull factors from the selected text (Source A).
- Each "expert" group will research their assigned push/pull factor and complete their designated section of a teacher-made graphic organizer for this activity. Graphic organizers should include the definition of the push/pull factor, the main components, and how the push/pull factor has impacted the economy of the state, province, or local area.
- Divide expert groups into smaller student groupings of three to four to share their research and provide peer support.
- Reorganize students into mixed groups where they teach each other about their researched push/pull factor.
- Review and discuss the concept of push/pull factors and provide information about how these migration factors have impacted the state, province, or local area.

The following scaffolds and other materials may be used to support students as they work with sources: The teacher can use visual learning aids, such as diagrams or flow charts, that outline local push/pull factors, structured group discussions and discussion prompts, peer teaching opportunities, and formative feedback to support student success.

The following source was selected to enhance understanding of the push/pull factors that impact the local area.
- **Source A:** District-approved state history social studies textbook or approved outside resource.
- The authors of this lesson used Burcar, C. (2019). *It happened in Michigan: Stories of events and people that shaped Great Lakes state history*. Globe Pequot Press.

Exit Ticket Suggestion:
After completing the activities outlined in Dimension 2, have students complete an exit ticket answering the prompt, "Identify two or three scenarios in which immigration and migration can occur and the effects of each."

Dimension 3

Supporting Question 1

Bell Ringer: Ask: "How would you define a trend?" Write down at least two characteristics a trend needs. This paragraph will be revisited at the conclusion of Dimension 3.

The first supporting question is "What role does immigration play in our community, and what evidence can we gather from it to support an argument?"

The formative task is as follows:
- Students will prepare and interview a community member who immigrated to discuss and analyze how immigration affects our community. Students will take notes as they interview the immigrant community member (Source A).
- Students will construct an argument based on the benefits of immigration as it pertains to gathering evidence to support the compelling question.
- The collected data will serve as the foundation for examining the costs and benefits of immigration and migration in Dimension 4.

Teachers may implement this task with the following procedures:
- Have students interview a member of the community who identifies as an immigrant (Source A). Students should ask the participant about their immigration experiences, the reason(s) why they immigrated to the community, and their beliefs concerning how immigration positively impacts the local community.
- Have students analyze the interview and locate evidence that helps answer supporting question 1.
- Have students construct an argument based on the benefits of immigration as it pertains to the information they learned from the interview.

The following scaffolds and other materials may be used to support students as they work with sources: Teachers can use a question list for students to ask the participant, cooperative grouping to conduct the interview, or whole class work through a guest speaker either in person or online.

The following source was selected to assist students in their understanding about the experiences of immigration.
- **Source A:** Immigrant community member interview
- For a pre-recorded option, see Not In Our Town. (2011, May 2). *New Immigrants Share Their Stories* [Video]. YouTube. www.youtube.com/watch?v=33OINi3xVbc

Supporting Question 2

The second supporting question is "How do we identify and explain trends of immigration and migration and gather evidence to support these trends?"

The formative task is as follows:
- Each continent group will focus on analyzing and predicting the past, present, and future of immigration and migration by completing a teacher-created WebQuest (Source A). They will work to identify where push/pull factors occurred over time based on the reading. The website should contain quantitative and qualitative data (Source B).
- Students will break into small groups of the world with one student representative from each continent. Each continent will take turns sharing their trends.
- Once all groups have shared their trends, the group will work together to create a line graph representing each continent with a different color. Each world group will focus on a specific push/pull factor assigned by the teacher.
- After creating their line graphs, the teacher will compile and display them in the hallway for students to share.

Teachers may implement this task with the following procedures:
- Place students back into their continent groups.
- Introduce students to the teacher-created WebQuest (Source A). Explain that students will use a website (Source B) to identify push/pull factors that have occurred over time in different continents. The website selected should include quantitative and qualitative data.
- Place students into different groups where each continent is represented. Have students share the trends they located for their continent.
- Guide students in developing line graphs that shows migration trends for each continent. Students should provide examples of the push/pull factors that are the cause of the migration patterns. After creating their line graphs, the teacher will compile and display them in the hallway for students to share.

The following scaffolds and other materials may be used to support students as they work with sources: Teachers can use cooperative grouping, peer review sessions, checklists for effective evidence, and examples of line graphs showing migration patterns of different world regions.

The following sources were selected to support students' understanding push/pull factors that have led to migration trends.
- **Source A:** Teacher-created WebQuest
- **Source B:** Migration Policy Institute. (n.d.). *Migration data hub.* www.migrationpolicy.org/programs/migration-data-hub

Supporting Question 3

The third supporting question is "How can students use their voice to educate others on the environmental impacts of immigration and migration?"

The formative task is as follows:
- Students will visit a local nature center (or a center's website) to learn about the migration of natural life while on a guided tour (Source B).
- As they do so, they intentionally investigate how various species migrate from place to place and how such migration impacts the environments inhabited, asking questions and taking notes as needed (Source A).
- Once returned to the classroom, students will discuss the data that they collected from the field trip and analyze the best strategies to share the information with another fourth-grade class.
- Lastly, students will revisit their previously taken notes on the sources from Dimension 2 and discuss possible ideas that they could incorporate into their multimedia sharings.

Teachers may implement this task with the following procedures:
- Have students visit a local nature center, have a representative from a local nation center speak to the class, or have students access the website of a local nature center (Source B).
- Provide students with a graphic organizer that helps them answer the questions "How do various species migrate from place to place?" and "What impacts do these species have on their new environments?" (Source A).
- Guide students in integrating the evidence they gathered from their field trip, speaker, or website.
- Conduct small discussions focusing on what they could share with another fourth-grade class.
- Encourage students to discuss possible ideas they could incorporate into a multimedia presentation about the topic.

The following scaffolds and other materials may be used to support students as they work with sources: Teachers can use cooperative grouping, writing organizers, and multimedia templates.

The following sources were selected to support students in researching the environmental impacts of migration.
- **Source A:** Social studies notebook Venn diagram
- **Source B:** Local nature centers *Search your specific state's nature centers on their state website*

Exit Ticket Suggestion:
After the students complete the activities outlined in Dimension 3, ask them to revisit their initial responses to "How would you define a trend?" Prompt students to reflect on their thoughts and whether their views have changed based on what they learned and discussed. Have students document their revised thoughts in their social studies notebooks.

Dimension 4

Overview

Dimension 4 of the C3 Framework emphasizes the importance of students communicating conclusions and taking informed action based on their civic knowledge. In the multidisciplinary lesson outlined, Dimension 4 activities are tailored to embody this focus, ensuring that students not only learn about the push/pull factors of migration but also actively participate by creating a multimedia presentation, participating in a class discussion, and contacting a state official about the impact of migration on the environment. These hands-on approaches allow students to present their understanding of the impacts of migrations in a variety of ways.

The structure of these activities supports the C3 Framework's goals by providing students with authentic experiences that enhance their understanding of the impact of push/pull factors on migration. In addition, they learn how the migration of a variety of species impacts the environment. Throughout this process, students are engaged in critical thinking, problem-solving, and collaborative decision-making, reflecting the core of active civic participation. The lessons also involve evaluating and reflecting on the effectiveness of their advocacy efforts, thereby fostering a deeper understanding of the civic processes and encouraging ongoing engagement. This aligns with the C3 Framework's aim to prepare students for active participation in civic life, making the activities in Dimension 4 not only educational but also transformative in equipping students with the skills necessary for informed civic action.

Supporting Question 1

The first supporting question is "In what ways does analyzing the community-level effects of immigration and migration contribute to our understanding of economic transformations?"

The formative task is that students will create a YouTube video to present their insights on how immigration and migration impacts their community. The video will include background information, highlights from a class interview with a local migrant (Sources A & B), and an analysis of changes in the local economy.

Teachers may implement this task with the following procedures:
- Guide students in preparing and developing their YouTube videos, focusing on clear articulation of their findings, justification using evidence, and persuasive techniques.
- Implement peer review sessions where groups evaluate the content of the YouTube videos, providing feedback for improvement.

The following scaffolds and other materials may be used to support students as they work with sources: The teacher can use guidelines for effective presentations, feedback forums, checklists for presentations components, and rubrics for peer feedback on effectiveness of the YouTube videos to support student success.

The following sources were selected to help ensure that the students' presentations are based on evidence from their research, which is essential for effective communication.
- **Source A:** Clips from class interview
- **Source B:** Notes from class interview from social studies notebook

Supporting Question 2

The second supporting question is "What factors should be considered when identifying trends of immigration and migration?"

The formative task is that students will collaboratively develop trend identification criteria and conduct trend analyses. Small groups will then present their chosen trends and apply the established criteria to evaluate each one. Each group will then develop personalized action plans based on their analysis. After peer review and feedback, groups will implement their plans with teacher monitoring. Finally, students will debrief their analyses and discuss real-world applications of these skills.

Teachers may implement this task with the following procedures:
- Facilitate a session where students brainstorm and agree on a set of criteria for analyzing trends in migrations. Provide guidance and examples of effective criteria to ensure the rubric is comprehensive and applicable.
- Allow small groups to present their chosen trends and apply the established criteria to evaluate trends. Then allow each group to developed personalized action plans based on their analysis.
- Conduct a peer review and feedback session where students evaluate their peers' action plans.
- Following the peer review session, students will discuss the real-word applications of their analytical skills.

The following scaffolds and other materials may be used to support students as they work with sources: The teacher can offer blank templates that students can take notes on the comments and feedback of their peers concerning their trend analyses.

The following sources were selected to foster critical thinking, decision-making, and analytical assessment.
- **Source A:** Migration Policy Institute. (n.d.). *Migration data hub.* www.migrationpolicy.org/programs/migration-data-hub
- **Source B:** Notes on trends from social studies notebook

Supporting Question 3

The third supporting question is "How can we show our support to those who dedicate their work to restoring populations such as sturgeons?"

The formative task is that students will write a handwritten letter to a key figure at their state Department of Natural Resources, sharing their experiences at their local nature center to express support for nature conservation efforts.

Teachers may implement this task with the following procedures:
- Provide examples of letters written to government officials.
- Allow students to receive feedback on letters emphasizing the importance of engaging with feedback to refine their communication skills.

The following scaffolds and other materials may be used to support students as they work with sources: The teacher can use cooperative grouping, sentence starters, examples of common language used in formal writing, and teacher conferences to support students in the development of their letters.

The following sources were selected to invite students to effectively reflect on the civic responsibility of contacting government officials.
- **Source A:** Key figure in state's Department of Natural Resources
- **Source B:** Notes from their social studies notebook on the field trip to the nature center

Summative Performance Task

In the summative performance task of this multi-disciplinary inquiry, students demonstrate their understanding of the population density, push/pull factors for migration, the impacts of migration on the local community, advocacy, and civic engagement by constructing educational multimedia projects and contacting local officials. They will then reflect on their learning process, participation, and the potential real-world impact of their projects. Each student group will present their ideas to their classmates, other classes, the local community, and government officials. Presentations and letters should include a detailed explanation of what they learned about these topics.

ARGUMENT Compose a written argument that enhances the compelling question by presenting specific claims and applicable evidence drawn from historical sources, all while recognizing different points of view. Students' arguments will likely vary, but could include any of the following: Migration and immigration have affected and continue to affect global growth in several ways such as making a contribution to a larger work force, boosting innovation, and stimulating economic activity while also considering the different perspectives of cultural and social impacts, environmental pressures, and short-term costs. To support students in their writing, teachers can provide students with a structured outline, use sentence stems, and engage them in diverse texts.

EXTENSION To extend their arguments, students will create a pamphlet detailing the outcome of migration into places of their choice, closing in on the impact on how land and resources were affected, as well as the dynamics of push/pull factors. Students may choose to use the information they had gathered through Dimension 3's formative assessment task and expand on what they learned to be included in their pamphlet

UNDERSTAND Students connect their learning about migration/immigration to current instances within their own community. This involves identifying ways in which their community is impacted by migrants and understanding how migration trends can be leveraged to make economic changes.

ASSESS Students examine the costs and benefits of immigration and migration. They will evaluate the potential impacts of trends in immigration and migration considering location and outcomes of implementing change.

ACT Students have the opportunity to Take Informed Action by engaging in hands-on approaches that will best allow them to present their understanding of the impacts of migrations. Students will write a letter to their local Department of Natural Resources (e.g., Randy Claramunt, the Chief of the Fisheries Division at the Michigan Department of Natural Resources), that outlines support for their efforts. Teachers should locate their own state's Department of Natural Resources to determine a significant role in which students can write a letter.

References

Burcar, C. (2019). *It happened in Michigan: Stories of events and people that shaped Great Lakes state history.* Globe Pequot Press.

CrashCourse. (2021, November 8). *How populations grow and change: Crash course geography #33* [Video]. YouTube. www.youtube.com/watch?v=JpAiBg0hrfQ

Dennis, E. (2022). *The boy from Mexico: An immigration story of bravery and determination.* Dragonfruit.

Grant, L., & Swan. (n.d.). *Inquiry Design Model (IDM)—At a glance.* https://c3teachers.org/idm/

KISM 9 NEWS. (2022, December 20). *Residents in South El Paso worry about impact of migrants on their neighborhood* [Video]. YouTube. www.youtube.com/watch?v=wqz1M8Rp7Lo

Lickley, D. (Director). (2008). *Mysteries of the Great Lakes* [Film]. Science North.

Migration Policy Institute. (n.d.). *Migration data hub.* www.migrationpolicy.org/programs/migration-data-hub

National Council for the Social Studies. (2010). *National curriculum standards for social studies: A framework for teaching, learning, and assessment.*

National Council for the Social Studies. (2013). *The college, career, and civic life (C3) framework for social studies state standards: Guidance for enhancing the rigor of K–12 civics, economics, geography, and history.*

Wedge, C. (Director). (2002). *Ice age* [Film]. Blue Sky Studies; 20th Century Fox Animation.

CAMERON PACK

High School World History

What did the Lost Generation lose?

Supporting Question Dimension 2
1. How did the experiences of World War I contribute to shaping the identity and values of the Lost Generation?

Supporting Questions Dimension 3
1. In what ways did the disillusionment with societal norms and institutions influence the artistic works produced by the Lost Generation?
2. How did the search for meaning in their experiences during World War I affect the Lost Generation?

Supporting Questions Dimension 4
1. Now that you have finished the unit, what are some contemporary issues that relate to our supporting questions?

High School World History

	What did the Lost Generation lose?
Standards and Content	**C3 Standards:** D2.His.12.9-12. Use questions generated about multiple historical sources to pursue further inquiry and investigate additional sources. D3.3.9-12. Identify evidence that draws information directly and substantially from multiple sources to detect inconsistencies in evidence in order to revise or strengthen claims D4.1.9-12. Construct arguments using precise and knowledgeable claims, with evidence from multiple sources, while acknowledging counterclaims and evidentiary weaknesses. **NCSS Themes:** ● People, Places, and Environments ● Individual Development and Identity
Staging the Compelling Question	**Dimension 1:** Define Generation Z. In groups, review teacher-made generation cards with traits and characteristics of different generations (Lost Generation, Greatest Generation, Silent Generation, Baby Boomers, Generation X, Millennials, Generation Z). Arrange the generations in chronological order based on birth years. Write a brief explanation of how they arrived at their conclusion. Match a generation-defining event (e.g., WWI, WWII, 9/11) with the corresponding generation. Hypothesize how each generation received its moniker, based on the defining event. Participate in a Teacher Talk about the importance of understanding generational perspectives and how historical events shape societal views.

Dimension 2

Supporting Question 1
How did the experiences of World War I contribute to shaping the identity and values of the Lost Generation?
Formative Performance Task
Annotate primary source documents to determine how World War I helped shape the collective identity of the Lost Generation. Analyze the experience of soldiers during this time.
Featured Sources
Source A: Interview with Andrew Johnson **Source B:** Interview with Conscientious Objector **Source C:** Harry L. Frieman Collection

Exit Ticket Suggestion: Using the 3-2-1 instructional strategy, have the students write down three things they learned in Dimension 2, two things they still have questions about, and one thing they need more help in understanding.

Dimension 3

Supporting Question 1	**Supporting Question 2**
In what ways did the disillusionment with societal norms and institutions influence the artistic works produced by the Lost Generation?	How did the search for meaning in their experiences during World War I affect the Lost Generation?
Formative Performance Task	**Formative Performance Task**
Watch *All Quiet on the Western Front* (1979) from 2:07:00 to 02:13:00 (the letter scene) and complete a Sticky-Note Storm. Participate in a Teacher Talk connecting experiences in war with forms of expression. In cooperative groups, read chapter 12 of the book *All Quiet on the Western Front* or the painting *Sunday Morning of Cunel*.	Complete a Poetry Gallery Walk in collaborative groups of four. Answer a teacher-made source guide
Featured Sources	**Featured Sources**
Source A: *Sunday Morning at Cunel* by Harvey Thomas Dunn (Painting) **Source B:** The letter scene (2:07:00–2:13:00) in *All Quiet on the Western Front* (Film) **Source C:** Chapter 12 in *All Quiet on the Western Front* by Erich Maria Remarque (Book)	**Source A:** "Trench Poets" by Edgell Rickword (Poem) **Source B:** "War and Peace" by Edgell Rickword (Poem) **Source C:** "Soldier From the Wars Returning" by A. E. Housman (Poem) **Source D:** "For a War Memorial" by G. K. Chesterton (Poem) **Source E:** "Laventie" by Ivor Gurney (Poem) **Source F:** Poems in *The Evening Herald*, May 6, 1919

Exit Ticket:
Have the students finish the prompt, "World War I veterans reflected their experiences through…"

Dimension 4

Supporting Question 1
Now that you have finished the unit, what are some contemporary issues that relate to our supporting questions?
Formative Performance Task
Make a list of things that Generation Z may have lost that former generations have or had. Determine ways to express their experiences of being Generation Z.
Featured Sources
All sources from Dimensions 1–3 can be used for this dimension.

Summative Performance Task	**ARGUMENT** *What did the Lost Generation lose?* Construct an argument in response to the compelling question consisting of claims with evidence that presents why the Lost Generation was called "lost"?
	EXTENSION Explore WWI biographies from the U.S. Department of Veterans Affairs **https://department.va.gov/history/**) and determine the similarities and differences among World War I veteran experiences.
Taking Informed Action	**UNDERSTAND** Connect historical content to contemporary issues by selecting what your generation has lost in comparison to previous generations. **ASSESS** Devise a comprehensive plan of action to express your experiences of being Generation Z. **ACT** Actively implement your action plan to express your experiences of being Generation Z.

Overview

Inquiry Description

This C3 inquiry guides students in examining the experiences of a generation during World War I, specifically the soldiers who participated in it. Students will analyze historical sources from World War I in order to determine how the battlefield experiences may have affected soldiers, how the war may have affected their generation, and how they found meaning to their lives afterward. Students then take this information and apply it to what their generation has experienced. Through analyzing primary and secondary documents, poetry, artwork, and films, students will assess how shared experiences can affect a generation.

Note. This inquiry is expected to take 9 days (50-minute class periods). Teachers can expand the inquiry process by adding extra elements like supporting questions, tasks, sources, writing tasks, or videos. It is advised that educators tailor the inquiry to suit their students' individual needs and interests. This framework encourages personalized learning and helps students enhance their historical thinking abilities by evaluating various sources critically.

Structure of the Inquiry

Dimension 1: The "hook" activity introduces students to the compelling question and a Reverse Frayer Model to gain understanding of different generational experiences and the monikers attached to them.
Dimension 2: Students analyze and annotate primary source documents to gain a deeper understanding of World War I veterans.
Dimension 3: This dimension will include an analysis and comparison of a film, book, and painting, along with a poetry Gallery Walk.
Dimension 4: Students will create an action plan and implement it with an authentic assessment.

Dimension 1

Staging the Compelling Question

Teachers may implement this task with the following procedures:
- On a whiteboard or smartboard, write the compelling question, "What did the Lost Generation lose?"
- On the whiteboard or smartboard, write the statement, "Define Generation Z."
- Divide the class into groups and hand out teacher-made generation cards, listing the traits and characteristics of each generation, but not the inclusive years. These generations include the Lost Generation, Greatest Generation, Silent Generation, Baby Boomers, Generation X, Millennials, and Generation Z.
- Students try to place the generations in the order that they were born and then write down how they arrived at this conclusion.
- Then, have them match a generation-defining event (i.e., WWI, WWII, 9/11) with the generation they believe corresponds with the event.
- Students then hypothesize how these generations received their monikers, based on the defining event that occurred. This instructional strategy is known as the Reverse Frayer Model, and another example of this strategy can be found on the Cult of Pedagogy's YouTube channel.

- Facilitate a Teacher Talk on the importance of understanding generational perspectives and the ways that historical events can shape societal views of different age groups.

Staging Exercise Source: Gonzalez, J. [Cult of Pedagogy]. (2014, September 17). *How to teach an inductive learning lesson* [Video]. YouTube. www.youtube.com/watch?v=-RlLVQYhJt8

Dimension 2

Supporting Question 1

Bell Ringer: Present the following question on a whiteboard or smartboard: "What shared trauma has your generation experienced?" Based on the students' answers, ask follow-up questions about how that event was traumatic and make a connection with a traumatic event from the teacher's generation (e.g., 9/11, Challenger Explosion, etc.). Your final question to the class should be "How might a world war affect a generation?"

The first supporting question is "How did the experiences of World War I contribute to shaping the identity and values of the Lost Generation?"

The formative task is as follows:
- Determine how World War I helped shape the collective identity of the Lost Generation by annotating primary source documents.
- Analyze the experience of soldiers during this time.

Teachers may implement this task with the following procedures:
- Divide the class into three cooperative groups. Each group will analyze and annotate a different primary source document. The annotation should be done individually with the students underlining the main point, circling words they do not know, and starring something they find interesting.
- Once they have completed the individual annotation, they share their annotations with the group. Then, the teacher facilitates by having the students answer each other's questions that they may have from the reading or unknown vocabulary words.
- The groups will rotate documents until each group has analyzed and annotated each document.
- Finish with a Teacher Talk about how these traumatic events were shared by young men and women from all the nations involved in World War I.

The following scaffolds and other materials may be used to support students as they work with sources: To assist students effectively, teachers can employ cooperative grouping or differentiation based on student need. Providing one-on-one instruction is also a viable approach within this lesson. Utilizing formative assessments to monitor progress toward objectives throughout the tasks can aid in maintaining student engagement and understanding.

The following sources were selected to complete the tasks:
- **Source A:** Hubert, L. C., & Johnson, A. (1938). [Andrew Johnson] [Interview Transcript]. Library of Congress. **https://**www.loc.gov/item/wpalh001413/
- **Source B:** Walden, W., & Turner, J. (1938). [Conscientious Objector] [Interview Transcript]. Library of Congress. https://www.loc.gov/item/wpalh001666/
- **Source C:** Frieman, J. & Frieman, H. L. (1917) Harry L. Frieman Collection. [Personal Narrative]. Library of Congress, https://www.loc.gov/item/afc2001001.23600/.

Dimension 3

Supporting Question 1

Bell Ringer:
- As the students walk in, play the song "Stick Season" by Noah Kahan. The students will sit and listen in silence. Once the song is complete, ask them which lyric informs people that the song was written after 2019. The lyric video will show the lyrics in the first verse.
- At this point the teacher can stop the song and reiterate the question. Students may mention that there are cars in the song, but given enough time, there is a high likelihood that the students will bring up the line about COVID-19.

Once this has been brought up, ask how this artist's music had been affected by a shared generational event.

Bell Ringer Source:
Kahan, N. (2022, July 8). *Noah Kahan - Stick Season (Official Lyric Video).* YouTube. www.youtube.com/watch?v=iWG6apzIWAk

The first supporting question is "In what ways did the disillusionment with societal norms and institutions influence the artistic works produced by the Lost Generation?"

The formative task is as follows: Using a Write Around instructional strategy, ask students to answer how World War I veterans reflected their experiences through works of art after the war. This will be done in three to four sentences.

These activities highlight different artistic works produced by members of the Lost Generation, especially those a part of the defining event of this generation: World War I. Based on the nature of the artwork, the students will determine if the art was affected by their disillusionment with the institutions that sent them to war.

Teachers may implement this task with the following procedures:
- Students will watch a scene from *All Quiet on the Western Front* (2:07:00-2:13:00; Source B) and complete a Sticky Note Storm over what they have watched. A Sticky Note Storm can be conducted by having students write down everything they noticed or thought of during the movie scene in two minutes on separate sticky notes. Their goal should be to cover their desks with thoughts in two minutes.
- The teacher should facilitate a conversation about the different ways experiences in war can affect art by connecting examples of living veterans and their effect on modern art. They can do this by exploring the Veteran Art Triennial (https://today.uic.edu/veteran-art-triennial-explores-the-transformative-power-of-art/).
- In cooperative groups, students will receive either a painting (Source A) or an excerpt from the book *All Quiet on the Western Front* (Chapter 12; Source C), based on the students' learning styles, in order to differentiate instruction. Make sure the students know these two works of art were created by veterans of World War I.
- Students finish the prompt, "World War I veterans reflected their experiences through..." with three to four sentences.

The following sources were selected to complete the tasks:
- **Source A:** Dunn, H. T. (2024). *Sunday Morning at Cunel* [Painting]. National Museum of American History, Smithsonian Institute. www.si.edu/es/object/sunday-morning-cunel:nmah_447412
- **Source B:** Mann, D. (1989). *All quiet on the western front* [Film]. Norman Rosemont Productions; Marble Arch Productions; ITC Entertainment.
- **Source C:** Remarque, E. M. (2025). *All quiet on the Western Front* (B. Murdoch, Trans.). Vintage. (Original work published 1929)

Supporting Question 2

Bell Ringer:
- Students freewrite for five minutes, creating a poem about something at school that affects them.
- Students share what they created.

The second supporting question is "How did the search for meaning in their experiences during World War One affect the Lost Generation?"

The formative task is as follows: In groups of four, students will complete a poetry Gallery Walk and answer a teacher-made source guide.

The following sources were selected to complete the tasks:
- **Source A:** Rickword, E. (1921a). *Trench poets.* Poetry Foundation. www.poetryfoundation.org/poems/57422/trench-poets
- **Source B:** Rickword, E. (1921b). *War and peace.* Poetry Foundation. www.poetryfoundation.org/poems/57421/war-and-peace-56d23aeecfe57
- **Source C:** Housman, A. E. (1922). *Soldier from the wars returning.* Poetry Foundation. www.poetryfoundation.org/poems/57367/soldier-from-the-wars-returning
- **Source D:** Chesterton, G. K. (1922). *For a war memorial.* Poetry Foundation. www.poetryfoundation.org/poems/48210/for-a-war-memorial

- Source E: Gurney, I. (n.d.). *Laventie*. Poetry Foundation. www.poetryfoundation.org/poems/57254/laventie
- Source F: *The evening herald*. (1919, May 6). Chronicling America, Section Two, Page Two. **https://chroniclingamerica.loc.gov/lccn/sn92070582/1919-05-06/ed-1/seq-8/**

Dimension 4

Overview

Dimension 4 helps students develop practical skills by connecting historical knowledge to modern contexts. Students take charge of their learning by creating their own inquiries, which promotes a sense of ownership. Teachers act as facilitators by guiding students through questioning instead of giving direct instructions. This phase highlights the significance of letting students lead their learning independently. By not giving direct answers and encouraging teamwork in problem solving, students can improve their skills in a supportive setting that values learning from errors and collaboration.

However, it is not the only way to have the students create an action plan and implement that plan. I recommend looking at inquiries on the C3 Teachers website (**https://c3teachers.org/inquiries/**) or in *Teaching the College, Career, and Civic Life (C3) Framework: Part Two* (Swan et al., 2018).

Summative Performance Task

Students are tasked with constructing a comprehensive, evidence-based argument in response to the compelling question: "What did the Lost Generation lose?" At this stage of inquiry, students have delved into the experiences and social issues faced by the Lost Generation and have traced both the intended and unintended consequences of their experiences and the ways they developed these experiences into works of art. Students are expected to showcase the depth of their comprehension and their ability to utilize evidence from diverse sources to bolster their individual claims. As students engage with the summative performance task, they are actively showcasing their proficiency in social studies skills such as gathering, utilizing, and interpreting evidence, as well as comparison and contextualization.

Prior to tackling the summative performance task, students may find it beneficial to revisit the provided sources from the previous dimensions. This review process can aid them in refining their assertions and pinpointing the pertinent evidence necessary to fortify their arguments.

While students' arguments may vary, they could potentially encompass viewpoints such as the following:
- The Lost Generation experienced significant losses as they were disillusioned by the aftermath of World War I, grappling with feelings of aimlessness and alienation.
- The Lost Generation lost their faith in traditional values and institutions, feeling disconnected from societal norms and cultural mores.
- The Lost Generation suffered the loss of innocence and optimism, as the horrors of war shattered their youthful idealism and optimism for the future.

Students can find validation for these arguments within the provided sources and through their meticulous analysis of the material.

References

Chesterton, G. K. (1922). *For a war memorial*. Poetry Foundation. www.poetryfoundation.org/poems/48210/for-a-war-memorial

Dunn, H. T. (2024). *Sunday Morning at Cunel* [Painting]. National Museum of American History, Smithsonian Institute. www.si.edu/es/object/sunday-morning-cunel:nmah_447412

The evening herald. (1919, May 6). Chronicling America, Section Two, Page Two. https://chroniclingamerica.loc.gov/lccn/sn92070582/1919-05-06/ed-1/seq-8/

Frieman, J., & Frieman, H. L. (1917). *Harry L. Frieman Collection*. Library of Congress. www.loc.gov/item/afc2001001.23600

Gonzalez, J. [Cult of Pedagogy]. (2014, September 17). *How to teach an inductive learning lesson* [Video]. YouTube. https://www.youtube.com/watch?v=-RlLVQYhJt8

Gurney, I. (n.d.). *Laventie*. Poetry Foundation. www.poetryfoundation.org/poems/57254/laventie

Housman, A. E. (1922). *Soldier from the wars returning*. Poetry Foundation. www.poetryfoundation.org/poems/57367/soldier-from-the-wars-returning

Hubert, L. C., & Johnson, A. (1938). [Andrew Johnson] [Interview Transcript]. Library of Congress. https://www.loc.gov/item/wpalh001413/

Kahan, N. (2022, July 8). *Noah Kahan – Stick Season (Official Lyric Video)*. YouTube. www.youtube.com/watch?v=iWG6apzIWAk

Mann, D. (1989). *All quiet on the western front* [Film]. Norman Rosemont Productions; Marble Arch Productions; ITC Entertainment.

Remarque, E. M. (2025). *All quiet on the Western Front* (B. Murdoch, Trans.). Vintage. (Original work published 1929)

Rickword, E. (1921a). *Trench poets*. Poetry Foundation. www.poetryfoundation.org/poems/57422/trench-poets

Rickword, E. (1921b). *War and peace*. Poetry Foundation. www.poetryfoundation.org/poems/57421/war-and-peace-56d23aeecfe57

UIC Today. (2023, April 14). *Veteran Art Triennial explores the "transformative power of art."* https://today.uic.edu/veteran-art-triennial-explores-the-transformative-power-of-art/

Walden, W., & Turner, J. (1938). [Conscientious Objector] [Interview Transcript]. Library of Congress. https://www.loc.gov/item/wpalh001666/

Jackson Magargee

High School World History

How did a vacation start a war?

Supporting Questions Dimension 2
1. Why was Europe on the brink of war?
2. Why did the war break out?
3. What were the results of fighting in 1914?

Supporting Questions Dimension 3
1. What makes a good historical source?
2. What primary sources are available that would provide insight into the events and perspectives leading up to the start of World War I?
3. Who is left out of the conversation when learning about World War I?

Supporting Questions Dimension 4
1. Using the new information from Dimensions 2 and 3, can we connect a current issue from our community that is similar to the unit?
2. As a class, describe a solution to the current issue.
3. As a class, design an action plan for the issue.

High School World History

	How did a vacation start a war?
Standards and Content	**C3 Framework:** D2.His.12.9-12. Use questions generated about multiple historical sources to pursue further inquiry and investigate additional sources. D3.3.9-12. Identify evidence that draws information directly and substantially from multiple sources to detect inconsistencies in evidence in order to revise or strengthen claims D4.1.9-12. Construct arguments using precise and knowledgeable claims, with evidence from multiple sources, while acknowledging counterclaims and evidentiary weaknesses. **NCSS Theme:** ❸ People, Places, and Environments
Staging the Compelling Question	**Dimension 1:** 1. Using the Quick Write Method, write a story (true or made up) answering the compelling question. 2. Using AI, ask "Could a vacation start a war?" 3. Complete a teacher-made graphic organizer and share with the class.

Dimension 2

Supporting Question 1	Supporting Question 2	Supporting Question 3
Why was Europe on the brink of war?	Why did the war break out?	What were the results of fighting in 1914?
Formative Performance Task	**Formative Performance Task**	**Formative Performance Task**
Watch the video (Source A) and complete the analysis tool (Source B). Complete a Frayer model (Source C) of vocabulary words concerning World War I (Source D): M.A.I.N. Militaristic Alliances Imperialism Nationalism	Watch the video (Source A) and answer the compelling question using evidence from the graphic organizer and today's video. Watch the video (Source B) and answer the supporting question using the evidence from their graphic organizer and today's new information to answer the supporting question.	In Jigsaw Groups, a. create your own map of Europe in World War I. b. describe the German Schlieffen Plan., c. discuss the western front, and d. discuss and in detail describe trench warfare.
Featured Sources	**Featured Sources**	**Featured Sources**
Source A: "6 Key Steps to World War One" (Video) **Source B:** Primary Source Analysis Tool, Library of Congress **Source C:** Frayer Model **Source D:** "The 4 M-A-I-N Causes of World War One" (article)	**Source A:** "How the assassination of Archduke Franz Ferdinand unfolded" (Video) **Source B:** "The 4 M-A-I-N Causes of World War One" (article)	**Source A:** Map from "The First World War in Europe, May 1917" **Source B:** Teacher-supplied map

Dimension 3

Suggested Bell Ringer:
1. Answer "What makes a good source?"
2. Describe characteristics of what is and is not a good source for learning.
3. Discuss what sources you have used and what constitutes those sources being good.
4. Transition to using AI to answer supporting question 1.

Supporting Question 1	Supporting Question 2	Supporting Question 3
What makes a good historical source?	What primary sources are available that would provide insight into the events and perspectives leading up to the start of World War I?	Who is left out of the conversation when learning about World War I?
Formative Performance Task	**Formative Performance Task**	**Formative Performance Task**
Observe the teacher using AI to model using the tool appropriately, asking a question to the AI tool, and clicking on the sources button. For the activity, go to one side of the room if you think the source is acceptable, and the other side if the source is unacceptable.	Read, source, contextualize and analyze primary sources from England prior to the war beginning (Sources A–E). Defend your stance to the teacher and other groups in the classroom.	Try to answer the supporting question using AI to research.
Featured Sources	**Featured Sources**	**Featured Sources**
Source A: AI tool (such as Perplexity, MagicSchool, ChatGPT, or SchoolAI)	**Source A:** MP Profiles **Source B:** Speech transcripts **Source C:** House of Commons Chamber, 1914 (Image) **Source D:** WWI Memorial, Westminster Hall (Image) **Source E:** Map of Europe, c. 1914	**Source A:** AI tool (such as Perplexity, MagicSchool, ChatGPT, or SchoolAI)

Dimension 4

Supporting Question 1	Supporting Question 2	Supporting Question 1
Using the new information from Dimensions 2 and 3, can we connect a current issue from our community that is similar to the unit?	As a class, describe a solution to the current issue.	As a class, design an action plan for the issue.
Formative Performance Task	**Formative Performance Task**	**Formative Performance Task**
Make a list of things you want to discuss in your community. Discuss how your topics relate to the content.	Make a list of solutions for their topic. Make sure you know the boundaries of the district and follow all school policies in your Action Plan.	Create an action plan.

	Featured Sources		Featured Sources		Featured Sources
	None		None		None

Summative Performance Task	**ARGUMENT** *How did a vacation start a war?* Using content from Dimensions 2 and 3, answer the compelling question in a P.E.E.L. paragraph using evidence.
	EXTENSION Explore the virtual exhibits from the World War I museum and write down what you notice, ranging from what you see, to what the videos say, to what takeaways you have (www.theworldwar.org/learn/educator-resource/immersive-tour-trenches-world-war-i). Watch the miniseries *37 Days* (2014) produced by BBC to help with the differing countries at play prior to the war breaking out. It shows the attitudes and reasons why the war started and also shows a lack of voice from anyone other than men in charge.
Taking Informed Action	**UNDERSTAND** Look at problems within your own school, local community, or state that can relate to the content from the unit.
	ASSESS Select a solution to an issue in the community or classroom.
	ACT Implement the solution with a student-led action plan.

Overview

Inquiry Description

This inquiry leads students through an investigation of the causes and buildup to World War I. Students are asked in Dimension 1, "How did a vacation start a war?" The students engage in an activity to hook them in to learn about WWI and to introduce the compelling question.

In Dimension 2, students will examine the supporting questions. (This will probably take two days of class for content). Students do this through two documentaries hosted by the historian Dan Snow. Students will work on Frayer models using the terms "militarism," "nationalism," "imperialism," and "alliances." These will be done in small groups for one term, and then the other groups will detail what they found and share with the class for all students to add to their models. Students then fill in a blank map provided by the teacher to fill in with the countries of Britain, France, Germany, Austria-Hungary, and Russia. Students will then use the reading from History Hit to discuss the Schlieffen plan and be asked if they thought it was a quality plan. Following that, they will then be told about the Western Front, be able to find it on a map, and be able to describe its importance (Jigsaw strategy is used).

Dimension 3 uses an AI chatbot like Perplexity. Making sure that students understand how to work the program is important, so the teacher should model it. Perplexity (**https://www.perplexity.ai/**) is suggested because it provides the sources on the same page as the answer so students can fact check. *Note.* Different AI programs that do not show the evidence can be used. However, by simply asking an AI chatbot "What sources did you use to provide this answer?" students can use that evidence to make a more informed analysis. Lastly with AI, students will ask it questions about some lesser-known people in World War I using Bloom's Taxonomy stems or quality questions.

In Dimension 4, students will take informed action in their community or classroom, and the P.E.E.L. or summative performance task is assigned. A P.E.E.L. paragraph is when the students write a paragraph making a point, using evidence, then explain their reasoning, and then link it to the content. Students will be asked to create a list of issues in their local community or classroom that have some connection to the content in the previous dimensions. The solutions must stay within reason and within the boundaries set by the district, principal, or department. Once a solution is selected, students must begin implementation. They will use their historical thinking skills to implement their plan that fits within policies and teacher facilitation.

Note. This inquiry should take 12–15 50-minute class periods. There is room for expanding the time frame if the teacher feels that students need additional class periods to grasp the concepts. Adding supporting questions or featuring different sources to better fit their class is encouraged. There are paths to differentiation in the inquiry using group work.

Structure of the Inquiry

Dimension 1: Introduction to the compelling question and staging activities
Dimension 2: Historical content (using C3 Framework, NCSS Themes, and state/district curriculum)
Dimension 3: Analyzing primary sources to formulate arguments related to the content
Dimension 4: Taking informed action through identifying a problem in the community and implementing a solution

Dimension 1

Staging the Compelling Question

Teachers may implement this task with the following procedures:
- Using the Quick Write Method, have the students write a story (true or fictional) answering the question, "Can a vacation start a war?" (15 minutes)
- Have some students share their stories with the class. (10 minutes)
- Have the students score the stories on a scale of 1-5: 1 being believable to 5 being total fiction. (5 minutes)
- Have the students ask the Quick Write question to an AI chatbot. Have the students share out what they found. (Perplexity is recommended.) (10 minutes)
- Using the student stories and AI information, ask "Was there a vacation that started a war?" (5 minutes)
- Students guess. The teacher will share the correct answer and give a short introduction. (5 minutes)

Note. The goal of the Teacher Talk in this staging activity is for the teacher to ask more questions to pull the terms from the teacher talk: "militarism," "nationalism," "alliances," and "imperialism."

Dimension 2

Supporting Question 1

The first supporting question is "Why was Europe on the brink of War in 1914?"

The formative task is as follows:
- Watch the video (Source A) and complete the analysis tool (Source B).
- Complete a Frayer model (Source C) of vocabulary words concerning World War I (Source D).

On day one, teachers may implement this task with the following procedures:
- Teachers will show the History Hit video (Source A).
- Have students fill out the Library of Congress Primary Source Analysis Tool (Source B) while watching the video in sections.
    - Introduction: 0:00–1:10
    - World of Empires: 1:11–8:56
    - Archduke: 8:57–11:06
    - Austria-Hungary: 11:07–15:16
    - Russia: 15:17–17:18
    - The War: 17:19–23:08
    - Conclusion: 23:09–end

- Students will watch the clips and then the teacher will conduct a teacher talk so the students fill out the appropriate section of the graphic organizer. Teachers will ask the students these questions after every clip.
    - Observe (Identifying details of the narration and sources on the screen):
        - Describe what you heard from the historian.
        - What did you see from the visuals?
        - How was the information/visuals arranged?
        - What are other details you need to add.
    - Reflect (Thinking about the source):
        - Who is the narrator?
- Is this a viable source?
- Are the primary sources in the video credible?
- What can you take away from this documentary?
    - Question (Observing the content of the video):
        - Who?
        - What?
        - When?
        - Where?
        - Why?
        - How?
    - Further Investigation:
        - What more do you need to know to answer the supporting question?
        - What are sources or tools we can turn to?

On day two, teachers may implement this task with the following procedures:
- Have the students get a sheet of notebook paper and a pencil to make a Frayer Model.
- Guide Students on how to make a Frayer Model using Source C. Make sure students only use half of the front page for the first one because they will make four in total (two per side).
- Groups of students will then be assigned one of the four terms: "militarism," "nationalism," "imperialism," or "alliances." Each group will be given one of the four terms for their Frayer Model.
- Allow students 10–12 minutes to fill out their Frayer Models. They should be using resources, such as Source D, technology, or a classroom textbook, to search for information.
- Then, convene as a class to Teacher Talk all four terms together. These will answer the supporting question by using the video and Frayer Models as evidence.
- *Note*. If there are more than four groups, more than one group can be working on a particular term.

The following scaffolds and other materials may be used to support students as they work with sources: Teachers have the option to use data-driven differentiation as well as formative assessments to check in on students throughout the lesson.

The following sources were selected to complete the tasks:
- **Source A:** History Hit. (2023, October 25). *6 Key Steps to World War One* [Video]. YouTube. www.youtube.com/watch?v=y-TmbOy4Jwg
- **Source B:** Library of Congress. (n.d.). *Primary source analysis tool for students*. www.loc.gov/programs/teachers/getting-started-with-primary-sources/guides/
- **Source C:** Wisconsin Department of Public Instruction. (n.d.). Frayer Model 6–12. https://dpi.wi.gov/reading/literacy-practices-bank
- **Source D:** Browne, A. (2021, September 28). *The 4 M-A-I-N causes of World War One*. History Hit. www.historyhit.com/the-4-m-a-i-n-causes-of-world-war-one/

Supporting Question 2

The second supporting question is "Why did the war break out?"

The formative task is to analyze the material, read and annotate readings and research, and use Teacher Talk to extract content from the students about the material.

Teachers may implement this task with the following procedures:
- Teachers will show the History Hit video (Source A).
- Teachers will ask the students "How did a vacation start a war?" Have the students share their thoughts using evidence from the graphic organizer (Source B in Supporting Question 1) and today's video.

- Students read the article from History Hit (Source B) aloud in a popcorn-style activity, and the teacher will ask the supporting question after each paragraph. Students use information from the Teacher Talk, evidence from their graphic organizer, and today's new information to answer the supporting question.
- Another method could be having the students read silently and use the sticky note strategy (see Scaffolds below) to take notes for discussion. The two reading options depend on your class. If many of the students have advanced literacy skills, the sticky note method may fit well. Classes with more auditory learners may need to read aloud using popcorn reading.
- The teacher will then hold a Teacher Talk after the conclusion of the reading by asking the compelling question again and ask if students would amend their answers from the beginning of class.

The following scaffolds and other materials may be used to support students as they work with sources:
- Teachers have the options to use data-driven differentiation, as well as implementing formative assessments to check in on students throughout the lesson.
- Reading techniques for teachers from https://www.cde.state.co.us/sites/default/files/documents/coloradoliteracy/clf/downloads/oral_reading_techniques.pdf
- Sticky note strategy for reading from Willis, J. (2018, January 8). *Aiding reading comprehension with post-its*. Edutopia. https://www.edutopia.org/article/aiding-reading-comprehension-post-its/

The following sources were selected to complete the tasks:
- **Source A:** History Hit. (2014, June 27). *How the assassination of Archduke Franz Ferdinand unfolded, with Dan Snow* [Video]. YouTube. www.youtube.com/watch?v=OfO7TduevHA
- **Source B:** Browne, A. (2021, September 28). *The 4 M-A-I-N causes of World War One*. History Hit. www.historyhit.com/the-4-m-a-i-n-causes-of-world-war-one/

Supporting Question 3

The third supporting question is "What were the results of fighting in 1914?"

The formative task is as follows:
- Use AI to model to the class how to use the tool appropriately.
- Look at the sources individually; usually there are between four and six sources.
- For the activity, have students go to one side of the room if they think the source is acceptable, and the other side if the source is unacceptable.
- The teacher will then have the students pull up an AI Chatbot for them to work with.
- Students will try to answer the supporting question using AI to research.

Teachers may implement this task with the following procedures:
- Students will look at a map of Europe in World War I (Source A).
- In Jigsaw Groups, the students will be asked to
    a) create their own map of Europe in World War I (A teacher-made map will need to be handed out to the students. Students will fill in the countries of France, Germany, Britain, Russia, Austria-Hungary. They will also label where the western front is on their maps),
    b) describe the German Schlieffen Plan,
    c) discuss the western front, and
    d) discuss and describe trench warfare in detail.
- There will be four expert groups that will be assigned a letter (activity) described above.
- Students will rotate to the Share Out Group where the other students teach their expertise.
- The teacher will conduct a Teacher Talk to make sure all content is correct. The teacher will fill in gaps of content or share other stories or sources as necessary.

The following scaffolds and other materials may be used to support students as they work with sources: Teachers have the options to use data-driven differentiation, as well as implementing formative assessments to check in on students throughout the lesson.

The following sources were selected to complete the tasks:
- **Source A:** Map from Netchev, S. (2023, November 3). *The First World War in Europe, May 1917*. World History Encyclopedia. www.worldhistory.org/image/18098/the-first-world-war-in-europe-may-1917/
- **Source B:** Teacher-supplied map

Dimension 3

Supporting Question 1

Suggested Bell Ringer:
- Ask "What makes a good source?" Have students describe characteristics of what is and is not a good source for learning. Ask "How do you know?" Then ask "How would you check if something is an accurate source?"
- Begin the lesson by saying, "Expanding on what was learned earlier about the causes of WWI, let's look at how to use primary sources to enhance our learning."

The first supporting question is "What makes a good historical source?"

The formative task is as follows:
- Use AI to model to the class how to use the tool appropriately.
- Have the teacher ask a question to the AI tool and click on the sources button.
- Look at the sources individually, usually there are between four and six sources.
- For the activity, have students go to one side of the room if they think the source is acceptable, and the other side if the source is unacceptable.

Teachers may implement this task with the following procedures:
- First, set up a projector to display Perplexity (**https://www.perplexity.ai/**) and get the class prepared to ask a question.
- Ask the AI tool a topical question about one of the causes of WWI.
- Use the *View More Sources* button to look at the sources individually. Usually there are about four to six different sources.
- For the activity, post the word "Acceptable" on one side of the room and "Not Acceptable" on the other side of the room.
- For each of the sources, click on the link to the source and look at it. Look at the url and the type of publication (journal, blog, book, etc.), compare it to other sources. After evaluating each source, have students go to the side of the room where they believe the source falls. Ask the students that group on one side "Why?" The teacher will confirm which type of source is acceptable or not.
- *Note.* Any sort of AI chatbot will work for this. Alternatives can be finding different sources through the AI tools to back up the statements that AI says about whatever question the class asks AI. If using an alternative AI source, ask the AI what sources it used to create the answer.

The following scaffolds and other materials may be used to support students as they work with sources: Teachers have the option to use data-driven differentiation as well as formative assessments to check in on students throughout the lesson.

The following source was selected to complete the tasks:
Source A: AI tool (such as Perplexity, MagicSchool, ChatGPT, or SchoolAI)

Supporting Question 2

The second supporting question is "What primary sources are available that would provide insight into the events and perspectives leading up to the start of World War I?"

The formative task is as follows:
- The teacher will follow the guide to create the lessons.
- Students will read, source, contextualize and analyze primary sources from England prior to the war beginning (Sources A-E).
- Students will defend their stance to the teacher and other groups in the classroom.
- The class should do this activity independently and then discuss their findings and sources at the end of class.

Teachers may implement this task with the following procedures:
- Follow the guide and resource pack "World War One and Parliament" from UK Parliament (**https://learning.parliament.uk/en/resources/world-war-one-and-parliament/**).
- Students should have skills now to identify quality sources, so create a graphic organizer asking where the publications were from, when the source was published, who the author is, etc.

- The teacher can provide the terms and have students find at least one publication for three of the terms used in the unit up to this point. The terms can be any of the following: "militarism," "nationalism," "alliances," "imperialism," "western front," "trench warfare."
- Students can use any of their resources to find these publications, but they must be able to find all the elements required on the teacher-made graphic organizer.

The following scaffolds and other materials may be used to support students as they work with sources: Teachers have the options to use data-driven differentiation as well as formative assessments to check in on students throughout the lesson.

The following sources were selected to complete the tasks. The sources are from the resource pack "World War One and Parliament" from UK Parliament (**https://learning.parliament.uk/en/resources/world-war-one-and-parliament/**):
- **Source A:** MP Profiles
- **Source B:** Speech transcripts
- **Source C:** House of Commons Chamber, 1914 (Image)
- **Source D:** WWI Memorial, Westminster Hall (Image)
- **Source E:** Map of Europe, c. 1914

Supporting Question 3

The third supporting question is "Who is left out of the conversation when learning about World War I?"

The formative task is as follows:
- The teacher will have the students pull up an AI Chatbot for them to work with.
- Students will try to answer the supporting question using AI to research.
- *Note.* The teachers can use Bloom's Taxonomy sentence starters on the AI. Teaching and modeling may help students dialogue to get better answers from AI. Using some of the sentence starters, the students will ask their own questions to the AI to explore and create individual inquiry.

Teachers may implement this task with the following procedures:
- The teacher will instruct the students to use their computers to pull up the AI tool of your choice. Perplexity (**https://www.perplexity.ai/**) is suggested for this lesson. Alternatives will be provided in the featured sources.
- Provide strict guidelines for this lesson. Students should have clear expectations of staying on topic and only looking up things that are related to the topic.
- Students will ask the following four questions using AI tools:
  - Who were important women in WWI?
  - Who were important children in WWI?
  - Who were important minorities in WWI?
  - What was the black hand's role in WWI?
- After each question, ask the students what their results were. Then use those results to make a small list on the board for the students to reference.
- After that, have students look up Bloom's Taxonomy sentence starters and then allow them to choose one from each of the five levels of Bloom's Taxonomy to ask their own questions to the AI to explore and create individual inquiry.
- *Note.* The teachers can use Bloom's Taxonomy sentence starters on the AI. Teaching and modeling may help students dialogue to get better answers from AI. Using some of the sentence starters, the students will ask their own questions to the AI to explore and create individual inquiry.

The following scaffolds and other materials may be used to support students as they work with sources: Teachers have the options to use data-driven differentiation as well as formative assessments to check in on students throughout the lesson.

The following source was selected to complete the tasks:
Source A: AI tool (such as Perplexity, MagicSchool, ChatGPT, or SchoolAI)

Dimension 4

Supporting Question 1

The first supporting question is "Using the new information from Dimensions 2 and 3, can we connect a current issue from our community that is similar to the unit?"

The formative task is to create topics to form an action plan in the community.

Teachers may implement this task with the following procedures:
- Ask the supporting question.
- Ask the students for ideas about issues either in their school or their local community.
- Have the students make a list of the issues they want to discuss.
- Have students discuss each issue and how it relates to the content of a particular unit.
- The list can be lengthy and allows students to provide any ideas they think relate and could be used.
- The teacher is the facilitator, not someone that gives answers and hints.

Supporting Question 2

The second supporting question is "As a class, describe a solution to the current issue."

The formative task is to pick a topic and brainstorm solutions to solve an issue.

Teachers may implement this task with the following procedures:
- Using the students' selected issues, they will look at options for solutions.
- Students will suggest different solutions, and the teacher will then make a list and help them narrow it down to a realistic solution.
- *Note:* Make sure students are aware of and know all the boundaries set by the school or district, the principal, and the department.

Supporting Question 3

The third supporting question is "As a class, design an action plan for the issue."

The formative task is to create and implement an action plan.

Teachers may implement this task with the following procedures:
- Using the class's solution, the students will create an action plan.
- This action plan is completely student-led. It is not a formula, but letting the students use their knowledge and letting student leaders emerge to find the best plan of action and to implement it.
- At the beginning of class, the teacher can inform the students that they must plan how to carry out their solution to the issue.
- Encourage the students but allow them to work and make their own decisions (within the boundaries provided by district, principal, or department).
- Once a plan is in place and approved, it can then be executed within the boundaries provided.

Summative Performance Task

The summative performance is a P.E.E.L. paragraph (or any other authentic assessment the teacher deems necessary for the students). In a P.E.E.L. paragraph, students write a paragraph making a point (P), using evidence (E), then explain (E) their reasoning, and then link (L) it to the content.

ARGUMENT *How did a vacation start a war?* Using content from Dimensions 2 and 3, answer the compelling question in a P.E.E.L. paragraph using evidence.

EXTENSION Explore the virtual exhibits from the World War I museum and write down what you notice, ranging from what you see, to what the videos say, to what takeaways you have (**www.theworldwar.org/learn/educator-resource/immersive-tour-trenches-world-war-i**).

Watch the miniseries *37 Days* (2014) produced by BBC to help with the differing countries at play prior to the war breaking out. It shows the attitudes and reasons why the war started and also shows a lack of voice from anyone other than men in charge.

UNDERSTAND Students will look at problems that can relate to the historical content from the unit.

ASSESS Students will select a solution to an issue in the community or classroom.

ACT Students will carry out their solution in a student-led action plan.

References

National WWI Museum and Memorial. (n.d.). *An immersive tour: Trenches of World War I*. www.theworldwar.org/learn/educator-resource/immersive-tour-trenches-world-war-i

Newcastle University. (n.d.). *Paragraphing*. www.ncl.ac.uk/academic-skills-kit/writing/academic-writing/paragraphing/

Volle, A. (n.d.). Western Front. *Encyclopedia Britannica*. www.britannica.com/event/Western-Front-World-War-I

Willis, J. (2018, January 8). *Aiding reading comprehension with Post-Its*. Edutopia. www.edutopia.org/article/aiding-reading-comprehension-post-its/

Wisconsin Department of Public Instruction (n.d.) *About the Strategy*. https://dpi.wi.gov/ela/instruction/reading-vocabulary-strategies

Wisconsin Department of Public Instruction (n.d). *Frayer Model*. https://dpi.wi.gov/sites/default/files/imce/ela/bank/6-12_L.VAU_Frayer_Model.pdf

STARLYNN NANCE AND KATIE ENGEMANN

High School History

Under what circumstances would breaking the law be justified?

Supporting Questions Dimension 2

1. Does a person's place matter?
2. What does it mean to have a courageous heart?

Supporting Question Dimension 3

1. Were some bystanders or upstanders neighbors?

Supporting Questions Dimension 4

1. How can Artificial Intelligence help us with real-world problems?
2. Does our society have bystanders and upstanders today?
3. How can we teach these issues to our community and solve the problem we see?

High School History

	Under what circumstances would breaking the law be justified?
Standards and Content	**C3 Standards:** D2.His.9.9-12. Analyze the relationship between historical sources and the secondary interpretations made from them. D2.His.12.9-12. Use questions generated about multiple historical sources to pursue further inquiry and investigate additional sources. D2.His.14.9-12. Analyze multiple and complex causes and effects of events in the past. **NCSS Themes:** ❷ Time, Continuity, and Change
Staging the Compelling Question	**Dimension 1:** Define "infringement" and share your definition with the class. Compare and contrast the dictionary definition with your prior knowledge. List infringements from history, the news, the community, etc. Is your example a true example of infringement? Explain why. Are there severities of infringement? Score the list from 1 (less severe) to 10 (more severe).

Dimension 2

Supporting Question 1	Supporting Question 2
Does a person's place matter?	What does it mean to have a courageous heart?
Formative Performance Task	**Formative Performance Task**
Define the assigned vocabulary work using the following activities: • Wraparound ("human rights") • Word Wall ("perpetrator" and "victim") • 3-2-1 ("bystander" and "upstander" or "rescuer") • 1-Minute Write ("resistance")	Watch the following clips from Source C and fill out the graphic organizer (Source B): • 0:00–2.53 (Introduction to story) • 10:40–13:08 (Jewish family home) • 13:25–16:01 (Health clinic) • 21:39–22:06 (Jewish son and dad) • 22:16–28:03 (Priest and Stefan) • 32:39–33:17 (Why?) • 35:21–35:54 (Nazis closing ghettoes) • 35:56–42:27 (Getting kids out & to families) • 43:27–46:05 (Jewish leader meeting) • 55:48–1:01:08 (Children taken by Nazis) • 1:18:21–1:21:00 (Arrested) • 1:30:01–1:32:52 (Escaped) • 1:32:59–1:34:13 (Primary Source)
Featured Sources	**Featured Sources**
Source A: Wraparound ("human rights") **Source B:** Word Wall ("perpetrator" and "victim") **Source C:** 3-2-1 ("bystander" and "upstander" or "rescuer") **Source D:** 1-Minute Write ("resistance")	**Source A:** Analyzing Motion Pictures Teacher's Guide, Library of Congress **Source B:** Primary Source Analysis Tool, Library of Congress **Source C:** *The Courageous Heart of Irena Sendler* (Film)

Dimension 3

Supporting Question 1
Were some bystanders or upstanders neighbors?
Formative Performance Task
Follow the lesson created by the U.S. Holocaust Memorial Museum (Source A).
Featured Sources
Source A: Some Were Neighbors Lesson Plan, U.S. Holocaust Memorial Museum

Dimension 4

Supporting Question 1	Supporting Question 2	Supporting Question 3
How can Artificial Intelligence help us with real-world problems?	Does our society have bystanders and upstanders today?	How can we teach these issues to our community and solve the problem we see?
Formative Performance Task	**Formative Performance Task**	**Formative Performance Task**
Practice asking quality questions and having dialogue with AI. *Note.* Other AI sites can be used to fit district policies, but some alterations may need to be made to get correct sources.	Have a dialogue with AI to discover if the vocabulary learned is a reality today. Dialogue with AI about real-life solutions. Use the AI website to decide on a solution to a problem they see in their community that correlates with the vocabulary taught.	Create a plan of action. Implement the plan or action. *Note.* Other AI sites can be used to fit district policies, but some alterations may need to be made to get correct sources.
Featured Sources	**Featured Sources**	**Featured Sources**
Source A: Perplexity.ai **Source B:** Bloom's Taxonomy Verbs	**Source A:** Perplexity.ai with Quality Questions to ask AI: a. Does our society have bystanders, etc. today? b. Can you give real-life contemporary example? c. Other questions created by the students to use with AI.	**Source A:** Perplexity.ai

Summative Performance Task	**ARGUMENT** *Under what circumstance would breaking the law be justified?* Construct an argument (e.g., detailed outline, poster, essay) that evaluates the need to study and remember what happened in the Holocaust. A P.E.E.L. paragraph is suggested as the model for writing an argument, but other ways of constructing an argument are available (e.g., iRead, H2W, CER).
	EXTENSION Teachers can design an extended IDM by incorporating more lessons from museums (and different programs from around the world). See the following links to expand students' knowledge about this time period in history: • U.S. Holocaust Memorial Museum, www.ushmm.org/ • The National Holocaust Centre and Museum, www.holocaust.org.uk/ • List of Holocaust Museums and Memorials from the United Nations, www.un.org/en/holocaustrememberance/additionalresources/museums
Taking Informed Action	**UNDERSTAND** Connect the vocabulary in Dimension 2 to the contemporary times and use AI to help develop an understanding of real-life examples of those vocabulary words. **ASSESS** Use your knowledge of vocabulary and real-world issues to develop a plan of action using AI to solve an issue you see with these vocabulary words in your community (e.g., school). **ACT** Follow through by implementing the plan and presenting it to the teacher and other stakeholders.

Overview

Inquiry Description

This inquiry leads students through an investigation of the bystanders, upstanders, and others who lived during the Nazi regime and knew about the treatment of Jews. This inquiry will bring those vocabulary words learned from the behaviors of regular people to the present, and students will ask themselves if these types of behaviors are seen today. Students will watch clips from a movie based on a true story of resistance and upstanders and analyze primary sources to help answer the compelling question.

This inquiry highlights the following standards:
- C3 Standards:
    - D2.His.9.9-12. Analyze the relationship between historical sources and the secondary interpretations made from them.
    - D2.His.12.9-12. Use questions generated about multiple historical sources to pursue further inquiry and investigate additional sources.
    - D2.His.14.9-12. Analyze multiple and complex causes and effects of events in the past.
- NCSS Themes:
    - ❷ Time, Continuity, and Change

It is important to note that this inquiry requires prerequisite knowledge of what, where, and when the Holocaust was during World War II.

Note. These series of lessons will be accomplished through four to six 90-minute class periods. During this inquiry-based unit, students will learn through activities and assessments (e.g., formative assessments, writing, and reviewing the film). This unit is intentionally designed to meet the needs of different learning styles in a classroom setting. This unit also works to bridge gaps within reading, collaboration, historical thinking, and self-reflection on the impact of a person's choice during the Holocaust.

Structure of the Inquiry

In addressing the compelling question, the students will go through each dimension of the C3 Framework's Inquiry Design Model (IDM).
Dimension 1: Hook and compelling question
Dimension 2: Vocabulary and film as examples of each vocabulary word
Dimension 3: Primary source analysis
Dimension 4: Plan of action/implementation

Dimension 1

Staging the Compelling Question

In staging the compelling question, ask the students to define "infringement." Have the students share out as the teacher writes a definition from the students on the board. After this, the teacher will post a dictionary definition for the students to compare. Have the students list infringements from history, the news, the community, etc. about which the students have prior knowledge. Have the students share out. After a student shares, the teacher will ask the students if the examples fit the definition of "infringement" on the board. From the list, ask the students if they think there are severities of infringements. Ask the students to score the list on a scale from 1 to 10: 1 for a less severe infringement to 10 for a severe infringement. Ask the students to get in a Think-Pair-Share group and answer the question, "If you see an infringement in public, are you going to get involved? Why? Why Not?" After this Teacher Talk is completed, ask the students if they can think of any historical events when there were people who got involved in severe infringements of other people. Students should explain their prior knowledge to the class. (The teacher will correct errors in content of the students' examples as necessary.)

Dimension 2

Supporting Question 1

The first supporting question is "Does a person's place matter?"

The formative task is as follows:
- Wraparound ("human rights")
- Word Wall ("perpetrator" and "victim")
- 3-2-1 ("bystander" and "upstander" or "rescuer")
- 1 Minute Write ("resistance")
- Teacher Talk

Teachers may implement this task with the following procedures:
- The teacher can decide to use small groups or cooperative groups with more than four students to work on the major vocabulary words for this inquiry.
- The teacher will facilitate and/or model each of the strategies. They will give the students the vocabulary words in sections of the lesson. The first word that will be posted is "human rights."
- Students will then participate in the Wraparound strategy to learn the word. After the students complete the strategy, the teacher will have a Teacher Talk to clarify the term, give examples, and ask follow-up questions to grasp if the students understand the term.
- The teacher will repeat this in sections two through four by posting the word(s), using the strategy, and having a Teacher Talk for clarification and examples.
- After the four sections have been completed, start a Teacher Talk asking the students questions like "How do the vocabulary words work together?" Have the students answer the supporting question as an Exit Ticket.

The scaffolds and other materials may be used to support students as they work with sources are working in different groups, formative assessments, and modeling for students.

The following sources were selected to use to learn the vocabulary words in the parentheses. These strategies engage the students to focus on the words singularly or in groups to understand how people behaved during the Holocaust.
- **Source A**: Wraparound ("human rights") from Facing History and Ourselves. (2020, August 28). *Wraparound.* www.facinghistory.org/resource-library/wraparound
- **Source B**: Word Wall ("perpetrator" and "victim") from Facing History and Ourselves. (2018, January 18). *Word wall.* www.facinghistory.org/resource-library/word-wall
- **Source C**: 3-2-1 ("bystander" and "upstander" or "rescuer") from Facing History and Ourselves. (2014, March 14). *3-2-1.* www.facinghistory.org/resource-library/3-2-1
- **Source D**: 1-Minute Write ("resistance") from page 18 of Regier, N., (2012). *60 formative assessment strategies.* Oklahoma CareerTech; Resource Center for CareerTech Advancement. **https://oklahoma.gov/careertech/educators/resource-center/teacher-trainer-tools/publications.html**

Supporting Question 2

The second supporting question is "What does it mean to have a courageous heart?"

The formative task is as follows:
- Analyzing Graphic Organizer
- Model Clip with all students to teach how to use the Graphic Organizer

Teachers may implement this task with the following procedures:
- Teachers will review the Teacher's Guide "Analyzing Motion Pictures" from the Library of Congress to have questions ready for the Teacher Talk after each clip.
- Teachers will discuss the difference between fact and fiction when watching a movie that is based on real events. It is still a fictional account.
- When using the film clips as evidence, show the students how to accurately write a paragraph answering the supporting and compelling questions (e.g., "As referenced in the film based on the story of..."). Make sure the students tell their audience that this example of upstanders is fiction.
- After watching each clip, have the students complete the Primary Source Analysis Tool using the teacher questions as a guide. Then have a Teacher Talk about the answers from the Primary Source Analysis Tool. Ask what vocabulary word they see in the clip and have the students justify their answers using the definitions. Do this for every clip. The Exit Ticket is answering the supporting question.

The scaffolds and other materials may be used to support students as they work with sources that have been altered for special education or differentiated for students' needs.

The following sources were selected to answer the supporting question and learn more in depth about the vocabulary words.
- **Source A:** Analyzing Motion Pictures Teacher's Guide, Library of Congress, www.loc.gov/programs/teachers/getting-started-with-primary-sources/guides/
- **Source B:** Primary Source Analysis Tool, Library of Congress, www.loc.gov/programs/teachers/getting-started-with-primary-sources/guides/
- **Source C:** Harrison, J. K. (Director). (2009). *The courageous heart of Irena Sendler* [Film]. Hallmark Hall of Fame.
- *Note.* The teacher can show the whole movie and then show the focus clips for the graphic organizer, but it is not necessary.

Dimension 3

Supporting Question 1

The first supporting question is "Were some bystanders or upstanders neighbors?"

The formative task is as follows: Use the lesson plan from the United States Holocaust Memorial Museum to answer the supporting question and learn more about the vocabulary words with primary sources.

Teachers may implement this task by following the prepared lesson.

The scaffolds and other materials may be used to support students as they work with sources include group work, differentiation, and modeling historical thinking skills.

The following source was selected to complete the task:
Source A: Some Were Neighbors Lesson Plan, U.S. Holocaust Memorial Museum **https://exhibitions.ushmm.org/some-were-neighbors/teacher-resources**

Dimension 4

Supporting Question 1

The first supporting question is "How can Artificial Intelligence help us with real-world problems?"

The formative task is as follows: Model how to use the Perplexity website (**www.perplexity.ai**) and have students practice asking quality questions and having a dialogue with the AI chatbot. The teacher should use direct teaching to show the students not only how to use the website but also how to vet the evidence the information comes from.

Teachers may implement this task by modeling and teaching the students how to develop quality questions to dialogue with AI.

The scaffolds and other materials may be used to support students as they work with sources by working as a whole group with the teacher using direct instruction.

The following sources were selected to teach students to appropriately dialogue with AI about historical content, to understand they need to ask good questions to get deeper understanding, and to understand that AI is not a search engine like Google and should be used to learn about the content and not to copy the answers.
- **Source A:** Perplexity.ai
- *Note.* Other AI websites can be used to fit district policies, but some alterations may need to be made to get correct sources.
- **Source B:** Bloom's Taxonomy Verbs (Students can use their own quality questions they create using Bloom's Taxonomy verbs)

Supporting Question 2

The second supporting question is "Does our society have bystanders and upstanders today?"

The formative task is as follows:
- Have a dialogue with AI to discover if the vocabulary learned is a reality today
- Have students dialogue with AI about real-life solutions
- Have students use the AI website to decide on a solution to a problem they see in their community that correlates with the vocabulary taught

Teachers may implement this task with the following procedures:
- Have the students create Quality Questions to dialogue with AI to answer the supporting question.
- Give the students autonomy to learn on their own and just facilitate the lesson, without sharing questions, hints, problems, or solutions.
- Have the students lean on each other, rather than the teacher, for help and assistance.

The scaffolds and other materials may be used to support students as they work with sources include working in groups and collaborating with the students in the class rather than the teacher.

The following sources were selected to use historical thinking skills to develop a plan of action and implement it with little to no teacher help.
Quality Questions to ask AI:
- Does our society have bystanders, etc. today?
- Can you give real-life contemporary example?
- Other questions created by the students to use with AI.

Supporting Question 3

The third supporting question is "How can we teach these issues to our community and solve the problem we see?"

The formative task is as follows: Create a plan of action to solve the problem the class came up with after studying Dimensions 1-4. Implement the plan of action following all school and district policies.

Teachers may implement this task by allowing the students to brainstorm using AI and to identify the problem and solution on their own. Teachers are just the facilitator at this time.

The scaffolds and other materials may be used to support students as they work with sources, work in groups, and collaborate with the students in the class rather than the teacher.

The following source was selected to use historical thinking skills, to develop a plan of action, and to implement it with little to no teacher help.
- **Source A:** Perplexity.ai
- *Note.* Other AI websites can be used to fit district policies, but some alterations may need to be made to get correct sources.

Summative Performance Task

At this point in the inquiry, students have examined the vocabulary, watched a fictional account of a real upstander, analyzed primary sources from all types of behaviors that meet the vocabulary definitions, and created and implemented a plan of action that brought the past to the present to compare history and the present.

Students should be expected to demonstrate the breadth of their understandings and their abilities to use evidence from multiple sources to support their claims. In this task, students will write a P.E.E.L. paragraph (recommended) or any other authentic assessment the teacher chooses.

Students' arguments will likely vary, but could include any of the following:
- No, there is no reason to break the law.
- Yes, there is reason to break the law with evidence used to answer either way.

To support students in their writing, they will learn to write the P.E.E.L. paragraph.

Students have the opportunity to Take Informed Action by using the past to inform the present. Students will develop a plan of action and implement it using the policies and guidelines of the school district and department.

ARGUMENT *Under what circumstance would breaking the law be justified?* Construct an argument (e.g., detailed outline, poster, essay) that evaluates the need to study, remember what happened in the Holocaust. A P.E.E.L. paragraph is recommended.

EXTENSION Teachers can design an extended IDM by incorporating more lessons from museums (and different programs from around the world). See the following links to expand students' knowledge about this time period in history:
- U.S. Holocaust Memorial Museum, **www.ushmm.org/**
- The National Holocaust Centre and Museum, **www.holocaust.org.uk/**
- List of Holocaust Museums and Memorials from the United Nations, **www.un.org/en/holocaustrememberance/additionalresources/museums**

UNDERSTAND Students will connect the vocabulary taught in Dimension 2 to the contemporary times and use AI to help develop an understanding of real-life examples of those vocabulary words.

ASSESS Students will use their knowledge of vocabulary and real-world issues to develop a plan of action using AI to solve an issue they see with these vocabulary words in their community (school).

ACT Students will follow through by implementing the plan and presenting it to the teacher and other stakeholders.

References

Facing History and Ourselves. (2014, March 14). *3-2-1.* **www.facinghistory.org/resource-library/3-2-1**

Facing History and Ourselves. (2018, January 18). *Word wall.* **www.facinghistory.org/resource-library/word-wall**

Facing History and Ourselves. (2020, August 28). *Wraparound.* **www.facinghistory.org/resource-library/wraparound**

Harrison, J. K. (Director). (2009). *The courageous heart of Irena Sendler* [Film]. Hallmark Hall of Fame.

Library of Congress. (n.d.-a). *Primary source analysis tool for students.* **www.loc.gov/programs/teachers/getting-started-with-primary-sources/guides/**

Library of Congress. (n.d.-b). *Teacher's guide: Analyzing motion pictures.* **www.loc.gov/programs/teachers/getting-started-with-primary-sources/guides/**

Regier, N., (2012). *60 formative assessment strategies.* Oklahoma CareerTech; Resource Center for CareerTech Advancement. **https://oklahoma.gov/careertech/educators/resource-center/teacher-trainer-tools/publications.html**

United States Holocaust Memorial Museum. (n.d.). *Teacher resources.* Some were neighbors: Choice, human behavior, and the Holocaust. **https://exhibitions.ushmm.org/some-were-neighbors/teacher-resources**

Index

Figures and tables are indicated by f and t following the page numbers.

A

Aboriginal Australians, 103
Acrostic poems, 63, 63f, 148
Advocacy
   lacrosse history lesson and, 52–54, 59
   legislation lesson and, 43. *See also*
       Legislation lesson
   migration lesson and, 203, 209
AI. *See* Artificial intelligence
All Quiet on the Western Front
   film (1979), 188, 218. *See also* World War I and
      Lost Generation lesson
   Remarque (book, 1928), 188, 218
American colonies. *See* Geography and early
   American colonies lesson
American Sociological Association, 96
"Analyzing Motion Pictures Teacher's Guide"
   (Library of Congress), 238
Anastasia, L., 77
Ancient history. *See* Silk Road lesson
Animal migrations, 205–206, 208–209. *See also*
   Migration lesson
Arrival of the Train at La Ciotat Station (film, 1896), 9
Artificial intelligence (AI)
   geography and early American colonies lesson
      and, 117
   Holocaust lesson and, 188, 239–240
   Silk Road lesson and, 154, 161, 163
   tools for, 163, 224, 228–229, 239
   WWI and Lost Generation lesson and, 188
   WWI causes lesson and, 224, 227–229
Artistic license, 190, 193
Assessments. *See* Formative assessments;
   Summative performance tasks
Asynchronous courses, 14, 110. *See also* Empathy
   lesson

B

Beauchamp, Meghan, 187, 199
Bell Ringers
   for geography and early American colonies
      lesson, 115, 119
   for Jamestown Colony lesson, 191, 192, 195, 196
   for lacrosse history lesson, 141, 145, 147
   for legislation lesson, 125, 132
   for migration lesson, 201, 207
   for Silk Road lesson, 153, 154, 158–159, 161
   for WWI and Lost Generation lesson, 217–218
   for WWI causes lesson, 223, 228
   for WWII economic dynamics lesson, 82, 86–88, 86f, 93, 171–172
Bias
   critical literacy and, 66, 83, 188
   in films, 20
Biden, Joe, 59
Blacksmith Scene (film, 1893), 9
Bloom's Taxonomy
   for Holocaust lesson, 239
   Silk Road lesson and, 70, 75–76, 161
   WWI causes lesson and, 224, 229
*The Boy from Mexico: An Immigration Story of
   Bravery and Determination* (Dennis, 2022), 204, 205
Boyle, Lori, 14–15, 28, 114
Boyle, Sean, 14–15, 28, 114
Branches of government, 44, 131. *See also*
   Legislation lesson
Breaking the law. *See* Holocaust lesson
Browne, A., 227
Buchanan, L. B., 19
Burcar, C., 207
Bystanders. *See* Holocaust lesson

C

Camel and Rider (Middlebury College Museum of Art), 152
*Canadian federal government apology to First
   Nations* (YouTube video), 183
Canadian residential schools, 96–97, 102–103, 183.
   See also Empathy lesson
Carey, Elaine, 24
CEE (Council for Economic Education), 70–71, 159
C.E.R. (Claim Evidence Reason), 184
Charts
   for geography and early American colonies
      lesson, 33, 119
   for legislation lesson, 124, 128–130
   for migration lesson, 205
China Blue (documentary, 2005), 15, 71, 160. *See
   also* Silk Road lesson
Choral Response, 157

Chronological reasoning, 24
Chronology of Powhatan Indian Activity (National Park Service), 195, 196
Circle of Knowledge, 50
Civic mindedness and citizenship skills, 20. *See also* Dimension 4, Communicating Conclusions and Taking Informed Action; Legislation lesson; Migration lesson
Civil Rights Movement, 19
Claim Evidence Reason (C.E.R.), 184
Close Read, 70, 160
College, Career, and Civic Life (C3) Framework
    Dimensions of, 23–24, 25*t*, 26. *See also specific Dimensions*
    films, choosing, 25–26
    goals emphasized in, 20
    Inquiry Arc, 10–11. *See also* Inquiry Design Model inquiry guides
    overview and purpose of, 13–14, 23
College, Career, and Civic Life (C3) Framework for Social Studies State Standards (NCSS)
    for empathy lesson, 107–109*t*, 177, 180
    for geography and early American colonies lesson, 31–32*t*, 115
    for Holocaust lesson, 234, 236
    for Jamestown Colony lesson, 190, 192
    for lacrosse history lesson, 54*t*, 140
    for legislation lesson, 42*t*, 124
    for migration lesson, 200
    overview, 10–11
    for Silk Road lesson, 66*f*, 152, 155
    for WWI and Lost Generation lesson, 214
    for WWI causes lesson, 222
    for WWII economic dynamics lesson, 84*t*, 167
Colonial America: 3 Regions of Colonies—U.S. History for Kids (YouTube video), 30–31, 118. *See also* Geography and early American colonies lesson
Colonialism. *See* Empathy lesson; Geography and early American colonies lesson; Jamestown Colony lesson; Lacrosse history lesson
Communicating conclusions. *See* Dimension 4, Communicating Conclusions and Taking Informed Action
Communication methods, 98–99
Comparing New England, Middle, and Southern British Colonies (YouTube video), 33, 119
Comparing the Lives of Native Peoples | Learn About the History and Culture of Native Peoples (YouTube video), 31, 118. *See also* Geography and early American colonies lesson
Compelling questions. *See also* Dimension 1, Developing Questions and Planning Inquiries
    development of, 26
    for empathy lesson, 99, 177, 180–181, 184
    for geography and early American colonies lesson, 28, 115, 117
    for Holocaust lesson, 234, 236–237
    for Jamestown Colony lesson, 190, 193
    for lacrosse history lesson, 63, 63*f*, 140, 143
    for legislation lesson, 40, 128
    for migration lesson, 200, 203
    overview of, 25*t*
    for Silk Road lesson, 65, 68, 152, 156–163
    for WWI and Lost Generation lesson, 214, 216, 219
    for WWI causes lesson, 222
    for WWII economic dynamics lesson, 82, 167, 170
Consitt, F., 9
Consumerism. *See* Silk Road lesson
Cornell Notes, 99, 105, 181
Council for Economic Education (CEE), 70–71, 159
The Courageous heart of Irena Sendler (film, 2009), 188, 238. *See also* Holocaust lesson
Critical literacy, 25, 66, 83, 96–97, 188
Critical thinking skills
    empathy lesson and, 97
    films as tool for, 11, 14, 20, 26
    geography and early American colonies lesson and, 30, 32
    lacrosse history lesson and, 63
    legislation lesson and, 46, 136
    migration lesson and, 209–210
    Silk Road lesson and, 66, 76
    WWII economic dynamics lesson and, 82–83, 89, 93, 94
Cross-curricular learning, 14. *See also* Legislation lesson; Migration lesson
C3 Framework. *See* College, Career, and Civic Life Framework
C3 Standards. *See* College, Career, and Civic Life Framework for Social Studies State Standards
Cult of Pedagogy (YouTube channel), 216
Cultural identity. *See* Empathy lesson; Lacrosse history lesson
Culture iceberg activity, 100–101, 101*f*, 181
Culture wars, 10–11, 18
Curiosity, 19, 28, 63
Curipod, 101

D

Dances with Wolves (film, 1990), 10
Definitions. *See* Vocabulary words
Democracy, 41. *See also* Civic mindedness and citizenship skills; Legislation lesson
Dennis, Edward, 204, 205
Difficult historical content, teaching, 19
Dimension 1, Developing Questions and Planning Inquiries
  development of, 26
  in empathy lesson, 98–99, 98t, 106t, 177, 180
  in geography and early American colonies lesson, 29–30, 31t, 35t, 115, 117
  in Holocaust lesson, 234
  in Jamestown Colony lesson, 189–190
  in lacrosse history lesson, 54t, 55–56, 60t, 140, 143
  in legislation lesson, 41–43, 42t, 48t
  for migration lesson, 199–200, 202–203, 209–211
  overview of, 23, 25t
  in Silk Road lesson, 67–68, 67t, 74t, 152, 156
  for WWI and Lost Generation lesson, 214, 216–217
  for WWI causes lesson, 225
  in WWII economic dynamics lesson, 84–85t, 86–87, 86f, 167, 170
Dimension 2, Applying Disciplinary Concepts and Tools
  development of, 26
  in empathy lesson, 98t, 99–102, 100–101f, 106–108t, 178, 181–182
  in geography and early American colonies lesson, 29, 30–32, 31t, 35t, 114–115, 117–118
  in Holocaust lesson, 233–234
  in Jamestown Colony lesson, 189–191, 193–194
  in lacrosse history lesson, 54t, 56–57, 61t, 138–140, 144–145
  in legislation lesson, 42t, 43–44, 48–49t, 123, 125
  in migration lesson, 199, 201, 205–207
  overview of, 23–24, 25t
  in Silk Road lesson, 67t, 68–70, 74t, 151–153, 157–158
  in WWI and Lost Generation lesson, 213–214, 217
  in WWI causes lesson, 221–222, 225–227
  in WWII economic dynamics lesson, 84–85t, 87–88, 88f, 166–167, 171
Dimension 3, Evaluating Sources and Using Evidence
  development of, 26
  in empathy lesson, 98t, 102–104, 104f, 108–109t, 178, 183–184
  in geography and early American colonies lesson, 29, 31t, 32–33, 35t, 114–116, 119–120
  in Holocaust lesson, 233, 235
  in Jamestown Colony lesson, 189, 191, 195–196
  in lacrosse history lesson, 54t, 57–58, 58f, 61t, 139, 141, 145–147
  in legislation lesson, 42t, 44–45, 45f, 49t, 123, 125–126
  in migration lesson, 199, 201–202, 207–209
  overview of, 23, 25t
  in Silk Road lesson, 67t, 70–72, 72f, 74t, 151, 153–154, 158–161
  in WWI and Lost Generation lesson, 213, 215, 217–219
  in WWI causes lesson, 221, 223, 228–229
  in WWII economic dynamics lesson, 84–85t, 88–91, 90f, 92f, 166, 168, 171–172
Dimension 4, Communicating Conclusions and Taking Informed Action
  development of, 26
  in empathy lesson, 98t, 104–105, 105f, 109t, 178, 184–185
  in geography and early American colonies lesson, 29, 31t, 33–34, 34f, 36t, 37, 37f, 114, 116, 120–121
  in Holocaust lesson, 233, 235–236
  in Jamestown Colony lesson, 189, 191, 196–197
  in lacrosse history lesson, 54t, 59–63, 62t, 63f, 139, 142, 147–149
  in legislation lesson, 42t, 46–47, 47f, 49t, 123, 126–128
  in migration lesson, 199, 202–203, 209–211
  overview of, 23–24, 25t
  in Silk Road lesson, 67t, 73–75, 74t, 151, 155–156, 162–163
  in WWI and Lost Generation lesson, 213, 215–216, 219
  in WWI causes lesson, 221, 223–224, 229–230
  in WWII economic dynamics lesson, 84–85t, 92, 166, 169, 173
Disciplinary concepts and tools. *See* Dimension 2, Applying Disciplinary Concepts and Tools
Discussion board posts, 98, 105, 177, 180
Dramatic license, 190, 193

E

Economics
  sociology and, 100, 181

trade and, 65–81. *See also* Silk Road lesson
war and, 82–95. *See also* World War II economic dynamics lesson
Edison, Thomas, 9, 19
e-Gallery Walks, 91, 93, 172
Elementary classrooms
    Civil Rights Movement, teaching through film, 19
    C3 Inquiry Framework and, 13–14
    geography and early American colonies lesson, 28–39. *See also* Geography and early American colonies lesson
    Jamestown Colony lesson, 189–199. *See also* Jamestown Colony lesson
    lacrosse history lesson, 52–64. *See also* Lacrosse history lesson
    legislation lesson, 40–51. *See also* Legislation lesson
    migration lesson, 199–212. *See also* Migration lesson
    social studies neglected in, 13, 18
Emojis, 99
Empathy lesson, 15, 96–112
    C3 Standards for, 98*t*, 107–109*t*, 177, 180
    Dimension 1, 98–99, 98*t*, 106*t*, 177, 180
    Dimension 2, 98*t*, 99–102, 100–101*f*, 106–108*t*, 178, 181–182
    Dimension 3, 98*t*, 102–104, 104*f*, 108–109*t*, 178, 183–184
    Dimension 4, 98*t*, 104–105, 105*f*, 109*t*, 178, 184–185
    extension activities for, 179
    IDM inquiry guide for, 176–186
    lessons overview, 96–97, 106–109*t*, 180
Empowerment
    empathy lesson and, 173
    geography and early American colonies lesson, 29
    lacrosse history lesson and, 59
    legislation lesson and, 41, 43, 45–47, 136–137
Engemann, Katie, 188, 233
Essays
    for empathy lesson, 105, 105*f*, 110, 185
    for Jamestown Colony lesson, 197
    for lacrosse history lesson, 63
    for legislation lesson, 137
    for Silk Road lesson, 73, 75–76
Ethical and moral issues. *See* Holocaust lesson; Silk Road lesson
Evidence. *See* Dimension 3, Evaluating Sources and Using Evidence; Featured sources; Primary source documents
The Execution of Mary Stuart (film, 1895), 9
Exit Tickets
    for empathy lesson, 181
    for Holocaust lesson, 237
    for Jamestown Colony lesson, 191, 194, 196
    for lacrosse history lesson, 141, 145, 146
    for legislation lesson, 124, 125, 126, 129–130, 132, 134
    for migration lesson, 201, 202, 205, 207, 209
    for Silk Road lesson, 68, 70, 78, 153, 154, 158, 161
    for WWI and Lost Generation lesson, 214, 215
    for WWII economic dynamics lesson, 87, 88, 92*f*, 93, 167, 171
Extension activities
    for empathy lesson, 179
    for geography and early American colonies lesson, 117
    for Holocaust lesson, 236, 240
    for Jamestown Colony lesson, 192
    for lacrosse history lesson, 142
    for legislation lesson, 127
    for migration lesson, 202, 211
    for Silk Road lesson, 77–78, 78*f*, 155, 163
    for WWI and Lost Generation lesson, 216
    for WWI causes lesson, 224, 231
    for WWII economic dynamics lesson, 169, 174

F

Facing History and Ourselves, 183, 237
Faivor, Samantha, 15, 40, 123
Fast fashion, 77–78, 78*f*. *See also* Silk Road lesson
Featured sources
    for empathy lesson, 177–184
    for geography and early American colonies lesson, 115–121
    for Holocaust lesson, 234–240
    for Jamestown Colony lesson, 190–197
    for lacrosse history lesson, 141–148
    for legislation lesson, 124–136
    for migration lesson, 199–210
    overview of, 24–26, 25*t*
    for Silk Road lesson, 152–163
    for WWI causes lesson, 222–230
    for WWII economic dynamics lesson, 168–173
"Filmmakers manipulate history? So did Shakespeare" (Toplin), 197
Films. *See also* YouTube videos; *specific film names*

benefits of using, 19
challenges of using, 20
choosing and pre-watching, 25–26
educational value of, 9–11, 14, 19–20, 26
film-centered guide, 25t
film clips, websites for, 19
history of, 9–10
rate of usage in classrooms, 19
Flow charts, 130
"For a war memorial" (Chesterton), 218
Formative assessments
for geography and early American colonies lesson, 32–33
for Holocaust lesson, 236–237
for Silk Road lesson, 71, 76, 157–158
for WWI and Lost Generation lesson, 217
for WWI causes lesson, 226–229
for WWII economic dynamics lesson, 171
Formative performance tasks
for empathy lesson, 178–184
for geography and early American colonies lesson, 32–33, 115–121
for Holocaust lesson, 234–235, 237–240
for Jamestown Colony lesson, 190–197
for lacrosse history lesson, 57, 140–148
for legislation lesson, 123–136
for migration lesson, 199–210
overview of, 25t, 26
for Silk Road lesson, 152–163
for WWI causes lesson, 222–230
for WWII economic dynamics lesson, 167–173
The 4 M-A-I-N causes of World War One (Browne, 2021), 226, 227. *See also* World War I causes lesson
Four Corners learning strategy, 70, 132, 153, 158
Frayer Model activities
for empathy lesson, 99–102, 100f, 181
for Silk Road lesson, 77–78, 78f, 161
for WWI and Lost Generation lesson, 216
for WWI causes lesson, 224, 226
for WWII economic dynamics lesson, 87–88, 88f, 171

G

Gallery Walks
for empathy lesson, 182
for legislation lesson, 50
for Silk Road lesson, 69, 77, 157, 161
for WWI and Lost Generation lesson, 218–219
for WWII economic dynamics lesson, 89, 90f, 91, 94, 172
Games and gamification in geography and early American colonies lesson, 29–30, 34, 115, 117, 120–121
legislation lesson and, 131–132, 135, 137
for WWII economic dynamics lesson, 93, 94
Gender equity in history, 19
Generational traits. *See* World War I and Lost Generation lesson
Geography and early American colonies lesson, 14–15, 28–39
C3 Standards for, 31–32t, 115
Dimension 1, 29–30, 31t, 35t, 115, 117
Dimension 2, 29, 30–32, 31t, 35t, 114–115, 117–118
Dimension 3, 9, 31t, 32–33, 35t, 114–116, 119–120
Dimension 4, 29, 31t, 33–34, 34f, 36t, 37, 114, 116, 120–121
IDM inquiry guide for, 114–122
lessons overview, 28–29, 35–36t, 117
Germany. *See* World War II economic dynamics lesson
Gladiator (film, 2000), 10
Globalization. *See* Silk Road lesson
Google Translate, 98, 177, 180
Graffiti Wall activity, 77–78, 78f, 161
Graphic organizers. *See also* T-chart activities; Venn diagrams
for empathy lesson, 99, 100f, 102, 181
for Holocaust lesson, 238
for lacrosse history lesson, 56–57, 144, 145
for legislation lesson, 129, 131, 136
for migration lesson, 205–207, 209
for Silk Road lesson, 67, 69, 156–160, 162
for WWI causes lesson, 226, 228–229
for WWII economic dynamics lesson, 87

H

Harris, Lauren, 10
Haudenosaunee Confederacy. *See* Lacrosse history lesson
Haudenosaunee Nationals keep Olympic dreams in focus (YouTube video), 147
Hawes-Guldenpfennig, Taylor, 15, 65, 96, 151, 176
High school. *See* Secondary school classrooms
Historical inaccuracies. *See* Jamestown Colony lesson
Historical thinking skills
for empathy lesson, 180

for geography and early American colonies lesson, 117
for Holocaust lesson, 236, 238–240
for Jamestown Colony lesson, 193
for Silk Road lesson, 67, 76, 156
for WWI and Lost Generation lesson, 216
for WWI causes lesson, 188, 224
for WWII economic dynamics lesson, 83, 170

Historical trauma. *See* Empathy lesson
History Hit, 188, 224, 225–227
Ho-Chunk Nation, 53, 60, 62–63, 147
Hollywood or History? (HOH) series, 13–14, 187
Holocaust education, 19
Holocaust lesson, 233–241
    C3 Standards for, 234, 236
    Dimension 1, 234
    Dimension 2, 233–234
    Dimension 3, 233, 235
    Dimension 4, 233, 235–236
    extension activities for, 240
    overview of, 236
    supporting questions for, 233–235, 237–239
The Home Front (Home Front History), 172
Hook. *See* Dimension 1, Developing Questions and Planning Inquiries
How populations grow and change: Crash course geography #33 (YouTube video), 204
How the Assassination of Archduke Franz Ferdinand Unfolded, with Dan Snow (documentary, 2014), 188, 227. *See also* World War I causes lesson
Human rights. *See* Empathy lesson

I

Ice Age (film, 2002), 187, 205–206. *See also* Migration lesson
Iceberg activity, 100–101, 101*f*, 181
Iceberg concept of culture (PBS Learning Media), 181
Identity, 181, 188. *See also* World War I and Lost Generation lesson
"I'm Just a Bill" (from *Schoolhouse Rock* film), 15, 41, 43–44, 130–132. *See also* Legislation lesson
Immigration. *See* Migration lesson
Imperialism, 182, 183–184. *See also* Empathy lesson
Inaccuracies in film, 20. *See also* Jamestown Colony lesson
Indian Removal Act (1830), 182
Indigenous peoples. *See* Empathy lesson; Geography and early American colonies lesson; Jamestown Colony lesson; Lacrosse history lesson

Inequality. *See* Empathy lesson
Informed action. *See* Dimension 4, Communicating Conclusions and Taking Informed Action
Inquiry Design Model (IDM) inquiry guides, 113–241
    for empathy lesson, 176–186
    for geography and early American colonies lesson, 114–122
    for Holocaust lesson, 233–241
    for Jamestown Colony lesson, 189–199
    for lacrosse history lesson, 139–150
    for legislation lesson, 123–138
    for migration lesson, 199–212
    overview of, 14
    for Silk Road lesson, 151–165
    for WWI and Lost Generation lesson, 213–220
    for WWI causes lesson, 221–232
    for WWII economic dynamics lesson, 166–175
Inquiry planning. *See* Dimension 1, Developing Questions and Planning Inquiries
It Happened in Michigan (Burcar, 2019), 207

J

Jamestown Colony lesson, 189–199
    C3 Standards for, 190, 192
    Dimension 1, 190, 193
    Dimension 2, 189–191, 193–194
    Dimension 3, 189, 191, 195–196
    Dimension 4, 189, 191, 196–197
    extension activities for, 192
    overview of, 192–193
    supporting questions for, 189–197
Japanese cinema, 9
Jewish people. *See* Holocaust lesson
Jigsaw instructional strategy, 44, 71, 131, 159, 227

K

Kahan, Noah, 217–218
Keywords. *See* Vocabulary words
Kurosawa, Akira, 9

L

Lacrosse history lesson, 15, 52–64
    C3 Standards for, 54*t*, 140
    Dimension 1, 54*t*, 55–56, 60*t*, 140, 143
    Dimension 2, 54*t*, 56–57, 61*t*, 138–140, 144–145
    Dimension 3, 54*t*, 57–58, 58*f*, 61*t*, 139, 141, 145–147
    Dimension 4, 54*t*, 59–63, 62*t*, 63*f*, 139, 142,

147–149
   extension activities for, 142
   IDM inquiry guide for, 139–150
   lessons overview, 53–54, 60–61*t*, 142
Language and culture. *See* Empathy lesson
Language arts inquiries, 14
Laventie (Gurney), 219
Laws. *See* Holocaust lesson; Legislation lesson
Learning management systems (LMSs), 98, 177, 180
Legislation lesson, 15, 40–51
   C3 Standards for, 42*t*, 124
   Dimension 1, 41–43, 42*t*, 48*t*, 123–124
   Dimension 2, 42*t*, 43–44, 48–49*t*, 123, 125
   Dimension 3, 42*t*, 44–45, 45*f*, 49*t*, 123, 125–126
   Dimension 4, 42*t*, 46–47, 47*f*, 49*t*, 123, 126–128
   extension activities for, 127
   IDM inquiry guide for, 123–138
   lessons overview, 41, 48–49*t*, 127
"Let it go" from Frozen according to Google Translate (Parody) (YouTube video), 98–99, 177, 180
Library of Congress
   "Analyzing Motion Pictures Teacher's Guide," 238
   interview transcripts, 217
   Primary Source Analysis Tool, 225–226, 238
LMSs (learning management systems), 98, 177, 180
"The Lonely Death of Chanie Wenjack" (Maclean's), 183
Lost Generation. *See* World War I and Lost Generation lesson
Lumière brothers, 9

M

Magargee, Jackson, 221
magicschool.ai/, 117
Map activities
   for empathy lesson, 182, 183
   for geography and early American colonies lesson, 34, 34*f*, 37, 37*f*, 117–118, 120–121
   for WWI causes lesson, 224, 227
Marcus, Alan, 10, 19
Margargee, Jackson, 187–188
"Mastodon Named State Fossil" (University Record Archives), 45, 132–133
McGowan, Shirley "Little Dove" Custalow, 191, 195
Mein Leben für Irland (film, 1941), 90–91, 172. *See also* World War II economic dynamics lesson
Méliès, Georges, 9
Metacognitive Markers, 70–71, 77, 159
Metamorphic thinking, 40

Metzger, Scott Alan, 9, 10
Michelin Man. *See* World War II economic dynamics lesson
Michigan Senate Bill 397, 45, 132–133
Michigan Social Studies Hub (Michigan Department of Education), 29–30
Middle school. *See* Secondary school classrooms
Migration lesson, 199–212
   C3 Standards for, 200
   Dimension 1, 199–200, 203–205
   Dimension 2, 199, 201, 205–207
   Dimension 3, 199, 201–202, 207–209
   Dimension 4, 199, 202–203, 209–211
   extension activities for, 202, 211
   overview of, 203
   supporting questions for, 199–210
Migration Policy Institute, 208, 210
Miller, Max, 86, 167, 170
Mind Maps
   for legislation lesson, 128
   for Silk Road lesson, 68, 70, 152, 156, 158
Moon, Poppy, 43, 130
Mysteries of the Great Lakes (documentary, 2008), 206

N

Nance, Starlynn, 10, 13–15, 23, 65, 151, 233
Napoleon (film, 2023), 20
National Council for the Social Studies (NCSS)
   C3 Framework. *See* College, Career, and Civic Life Framework
   on civics, 44
   C3 Standards. *See College, Career, and Civic Life Framework for Social Studies State Standards*
   Hollywood or History? series and, 13
   National Curriculum Standards for Social Studies, 65, 83
   on purpose of social studies, 65, 82
   themes. *See* NCSS Themes
National Curriculum Standards for Social Studies (NCSS), 65, 83
National Holocaust Centre and Museum, United Kingdom, 236, 240
Native Americans. *See* Empathy lesson; Geography and early American colonies lesson; Jamestown Colony lesson; Lacrosse history lesson
Nazi posters: 1939–1945 (German Propaganda Archive), 172
Nazi propaganda materials, 9, 90–92, 172. *See also* World War II economic dynamics lesson

NCSS. *See* National Council for the Social Studies
NCSS Themes
  for empathy lesson, 177, 180
  for geography and early American colonies lesson, 115
  for Holocaust lesson, 234, 236
  for Jamestown Colony lesson, 190, 192
  for lacrosse history lesson, 140
  for legislation lesson, 124
  for migration lesson, 200
  for Silk Road lesson, 152
  for WWI and Lost Generation lesson, 214
  for WWI causes lesson, 222
  for WWII economic dynamics lesson, 167
Netflix, 9
New Immigrants Share Their Stories (YouTube video), 208
Noah Kahan – Stick Season (Official Lyric Video) (YouTube video), 217–218
North American Indigenous Athletics Hall of Fame, 62, 149
North American Indigenous Games, 62
Note taking
  for empathy lesson, 99, 105, 181
  for Jamestown Colony lesson, 193–194, 196

O

Olympic Games, 59, 147
Oneida Nation, 53
Online courses, 14, 110. *See also* Empathy lesson
Oppenheimer (film, 2023), 20

P

Pack, Cameron, 15, 82, 158, 187–188, 213
Padlet, 77, 101
Parent-Teacher Organizations (PTOs), 46, 137
Paxton, Richard, 10
P.E.E.L. (Point, Evidence, Explain, Link) paragraphs
  for empathy lesson, 103, 104f, 184
  for Holocaust lesson, 240
  for Silk Road lesson, 73, 75, 163
  for WWI causes lesson, 224, 230–231
  for WWII economic dynamics lesson, 88, 91, 167, 171, 174
Peer-to-peer learning strategies, 44, 135
Perez, Tom, 59
Performance tasks. *See* Formative performance tasks; Summative performance tasks
Perplexity.ai, 163, 224, 228–229, 239
Perspective taking, 24

Persuasive writing, 45–46, 134
Pocahontas (film, 1995), 187, 192–194, 196–197. *See also* Jamestown Colony lesson
Pocahontas: Her life and legend (National Park Service), 194
Pocahontas and the Powhatan dilemma (Townsend, 2005), 196
Poetry
  lacrosse lesson, 63, 63f, 148
  WWI and Lost Generation lesson, 216, 218–219
Poetry Foundation, 218
Point, Evidence, Explain, Link paragraphs. *See* P.E.E.L. paragraphs
Political cartoons, 182
Political polarization, 10–11, 18
Population density. *See* Migration lesson
Pre-service teachers, 13–14, 19
Primary source documents
  choosing films and, 26
  for Holocaust lesson, 236, 238
  for Silk Road lesson, 71
  for WWI and Lost Generation lesson, 217
  for WWI causes lesson, 225–226, 228
Propaganda materials, 9, 84, 89–92. *See also* World War II economic dynamics lesson
PTOs (Parent-Teacher Organizations), 46, 137
Public service announcements (PSAs), 73–75

Q

Quality questions, 70, 75, 86, 188, 239
Questions. *See* Compelling questions; Dimension 1, Developing Questions and Planning Inquiries; Supporting questions
Quick Write activities
  for geography and early American colonies lesson, 32–33, 115, 119
  for legislation lesson, 124
  for WWI causes lesson, 222, 225

R

Reading
  Close Read, 70, 160
  Read Aloud strategies, 70–71
"The Real Cost of Fast Fashion" (Anastasia, 2017), 77
Residential schools. *See* Empathy lesson
Residents in South El Paso worry about impact of migrants on their neighborhood (YouTube video), 205
Reverse Frayer Model, 216

Rewriting history through film. *See* Jamestown Colony lesson
Riefenstahl, Leni, 9
Roberts, Scott L., 10, 13–14, 18, 187
Roots: Exploring the History of Lacrosse (film, 2020), 56, 57, 60, 143–144, 146–147. *See also* Lacrosse history lesson
Rubrics
　for empathy lessons, 105, 110
　for legislation lesson, 135–136
　for WWII economic dynamics lesson, 92
Russell, W. B., 19

S

Sabzalian, L., 60
Sardone, Nancy B., 187, 189
Saving Private Ryan (film), 10
Scaffolds
　for empathy lesson, 181, 182, 184
　for Holocaust lesson, 237–240
　for Jamestown Colony lesson, 194, 195
　for lacrosse history lesson, 144–148
　for legislation lesson, 128–135, 137
　for migration lesson, 204–205, 207–210
　for Silk Road lesson, 157–160
　for WWI and Lost Generation lesson, 217
　for WWI causes lesson, 228
　for WWII economic dynamics lesson, 171
Scheiner-Fischer, C., 19
Schindler's List (film, 1993), 10
Schoolhouse Rock, 15, 41, 43–44, 130–132
School improvement proposals, 45, 45*f*
The School with No Rules (Moon, 2014), 43, 130
Scientific method, 97
Secondary school classrooms
　civics education in, 41
　empathy lesson, 96–112. *See also* Empathy lesson
　Holocaust lesson, 233–241. *See also* Holocaust lesson
　ineffective teaching practices in, 18
　Jamestown Colony lesson, 189–199. *See also* Jamestown Colony lesson
　Silk Road lesson, 65–81. *See also* Silk Road lesson
　WWI and Lost Generation lesson, 213–220. *See also* World War I and Lost Generation lesson
　WWI causes lesson, 221–232. *See also* World War I causes lesson
　WWII economic dynamics lesson, 82–95. *See also* World War II economic dynamics lesson

Seeing world through another's eyes. *See* Empathy lesson
Seixas, Peter, 10
Sierra, A., 111
SignUpGenius, 103
Silk Road lesson, 15, 65–81
　C3 Standards for, 66*f*, 152, 155
　Dimension 1, 67–68, 67*t*, 74*t*, 152, 156
　Dimension 2, 67*t*, 68–70, 74*t*, 151–153, 157–158
　Dimension 3, 67*t*, 70–72, 72*f*, 74*t*, 151, 153–154, 158–161
　Dimension 4, 67*t*, 73–75, 74*t*, 151, 155–156, 162–163
　enhancement lessons, 77–78, 78*f*, 154, 161
　extension activities for, 155, 163
　IDM inquiry guide for, 151–165
　lessons overview, 65–67, 74*t*, 155
　tips and tricks, 75–76
Simon Partner: The WWII Home Front in Japan (lecture), 172
Simulation activities. *See* Games and gamification
6 Key Steps to World War One (YouTube video), 188, 226
Smith, John. *See* Jamestown Colony lesson
Smithsonian National Museum of the American Indian, 118
Snow, Dan, 188, 224, 227
Sociology. *See* Empathy lesson
"Soldier from the wars returning" (Housman, 1922), 218
Some Were Neighbors Lesson Plan, U.S. Holocaust Memorial Museum, 238
Sources and evidence. *See* Dimension 3, Evaluating Sources and Using Evidence; Featured sources; Primary source documents
Sourcing skills, 24
Specialized Professional Associations (SPAs), 13
Spirit Game: Pride of a Nation (film, 2013), 53, 56, 58, 143–144, 146. *See also* Lacrosse history lesson
Sports. *See* Lacrosse history lesson
Standards
　C3 standards. *See* College, Career, and Civic Life Framework for Social Studies State Standards
　National Curriculum Standards for Social Studies, 65, 83
"Stick Season" (Kahan, 2022), 217–218
Sticky Note Storm, 218
Stoddard, J. D., 10, 19
The stomach for the fight: the food policies used by the Nazis to maintain control in the Third Reich

(History Extra), 172
Student-created videos, 209–210
Student-drafted bills. *See* Legislation lesson
Student supports. *See* Scaffolds
Summative performance tasks
    for empathy lesson, 105, 105f, 179, 184
    for geography and early American colonies lesson, 116, 121
    for Holocaust lesson, 236, 240
    for Jamestown Colony lesson, 192, 197
    for lacrosse history lesson, 63, 142, 148–149
    for legislation lesson, 127, 137
    for migration lesson, 202, 211
    overview of, 25f
    for Silk Road lesson, 155, 163
    for WWI and Lost Generation lesson, 216, 219
    for WWI causes lesson, 224, 230–231
    for WWII economic dynamics lesson, 169, 174
Supporting questions
    development of, 26
    for empathy lesson, 176–184
    for geography and early American colonies lesson, 114–121
    for Holocaust lesson, 233–235, 237–239
    for Jamestown Colony lesson, 189–197
    for lacrosse history lesson, 139–148
    for legislation lesson, 123–136
    for migration lesson, 199–210
    overview of, 25t, 26
    for Silk Road lesson, 68–72, 151–163
    for WWI and Lost Generation lesson, 213–218
    for WWI causes lesson, 221–230
    for WWII economic dynamics lesson, 166–173
Swan, K., 26, 173
Sweatshops. *See* Silk Road lesson

T

"Talk with the Text" activities, 132
Tasting History, 86, 167, 170
T-chart activities
    for geography and early American colonies lesson, 33, 119
    for legislation lesson, 124, 128–129
    for migration lesson, 205
Teacher Talks (TT)
    for Holocaust lesson, 237
    for Silk Road lesson, 68–69, 71, 76, 156, 157, 159, 160, 162
    for WWI and Lost Generation lesson, 214, 217
    for WWI causes lesson, 225–226
    for WWII economic dynamics lesson, 86, 88–89, 92, 172, 173
Teaching and Learning Like a Historian: The C3's Dimension 2 (Carey, 2015), 24
Teaching the College, Career, and Civic Life (C3) Framework: Part Two (Swan, 2018), 173, 219
Teaching the ethical foundations of economics (National Council on Economic Education), 156, 159–160
"10 historical movies criticized for their accuracy & realism" (Mutuc, 2023), 197
Think Aloud strategies, 70
Think-Pair-Share (TPS)
    for Holocaust lesson, 237
    for legislation lesson, 124, 128–130
    for migration lesson, 200, 203, 204, 206
    for Silk Road lesson, 68, 152, 156
    for WWII economic dynamics lesson, 87, 91, 167, 170, 172
Thompson, Chloe, 187, 199
Trade. *See* Silk Road lesson
Traditions. *See* Lacrosse history lesson
"Trench poets" (Rickword, 1921), 218
Tribal sovereignty. *See* Lacrosse history lesson
A Trip to the Moon (film, 1902), 9
A True Relation (Wiggin & Lunt, 1608), 195

U

United Kingdom. *See* World War II economic dynamics lesson
United Nations
    inequality data from, 102, 181–182
    List of Holocaust Museums and Memorials, 236, 240
United States Holocaust Memorial Museum, 188, 236, 238, 240
"Until there is not a single Indian in Canada" (Facing History & Ourselves), 183
Upstanders. *See* Holocaust lesson

V

The Value of Films in History Teaching (Consitt, 1931), 9
Van Haren, Kate, 15, 52, 139
Venn diagrams
    for geography and early American colonies lesson, 31, 118
    for lacrosse history lesson, 58, 58f, 146–148
    for migration lesson, 206
Veteran Art Triennial, 218

Videos. *See* Films; YouTube videos
Virginia Historical Society, 191, 195–196
Vocabulary words. *See also* Graffiti Wall activity
   for empathy lesson, 99–102, 100f, 180–182
   for Holocaust lesson, 234, 237, 238
   for lacrosse history lesson, 63, 63f, 148
   for legislation lesson, 128
   for migration lesson, 204
   for Silk Road lesson, 68, 70–71, 77–78, 78f, 156, 161
   for WWI and Lost Generation lesson, 216
   for WWI causes lesson, 224–226, 229
   for WWII economic dynamics lesson, 87–88, 88f, 167, 171
The Voice That Won the Vote (Boxer, 2020), 43, 129

W

"War and peace" (Rickword), 218
WebQuest, 208
We Were Children (film, 2012), 15, 97, 102, 183. *See also* Empathy lesson
"Where should we locate our colonial town?" game, 29–30, 34, 117
Why a Tire Company Gives Out Food's Most Famous Award (YouTube video), 86–87, 167, 170
Why is it important to say "settler colonialism" instead of "westward expansion"? (Choices Program video), 182
Wildlife. *See* Migration lesson
The Wiley International Handbook of History Teaching and Learning (Metzger & Harris, 2018), 10
World War I and Lost Generation lesson, 213–220
   C3 Standards for, 214
   Dimension 1, 214, 216–217
   Dimension 2, 213–214, 217
   Dimension 3, 213, 215, 217–219
   Dimension 4, 213, 215–216, 219
   extension activities for, 216
   overview of, 213–220
   supporting questions for, 213–218
World War I causes lesson, 221–232
   C3 Standards for, 222
   Dimension 1, 225
   Dimension 2, 221–222, 225–227
   Dimension 3, 221, 223, 228–229
   Dimension 4, 221, 223–224, 229–230
   extension activities for, 224, 231
   overview, 224–225
   supporting questions for, 221–230

World War II and Holocaust. *See* Holocaust lesson
World War II economic dynamics lesson, 15, 82–95
   C3 Standards for, 84t, 167
   Dimension 1, 84–85t, 86–87, 86f, 167, 170
   Dimension 2, 84–85t, 87–88, 88f, 166–167, 171
   Dimension 3, 84–85t, 88–91, 90f, 92f, 166, 168, 171–172
   Dimension 4, 84–85t, 92, 166, 169, 173
   extension activities for, 169, 174
   IDM inquiry guide for, 166–175
   lessons overview, 83–84, 85t, 170
"World War One and Parliament" (UK Parliament), 228–229
Write Around strategy, 218
Writing exercises. *See also* Essays; P.E.E.L. paragraphs; Quick Write activities; Scaffolds
   for empathy lesson, 184
   for geography and early American colonies lesson, 32–33
   for Holocaust lesson, 237
   for Jamestown Colony lesson, 197
   for legislation lesson, 45–46, 134
   for migration lesson, 203, 211
   for WWI and Lost Generation lesson, 217–219
   for WWI causes lesson, 225, 230–231
Writing rubrics, 184

Y

YouTube videos, 209–210. *See also specific videos*

www.ingramcontent.com/pod-product-compliance
Lightning Source LLC
Chambersburg PA
CBHW060235240426
43663CB00040B/2743